CONSERVATIVE PARTY

CONSERVATIVE PARTY POLITICS

Edited by
Zig Layton-Henry
Lecturer in Politics
University of Warwick

Foreword by
Sir Ian Gilmour, M.P.

First published 1980 by
THE MACMILLAN PRESS LTD
London and Basingstoke
Associated companies in Delhi
Dublin Hong Kong Johannesburg Lagos
Melbourne New York Singapore Tokyo

Printed in Great Britain by
Billing and Sons Ltd,
Guildford, Worcester and London

British Library Cataloguing in Publication Data

Conservative Party politics
  1. Conservative and Unionist Party
  I. Layton-Henry, Zig
  329.9′41   JN1129.C7

ISBN 0-333-26601-3
ISBN 0-333-26602-1 (Paper)

For Barbara

Contents

Foreword

The British Conservative Party is a very peculiar institution, and British Conservatism is scarcely less distinctive.

In the sense of gaining votes from all sections of the community, the Tories were, even in October 1974, still the most representative of the parties.[1] Except in views, however, the Conservative party in Parliament, as David Butler and Michael Pinto-Duschinsky emphasise, is unrepresentative of Conservative voters in the country. That is, of course, to some extent true of all parliamentary parties. Labour MPs are now more likely to be polytechnic lecturers than anything else. Parliamentary parties abroad are in occupation and class also unrepresentative of their voters. Lawyers are very thick on the parliamentary ground in practically every democratic country, especially in the United States. The only so-called parliament that provides a mirror image of the electorate is the East German, which is not in other respects the model of a democratic assembly.

Nevertheless, the British Conservative party is even more unrepresentative socially than most other democratic parliamentary parties, though this is at least partly explained by the tying of the trade union movement to the Labour party. Furthermore, it has a larger mass organisation than most do, and it gives greater power to its leader. In addition, it has been more successful electorally, at least until recent times, than its nearest equivalent elsewhere. Finally, it has had no consistent body of doctrine and its policies have widely varied from time to time.

For reasons connected with all this, British Conservatism is very different from any other conservatism. Indeed the word Conservative has a different meaning in Europe from what it has here. Yet French, German and British Conservatism all had a

---

1. *Financial Times*, 25 October 1974 (Harris poll reproduced and commented upon by David Watt).

common origin in reaction to the French Revolution.

French Conservatism soon got mixed up with the ideal of a united Christendom under a united Church. French Conservatives believed that spiritual unity was the basis of political order, and that that unity must be complete. Hence, there was no room for moderation or for the sometimes messy compromises of democracy or liberty. Plainly unity in that sense is either there or it is not; there can be no partial unity. And equally plainly, democracy and liberty necessarily lead to a breaking up of that unity. Therefore, liberty and democracy are incompatible with the French Conservative ideal. In consequence, French Conservatism ended up, paradoxically, far closer to Rousseau than to Burke. And its version of harmony and unity made it Utopian, which to the eyes of British Conservatives is the very opposite of Conservatism.

German Conservatism got into even bigger trouble. It soon became associated with a very high view of the State. According to German Conservatives, the State was more real and more rational than its individual members. Only the organic state was fully rational, and it was more real than the individual in the same way that the whole is more real than its parts. And we all know where that idea ended up.[2]

British Conservatism also dates from the French Revolution, but it avoided the excesses of French and German Conservatism for a variety of reasons. Firstly, there was no revolution or foreign conquest. It is very difficult to be Conservative in the British sense after a revolution. Secondly, the British State was just about the oldest and best established in Europe. Thirdly, Britain had a settled if continually changing constitution and a living and unbroken political tradition.

British Conservatism thus never sought to restore something that had been lost or to return to a previous allegedly golden age, or to move into a new idyllic condition of things. In contrast, the French Conservatives wanted to restore something that had not existed under the *Ancien Régime* — a united Christendom — and the Germans wanted to establish something they had never possessed — a single powerful state, governing all the German peoples. Had they ever possessed such a State, they would not have taken such an exalted view of it.

2. For my remarks on French and German Conservatism I am indebted to Noël O'Sullivan's *Conservatism*.

As a result, neither the ideas of the French Revolution, nor the ideas of the reaction to the French Revolution, had as much impact here as they had elsewhere. There were breakwaters in Britain against the waves of new ideas which did not exist in other countries. Thus the younger Pitt, who was, after all, running the country at the time, said of Burke's writings on the French Revolution that he saw in them much to admire and nothing to agree with. Burke himself took a high view of the State, — 'the State is a partnership in all perfection' — but he did not hold the organic theory of the State. The State, he believed, was in some ways like an organism, but it was not one. And while he was highly religious, he did not believe that spiritual or ecclesiastical unity could or should be enforced.

Because of its origins, because Conservatism did not in England fall on virgin ground but in an established political tradition, and because Burke was a very much wiser man than any of his continental equivalents, English Conservatism has always been very different from any other version and the Conservative party different from other parties. Burke did not seek to erect a complete philosophical system. Indeed he eloquently denounced the French Revolutionaries as ideologues, and he was unalterably opposed to metaphysical speculation in politics. Like Halifax and Hume before him, he stressed the overriding importance of 'circumstances'. No rational man, he pointed out, governed himself 'by abstractions and universals'.

Hence, political ideas should be judged not by their speculative attractiveness, but by their 'practical consequences'. Political problems, Burke said, do not 'primarily concern truth or falsehood. They relate to good or evil. What in the result is likely to produce evil is politically false, that which is productive of good, politically true'. Thus for Burke, 'expediency' is not in opposition to 'right'. What is expedient is right. 'Expedience is that which is good for the community and good for every individual in it. . . . ' The test is a practical one. Does it work?

'Prudence', Burke thought, was 'not only the first in rank of the virtues, political and moral, but she is the director, the regulator, the standard of them all'. He combined this 'prudence' with a strong defence of property and liberty. But it was 'liberty connected with order'. Not even liberty, then, can be pursued as an end in itself.

Burke reflected the long-standing practice of British politics, and by his moderate theory or theories he helped to perpetuate them. The fact that British Conservatism has never been a system or an ideology has had profound consequences. In Britain, on the Right but not on the Left, there has been little tension between theory and practice. And since British Conservatism is not a system, balance and moderation have been an important element in it. If you have a system, you do not need balance and moderation. Your system is, by definition, right and you do not want to modify it, since that would make it imperfect.

But British Conservatism is admittedly imperfect; it accepts diversity and imperfection. If you do not have a system, you have to be empirical and you have to take circumstances into account. You have no 'crib', to use Oakeshott's word, to help you steer through every conceivable difficulty. You have, therefore, to judge issues on their merits and not by doctrine. This means, too, or it should mean, that means are distinguished from ends and are not erected into ends. Thus, while patriotism and a belief in the national identity have always been at the heart of Conservatism, they did not stop the Conservative party, in response to a change of circumstances, from being strongly in favour of joining Europe.

Two other important features of the Conservative party stem from Disraeli. They are that the party must be a national party and that 'the condition of the people' must be its abiding concern. These themes were present before Disraeli — Peel in rather a different fashion understood and used them — but they are with reason particularly associated with Disraeli. And since his day, with only occasional backsliding, the Tory party has always been a national party, appealing to all classes, and nowadays to be so is a condition of survival.

Yet, as the editor points out in his introduction, in March 1979 the Conservatives had lost four out of five successive elections. Admittedly Labour's first two victories gave the party less than six years of power, and its second two only a little more than five. The virtual monopoly of power by the Tories in the inter-war years is not something they could expect often to repeat, and by 1979 the major parties had since the end of the wartime coalition been in office for roughly equal periods. Even so, the Conservatives' recent electoral record has been dispiriting.

Certainly the Tories are as avid for office as any other party[3]. But it is less their electoral failure than the observed results of Labour rule that has caused Tory disquiet. After all there was a not

3. This foreword was written before the recent general election.

dissimilar Conservative unease in the early years of this century—
under a Conservative Government. Had the consequences of
Labour dominance for eleven out of the last fourteen years been a
thriving economy and social peace, the Conservative attitude
would have been at worst tolerance and at best admiration. But
Anthony Crosland was frank enough to admit the failure of the first
Wilson Government of 1964–70, and a similarly harsh verdict on
1974–9 seems inescapable.

So the Conservative malaise has far deeper causes than mere
electoral disappointment. These are in essence: Britain's economic
decline in comparison with our friends and neighbours; and the
threat to the constitution presented by Labour's flouting of the
constitutional and political conventions during the seventies.
(Conservative anxiety on these matters does not presuppose that the
Tory party is itself entirely blameless.) Both the economic sickness
and the constitutional threat posed a challenge to traditional
Conservatism.

Britain's economic decay suggested that we could not long go on
as we were, and Labour's breaking of the post-war consensus after
1970 revealed that the British constitution based as it is largely on
convention and containing few legal curbs on the activities of a
temporary majority of the House of Commons, even one elected by
only a small minority of the electorate, was something of a hangover
from more scrupulous days and less dogmatic politics. Yet the Tory
emphasis on the virtue of gradual change and on the national
advantage to be gained from each party generally accepting the
work in government of its opponents assumes that the country will
be reasonably well governed whichever party is in power and that
there will be no massive deterioration in the economic or social
fabric. If on the contrary the other party has not observed the
constitutional conventions and unmistakeable damage has been
done to the economy, mere passive acceptance of such a legacy is
clearly not a particularly seductive option for an incoming
Conservative government. For the Tory party to be the guardian of
national continuity is one thing; for it to be the guardian of national
failure is quite another.

Although Disraeli put the maintenance of the country's institutions on the same level of importance as the economic well-
being of the people, the party's response to the economic problem
has been very different from its response to the constitutional one.
During the last few years, there has been intense discussion of the

economy within the party and a reasonable measure of agreement on a change of course though not a violent one. But there has been relatively little discussion of the constitution and no agreement. Our institutions are in palpable disrepair, and Britain is less well protected than any other democratic country against the arbitrary actions of a temporary parliamentary majority. Yet, although Nevil Johnson is no doubt right in saying that piecemeal reform of the constitution is now difficult, it is surely remarkable that there is within the party no consensus even on one measure of piecemeal reform. There is not even a consensus on the reform that seems the most obvious and the easiest: to make the House of Lords an elected instead of an hereditary and an appointed Chamber.

Thus the Tory party has dealt with the economic problem in a fairly traditional manner, and it has shirked dealing with the constitutional problem also in a fairly traditional manner. Or to put it in another way, while the economic policies of the next Conservative government have been largely decided, constitutional reforms to prevent the next Labour government, with little popular support, wrecking those policies and much else besides have been neglected. This suggests either a touching Tory confidence in uninterrupted Conservative rule or an equally touching faith in the Labour party's capacity for repentance and redemption.

Like all political parties, the Conservative party has many defects, as these essays make clear. Yet by being a truly national party, which means amongst other things being concerned to represent the British people's hopes and aspirations and to preserve the unity and continuity of the country, rather than being concerned to execute a set of doctrinaire schemes and theories, the Conservative party has been the most successful right of centre party in the world. It has achieved that success because it has almost never been reactionary.

Zig Layton-Henry is much to be congratulated both on the distinguished contributors he has collected and on the quality of their contributions. These essays will not make the Conservative party seem any less peculiar; they will certainly make it more understandable.

Ian Gilmour

Acknowledgements

This volume is based on a conference which was sponsored by the Social Science Research Council and was held at Nuffield College, Oxford, in July 1978. The development of the book has been assisted by generous help and encouragement from colleagues and friends, especially David Butler, Jack Lively, Lewis Minkin, and Willie Paterson. I also wish to thank Daniel Lawrence and Bob Miles for their helpful comments on Chapter 3, and Wyn Grant and Jim Bulpitt for sharing their ideas and enthusiasm. I am indebted to Ann Clark and Iris Host for their efficient secretarial assistance.

Z. L.-H.

Notes on the Contributors

NIGEL ASHFORD is a graduate student at the University of Warwick, carrying out research on the Conservative party and European unity. He was Secretary-General of European Democrat Students for two years.

VERNON BOGDANOR is Fellow and Tutor in Politics at Brasenose College, Oxford. He is author of *Devolution*, editor and contributor to *The Age of Affluence 1951–64*, and editor of Disraeli's *Lothair*.

MARTIN BURCH studied at the Universities of Hull and Glasgow and at the latter completed his doctorate on Conservative party politics in the 1960s. Since 1974 he has been a Lecturer in the Department of Government at the University of Manchester, where he specialises in policy analysis.

DAVID BUTLER is Fellow of Nuffield College, Oxford. He is author of numerous books on electoral politics, including the Nuffield studies of British General Elections. He is co-author of *Political Change in Britain* and his more recent publications include *The Canberra Model* and *Coalitions in British Politics*.

IVOR CREWE is Director of the SSRC Survey Archive and Co-Director of the British Election Study, both at the University of Essex. He is currently editor of the *British Journal of Political Science*. His publications include numerous articles on electoral behaviour and public opinion in Britain and the co-editorship of *Party Identification and Beyond*.

ANDREW GAMBLE is lecturer in modern British political economy at the University of Sheffield. He is author of *The Conservative Nation* and co-author of *Capitalism in Crisis*.

NEVIL JOHNSON has been Nuffield Reader in the Comparative Study of Institutions at Oxford since 1969 and is a Fellow of Nuffield College. He is the author of *Parliament and Administration: The Estimates Committee 1945–65* (1966), *Government in the Federal Republic of Germany* (1974) and *In Search of the Constitution* (1977). He has been honorary editor of the journal *Public Administration* since 1967.

ZIG LAYTON-HENRY is Lecturer in Politics at the University of Warwick, and author of numerous articles on political youth movements, the Conservative party, and the politics of race in Britain.

CHRIS PATTEN was the Director of the Conservative Research Department and is now M.P. for Bath.

MICHAEL PINTO-DUSCHINSKY is Lecturer in Government at Brunel University and Secretary to the International Political Science Association's Study Group on Political Finance and Corruption. He is author of *The Political Thought of Lord Salisbury 1854–68*, co-author of *The British General Election of 1970*, and author of a forthcoming book on *British Political Finance*.

ANDREW ROWE was a Lecturer at Edinburgh University before becoming Director of the Department of Community Affairs at Conservative Central Office. His responsibilities include the Conservative Trade Unionist Organisation. He is author of *Democracy Renewed*.

BO SÄRLVIK is Professor of Government at the University of Essex and author of Opinionsbildningen vid folkomröstningen (1957, 1959), and also of numerous articles on electoral behaviour.

PATRICK SEYD is Lecturer in Modern British Politics at the University of Sheffield. His main research interest is the British party system and he has published numerous articles on aspects of party politics.

Introduction

The decisive victory in the general election of 3 May 1979 has ended a period of considerable frustration and uncertainty for members of the Conservative party. The euphoria of victory and the practical problems of government have caused a reassertion of party unity behind Mrs Thatcher's leadership and her new administration. It has also caused a revival of confidence in the success of the party and in hopes for the future. This new mood of optimism is in marked contrast to the doubts and uncertainties which assailed many Conservatives only a few months ago, and which may do so again if the new administration is unable to arrest Britain's economic decline and realise the expectations of economic expansion and growth that Conservative leaders have promised the electorate.

The post-war period has witnessed considerable fluctuations in the fortunes of the major political parties. For those who are able to remember the Conservative ascendancy before the Second World War and witnessed the Conservative recovery from post-war defeat, the Labour government of 1945–51 must have appeared as an interlude of opposition for the 'natural' party of government. It was an interlude from which the Conservative party emerged refreshed and revitalised, having reformed its policies, overhauled its organisation and refurbished its image. In contrast the more recent period from October 1964 to May 1979 has been one of Labour party ascendancy during which the Conservative government of 1970–4 appears as a short, traumatic interlude. During this period the Labour party won four out of five general elections in the sense that it emerged as the largest party and formed the government. Labour held office for eleven of these fifteen years.

The Conservative party has been deeply influenced by this long period in opposition. Many leading Conservatives have become increasingly dissatisfied with economic and social trends in society and were frustrated by their inability to influence events. They became less and less satisfied with policies that merely sought to conserve and increasingly wished to roll back and dismantle parts of the social democratic, welfare state which had been created and extended by both Conservative and Labour governments since the war. The Heath government of 1970–4 was influenced by a similar mood and came to office committed to a wide range of new initiatives and reforms. Some of these reforms, like the taxation proposals, were associated with the commitment to join the EEC, while others reflected a 'non-conservative' determination to reform inefficient and outdated institutions and practices such as the commitments to reform industrial relations and local government. The failures of the Heath government to achieve the economic investment and expansion it hoped for and its failure to reform industrial relations led to a serious debate in the party between those who wished to restore the foundations of a free market economy and those who accepted the necessity for widespread government intervention. Gamble argues that the supporters of a social market economy are only a minority among the Conservative leadership and that the first priority for the new government will be to promote economic growth. Free market policies are likely to be applied selectively to encourage changes in attitudes and behaviour favourable to a more efficient economy but there will be enormous pressures on the government to adopt a cautious approach. These constraints will be imposed partly by the difficulties of managing the economy in a period of world economic uncertainty and recession and partly by the pressures from a large public sector and a powerful trade union movement. Also many industrialists, especially those managing large companies, favour certain forms of government intervention and help for industry, and would not support a sharp move towards a free market economy.

This debate over economic policy is reflected in debates in other areas of policy in the Conservative party. In opposition a party is inevitably deeply involved in re-examining its policies as part of its strategy to regain office. Patten shows how in opposition recent party leaders have involved wide sections of the party in policy discussions and challenges the view that the Conservative party leader has a high degree of autonomy in determining party policy. He argues that the shadow cabinet is the collective policy-making body in opposition and that to some extent the party manifesto and other policy statements can be regarded as treaties between different groups in the party. The debates over economic policy in the party and the compromise documents that have emerged like

The Right Approach and *The Right Approach to the Economy* are good illustrations of this process. This is not to say that the leader cannot take major policy initiatives but to be successful they do need substantial support in the party. Ashford argues, for example, that Macmillan's initiative to apply for membership of the EEC was not as radical as it appeared because many groups in the party and interests associated with Conservatism were already in favour of membership of the EEC. It was, therefore, not difficult to mobilise a substantial majority in the party behind his initiative. On devolution in Scotland, the party has been much less certain, and Heath's initiative in supporting a devolved Scottish assembly at Perth in 1968 did not rouse strong feelings for or against in the party. Gradually opinion among English back-bench Tories has hardened against devolution during a period when Scottish Conservatism has been in rapid decline. Scottish Conservatives are seriously divided on the issue and the prospects for a firmly-based Conservative revival in Scotland look bleak, in spite of the recent gains from the Scottish Nationalists. Bogdanor feels that the weakness of the Conservative party in Scotland may lessen the ability of a Conservative government to manage Scottish affairs. The decline of Scottish Conservatism and the break with the Ulster Unionists has also weakened Conservative claims to be the party of the United Kingdom as it has become more dependent on its suburban and rural strength in southern and central England.

The analysis of Conservative policy on immigration illustrates how the failure of party leaders to take early action can reduce their autonomy in determining party policy. If members of the cabinet in the early 1950s had foreseen the reaction to coloured immigration they might have initiated policies that would have aided the integration of members of the new ethnic minorities. Instead immigration was ignored until the campaign for immigration control was well advanced. Party leaders were then panicked into hurried measures by a combination of pressures within and without the party demanding control and also by a large increase in immigration which itself was partly a response to the campaign for control. Since 1962 immigration policy has been determined largely by calculations of electoral advantage, and paradoxically the growing electoral importance of Asian and West Indian voters may push a reluctant Conservative party towards more positive policies in the areas of race relations and racial discrimination.

Nevil Johnson discusses the dilemma facing Conservatives who are no longer confident that 'whichever party is in office, the Conservatives are always in power'. Should Conservatives support constitutional reform in order to preserve the constitution? The growing support in the Conservative party for a Bill of Rights and for electoral reform reflects a fear that a future Labour government, elected on a minority vote but with a majority in the Commons, might introduce radical constitutional reforms which the opposition would be powerless to resist, because of the sovereignty of the Commons. The crisis in Ulster, the question of devolution for Scotland and Wales, the demands for reform of the House of Lords and entry into the EEC have made constitutional issues of central importance once again even though these issues tend to be pushed aside by the more immediate importance of economic problems.

Crewe suggests that when a major party goes into opposition a battle frequently commences between those fundamentalists who wish to return to the first principles of the party, and those with experience of office who wish to maintain a pragmatic approach. Burch makes a similar distinction when he compares the critical approach to opposition with the alternative government approach. As he regards Heath as the exemplar of the credible alternative government approach, perhaps it is not surprising that Mrs Thatcher should have emphasised party principles and followed the path of leading a critical opposition rather more than her predecessor. This style of leadership in opposition is certainly more suited to a politician of conviction. As leader of the Conservative party before 1970 Mr Heath cultivated an alternative government approach to opposition and ran the Conservative party as an alternative prime minister insisting, for example, on collective responsibility for members of the shadow cabinet. This style of leadership continued after 1970 and Heath's premiership has been described as a paradigm of 'prime ministerial government'. Mr Heath received much of the credit for the unexpected Conservative victory in 1970 but his style of leadership antagonised many back-bench MPs who became increasingly ready to dissent in the division lobbies and who were only too ready to blame him for the electoral defeats of 1974. The bitterness of the ensuing leadership struggle is only gradually subsiding and is not yet fully healed as Mr Heath's exclusion from the cabinet shows. Mrs Thatcher has been more careful to keep in close touch with back-bench opinion and to involve backbenchers in policy-making. This is partly a natural consequence of opposition when defeat is often attributed to the failure of party leaders to remain in contact with grass roots opinion in the party but it is also due to the manner of Mrs Thatcher's election to the leadership which was the result of a back-bench revolt. It is also on the back benches that many of her strongest supporters are to be found. As Prime Minister, Mrs Thatcher is likely to be much more attentive to back-bench opinion than her predecessor. Seyd is also concerned with the growing incidence of conflict and factionalism in the party and argues that this is largely due to the lengthy period of opposition the Tories have experienced since 1964. He argues that the achievement of office is likely to reduce the incidence of factionalism as party members concentrate on the 'realities of government'. However, the level of Conservative dissent in parliament was substantial during the Heath government and its level is likely to depend as much on the success of Mrs Thatcher's policies as on her ability to manage back-bench opinion.

The problems of electoral strategy facing the Conservative party are considered by a number of contributors. Crewe analyses the most rational electoral strategy for the Conservatives in relation to socioeconomic and popular authoritarian issues. He suggests that a fundamentalist electoral strategy appears more promising on matters of law and order and traditional morality than it does on issues of race where, while the electorate supports strong immigration controls, it is divided and moderate. Crewe argues that the Conservative party may be tempted to exploit popular authoritarian issues in a situation where it may not be able to offer the electorate substantial hopes of economic improvement or more competent leadership. Butler and Pinto-Duschinsky examine the composition of the Conservative elite in parliament and in the constituency parties and suggest reasons why the restricted social composition of the party elites may make it less attractive electorally, and may weaken its ability to develop an understanding with the trade union movement. The ability of the new Conservative administration to work with the trade unions and gain their acceptance of, or acquiescence to, Conservative policies, especially those concerned to reform trade union law, will be a major test facing the government. The electoral importance of the trade unions appeared to have changed considerably after the election of February 1974. Before that election, the links between the Labour party and the trade unions were widely regarded as an electoral disadvantage for the Labour party. After the election this seemed less certain and it appeared that the Conservative party's difficulties in working with the trade unions might be a source of electoral weakness. The strikes of last winter and the failure of Mr Healey's 5 per cent incomes policy showed that neither party had a monopoly of trade union goodwill. Nevertheless it was surprising that Mrs Thatcher did not make more public efforts to conciliate trade union leaders before the general election. The chapter by Rowe shows that party leaders and officials are well aware of the need to come to terms with the growth in trade union membership and influence, and to educate party members about trade union values, assumptions and practices. The revival of the Conservative trade union organisation has been dramatic and they held a well-publicised rally during the general election campaign. However, Rowe's ideas about the role of Conservative trade unionists and their long term objectives may well cause the established Labour leaders of the trade unions to feel that organised Conservative trade unionists would be a Trojan Horse in their midst.

This book is largely, though not exclusively, concerned with the Conservative party as a party in opposition, which has been their role for most of the last fifteen years. The impact of opposition can be seen in the internal divisions over policy, the conflict over the leadership and the growth in factional activity. The achievement of office with a substantial majority has, however, endorsed Mrs Thatcher's leadership with the imprimatur of success and has reduced many of the reasons for dissent and dissatisfaction. It has also provided her with the opportunity to show whether the politics of conviction can be as successful as the politics of compromise. Mrs Thatcher and her colleagues will be judged on their ability to return to an economy of free enterprise and profitability, to restrict the excesses of trade union power, to make a success of Britain's membership of the EEC and to manage the other major issues that confront them such as Rhodesia and Ulster. The success with which the new government tackles these problems will determine whether the party returns to opposition after another interlude in office or whether the victory of 3 May is the beginning of another period of Conservative ascendancy in British politics.

PART ONE

POLICY MAKING

1 Policy Making in Opposition[1]

Chris Patten

I INTRODUCTION

The study of the way in which the Conservative party makes policy, and of the pressures which help to determine what that policy should be, is clearly of the greatest importance. No-one, for example, could properly consider the history of the Conservative government from 1970–4 without examining how and why it came to office with the particular commitments on industrial relations, tax, housing finance and so on, which helped both to shape its life and precipitate its death.

Yet the literature on this subject is not as extensive as one might expect. J. D. Hoffman[2] and R. M. Punnett[3] admittedly look at policy making in some detail, and there is a scattering of references in general works on politics (like the Nuffield Election Studies[4]) and a good essay by Anthony King in *New Society*.[5] But otherwise the student of politics has to rely on references of a more or less anecdotal nature in politicians' biographies (of which the most useful is Lord Butler's[6]) and journalists' gleanings, based on the indiscretions of politicians and the more discreet guidance of officials.[7]

The main reason why there is not more published work on policy-making may lie in the natural reluctance of officials and even, perhaps more surprisingly, of front-bench politicians to disclose exactly what happens. The caution of these first-hand sources is understandable. Some of the pressures which produce a particular policy response may not look very attractive to the electorate and the occasional flimsiness of the research behind a new policy

9

initiative could be equally embarrassing. Politicians are not unique in wishing to appear more rational, high-minded and well-organised than circumstances or personalities often allow any of us to be. In addition, those from outside the political arena who play a part in policy-making may wish to draw a veil over their political activities, and those most closely involved as officials have usually taken a lead from the party's most distinguished post-war civil servant, Lord Fraser of Kilmorack,[8] who once observed that the correct place for backroom boys is in the back room. But in fact the process of policy making is on the whole—as I shall attempt to show—much more thorough, respectable and responsible, and much less conspiratorial, partisan and superficial, than this political reticence might make some observers suppose.

An examination of the business of making policy inevitably concentrates on periods when the Conservative party is in opposition. In government the parliamentary party, the party organisation, and the party conference naturally make some contribution to policy, and the machinery for sounding opinion, mobilising arguments and producing documents still operates. But most policy work during these periods is done by ministers and officials; it emerges very largely from reactions to events, from tackling the problems of governing the country.

In or out of office, as Hoffman has argued, 'the party constitution accords what appear to be very close to dictatorial powers to the leader of the party in the matter of policy-making'.[9] In practice, the leader carries out this work in consultation with his or her chosen close colleagues in the cabinet or the shadow cabinet, and with members of the parliamentary party. The leader must also take account of the views of the party outside parliament, as expressed, for example, at the party conference, though this body does not have the same quasi-democratic binding role as the Labour party conference in determining policy. The leader is assisted by two bodies specifically established for the purpose.

The first is the Advisory Committee on Policy. This committee was one of the fruits of the Maxwell-Fyfe Committee on the Party Organisation, whose report was passed by the Central Council on 15 July 1949. It replaced the Advisory Committee on Policy and Political Education—set up in 1945 as part of the party's post-war reconstruction—but the change was greater than the modification of the committee's name would suggest since henceforth the Advisory Committee on Policy was to be directly responsible to the leader, who was to appoint the chairman and vice-chairman, and not to the National Union.

The current composition of the Advisory Committee on Policy under its chairman, Sir Keith Joseph, is:

Parliamentary Party:	two from the House of Lords and five (appointed by the 1922 Committee) from the House of Commons;
National Union:	eight, of whom four are ex-officio, including, invariably, the chairman of the Young Conservatives, and four elected;
Five ex-officio members:	the chairman and deputy chairmen of the party, the director of the Research Department, and the director of the Conservative Political Centre;
Up to six co-opted members	who include, by tradition, the chairman of the Federation of Conservative Students
The secretary of the Advisory Committee on Policy,	who has always been a member of the Conservative Research Department

The Advisory Committee on Policy meets about once a month when parliament is sitting and discusses some aspects of policy often prepared by one of the party's policy groups. It also considers the reports of Conservative Political Centre discussion groups and, when in office, trends in departmental policies. The discussion is usually introduced by a shadow minister (or minister). In addition, the committee discusses, and may suggest amendments to, the party's manifestos and other policy documents. It acts as a sounding-board on policy for the party leadership. Anthony King has noted that 'Unlike Labour's NEC, the Advisory Committee on Policy has no formal policy-making status; but it does have a traditional claim to be consulted, to advise, and to warn'.[10]

The second body, which has a central role in policy work, is the Conservative Research Department.[11] This was set up, independent of the Central Office, in 1929 or 1930 by Neville Chamberlain or Viscount Davidson (the adjudication on year of birth and paternity must await John Ramsden's further researches). The department is physically separate from the party headquarters with offices in Old Queen Street near Parliament Square. It is usually chaired by a senior politician, at present Mr Angus Maude, who is also deputy chairman of the party. It has four principal roles. It provides a secretariat for the shadow cabinet with individual members acting as research assistants to front-bench spokesmen. Its director and senior officials also attend and service the meetings of the shadow cabinet, preparing papers and arranging the agenda. (In government, the relationship with ministers is obviously looser, but members still provide help with party political tasks.) The second role is to provide the official 'civil service' support for policy work—for example, servicing the Advisory Committee on Policy, and individual policy groups. The department's desk officers act, in Richard Rose's words, as 'not so much innovators as brokers between MPs concerned with day-to-day parliamentary problems and experts outside Westminster, whether in the universities, business and industry, professions, or trade unions'.[12] Thirdly, the Research Department briefs the parliamentary party as a whole, with officials acting as secretaries of the back-bench subject committees. Fourthly, it produces a series of information publications for the whole party and a wider audience, most notably its regular fortnightly journal *Politics Today* and the *Campaign Guides*, a series of unique reference books prepared before general election campaigns.

The Research Department usually employs up to 35 graduates in opposition (the number falls in government when the burdens are lighter). There is a supporting staff of about 30. Many members go on to a career in the House of Commons. There are today 21 ex-Research Department officers there.

II POLICY MAKING 1945–51

Under Lord Butler's chairmanship after the war, the department was the boiler-room in the work of restating policy for the 1950 and 1951 elections. There was initially some resistance to doing this at all. The leader of the party, Winston Churchill, never disguised his doubts about the wisdom of the party trying to make policy while in opposition. 'When an opposition spells out its policy in detail . . . having failed to win the sweets of Office, it fails equally to enjoy the benefits of being out of Office.'[13] However, as Lord Butler, who quotes this statement, goes on, 'The 1946 Party Conference at Blackpool had overwhelmingly demanded some re-formulation of our policy and Churchill moved to meet this demand soon after'.[14] Lord Woolton, the party chairman from 1946 to 1955, gave the main reason for this demand in his *Memoirs*: 'It is always dangerous in politics to be committed to detail in any programme. But I concluded it was at least as dangerous to be so vague that the nation would think that the Conservatism that we were expounding would be no different from the Conservatism of the thirties. We therefore decided to take the risk of defining in terms the policies we would encourage the nation to undertake.'[15]

The main policy statements of that period were *The Industrial Charter* (1947), *The Agricultural Charter* (1948), *The Conservative Policy for Wales and Monmouthshire, Imperial Policy, Scottish Control of Scottish Affairs*, and a synoptic policy document, *The Right Road for Britain* (all published in 1949). The party's manifestos in 1950 and 1951 drew heavily on these documents.

While the leader was closely consulted about these statements and left his unmistakeable imprint on some of them, they were usually the product of small committees of his senior colleagues aided by a few backbenchers and the staff of the Research Department. Each of the charters was presented to, and approved by, the annual party conference.

The differences with the policy exercise of 1964–70 are quite extensive. First, the total scope of the exercise was much more limited. There was a handful of wide-ranging committees or groups instead of some 30 or more dealing with fairly specific detailed questions.

Secondly, even on the subjects covered, the policy recommendations in the earlier period were much less detailed, or as Lord Butler puts it, 'more impressionistic'.[16] Contrary to some reports, the policy work of 1964–70 was never developed to the point where draft legislation was prepared. Nevertheless, in many fields (notably industrial relations, housing finance, tax reform and the structure of central government) very detailed reports were produced which were made available to ministers when the party took office. These could serve as blueprints for legislation or administrative arrangements. After 1951, civil servants would have had little more than a general impression of the attitude that the new government would adopt to the problems confronting it.

Thirdly, although back-bench MPs were associated with the work in the earlier period, 'for the most part', as Punnett points out, 'the members of the Shadow Cabinet were the dominant figures of the committees'.[17] Equally important, the very small number of committees enabled each one to include a fairly wide range of front-benchers. It could act as a genuine sub-committee of the shadow cabinet with additions from the back benches; in 1964–70, most committees were made up of a single shadow minister with back-bench and non-parliamentary members.

Fourthly, there does not seem to have been a very organised or systematic arrangement for tapping expert opinion. The Research Department officers who serviced the committees would certainly draw on their contacts in the academic, business and professional worlds for expert advice when required, and distinguished outsiders would have been consulted by members of the committee. But from 1964–70 non-parliamentary members contributed more directly to the work.

It seems probable that after the war there was, in fact, a fairly wide technical consensus, at least among 'informed opinion'. The main lines, or at least general direction, of policy over a large area—education, full employment, social services, the health service, etc.—had been developed in the closing years of the war in a largely bipartisan spirit by a variety of Royal Commissions, inter-departmental committees and the like. Butler himself seems to have regarded the party's Advisory Committee on Policy as an extension into conditions of opposition of the previous Conservative 'caretaker' government's Post-War Problems Committee, which itself had its origins under the wartime coalition. In effect, the job of party policy formation was to draw on this body of 'sound' economic and administrative principles, weaving together a programme that would conform to Conservative philosophy and would be accepted—or could be rendered acceptable—to the party.

A good deal of emphasis throughout this period seems to have been placed on 'political education',[18] meaning the education of the party itself into the ideas of a post-Beveridge, post-Keynes epoch. The work was successful and proved highly effective politically because the party realised, in a way the Labour party failed to do, the potential of these new ideas. Labour certainly accepted the Keynesian analysis, but the Conservatives saw that the shift to macro-economics opened the way for a return to the liberal economic values that had been in eclipse since the early years of the century, and rendered unnecessary the detailed micro-economic controls that the Labour government were reluctant to abandon and which had been by and large the orthodoxy for some years. By offering an alternative cure to the scourge of unemployment, Conservatives were able responsibly to claim that in government they could 'Set the People Free'.

III POLICY MAKING 1964–70

In 1964–70 there was not the same need for a fundamental shift in the attitudes of the party. But after thirteen years of office, it had grown stale. It had exhausted the intellectual capital with which it arrived in government in 1951, and become captured by the negative attitude of the Whitehall machine, which is usually more conscious of the difficulties of any departure from the existing way of doing things than of the benefits of new ideas. Unlike the situation in 1945, there were no powerful voices raised to oppose the idea of detailed policy work. On the contrary, fairly soon after the 1964 defeat, Sir Alec Douglas-Home asked Mr Heath, as chairman of the Advisory Committee on Policy, to set in motion a review of policy in all the main fields.

The instrument chosen for this review was a series of policy study groups that at one stage numbered more than 30. The chairman (normally the appropriate shadow minister) and each member of a policy group was personally appointed from the start by the chairman of the Advisory Committee on Policy 'with the agreement of the leader of the party' before he himself became leader. The typical policy group consisted of a chairman, half a dozen backbench MPs, and an equivalent number of experts from outside the parliamentary party, including representatives from the National Union. The back-bench parliamentary MPs were chosen from those who had been most actively interested in the subject and in such a way as to cover, as far as possible, the spectrum of views inside the parliamentary party. Each policy group was serviced by the appropriate Research Department officer, who also remained responsible for parliamentary briefing on the subject and for looking after the relevant back-bench parliamentary committee. So there was very close correspondence between the short-term parliamentary work and the longer-term policy work. Thus the pledge to abolish SET came first, and what this meant in terms of a complete restructuring of indirect taxation developed from that decision.

The main policy documents during this period were the synoptic *Putting Britain Ahead* (1965) on which the 1966 manifesto was based, *Fair Deal at Work* (1968) which set out the party's proposals on industrial relations reform, and *Make Life Better* (1968) which was presented to the party conference as a general statement of policy. As with any large-scale voluntary effort, the results of all this policy work were uneven. Some groups had relatively little to show for their efforts. Others produced reforms like the restructuring of the taxation system, which was by any standards a considerable achievement. The beginning of the concept of the Tax Credit Scheme can also be traced to work at this time on what was then called Negative Income Tax. Other projects—like the reforms of industrial relations and housing finance—seemed equally impressive at the time. The subsequent political difficulties to which they led may be blamed on ill-judged implementation, on the strength of the forces which they were trying to reform, on the irresponsibility of Labour in opposition, or on sheer bad luck, but it cannot be said that they were caused by inadequate preparation.

Some observers find it impossible to be equally charitable about other areas of policy. Whatever else can be said in its favour, the re-organisation of local government does not appear to have been successfully thought through and argued out within the party before 1970. Other more serious criticisms have been made about concentration on institutional reform at the expense of hammering out a coherent and detailed approach to economic policy. An unnamed critic, quoted by Butler and Pinto-Duschinsky, argued in 1970, for instance, 'I have been saying for years that we have been making too much policy. We have come out with a glorious set of platitudes and have avoided having a detailed set of economic policies.'[19] In later years, others were to echo this view. But the most serious criticism that is made about the policy work of 1964–70 is of the eclecticism which was probably fostered to some extent by the emphasis placed on problem-solving and by the structure of distinct, separate policy groups. The principle of collective shadow cabinet responsibility was maintained and policies were not accepted until they had been discussed and agreed by the whole shadow cabinet. This, however,—according to the critics—may have been more a matter of arguing a case for specific policy recommendations than agreeing a general approach to policy.

Even the very full and lengthy discussions that took place over a whole weekend at the Selsdon Park Hotel in 1970 did not, as popular mythology would have us believe, result in the formulation of some general concept which could be termed 'Selsdon Man'. This conference remained a series of discussions—often in very considerable detail—on a collection of specific policies listed for inclusion in the draft manifesto. The 'general concept' which achieved notoriety was the result of Sir Harold Wilson's fertile political mind.

This acceptance of the principle of collective shadow cabinet responsibility, which can be argued to be something of a constitutional innovation, did not prevent the persistence of some underlying divisions of opinion, at least of a technical nature. Of these, the most important—recognised to a limited extent at the time, but more obvious in the light of subsequent events—was the difference of emphasis about the relative importance of monetary and competition policy on the one hand and some, not necessarily statutory, form of incomes policy on the other.

IV POLICY MAKING 1974–9

Policy work in the immediate aftermath of the defeat in February 1974 was largely governed by the circumstances of that election and the imminence of another campaign. The main problem was not to show that the Conservative party had built up a new stock of ideas for governing the country, but in the wake of the miners' strike and the 'Who Governs?' campaign that it was capable of running the country at all. In addition, it was believed that the electorate had been offered too harsh a choice by Conservatives in February. Though the economic consequences of the four-fold increase in the price of oil limited the number of attractive policies which could be included responsibly in the manifesto for protecting or raising the standard of living of particular groups, it was felt that it should contain more than the prospect of 'blood, sweat and tears'.

One other factor helped to determine the outcome of the policy work. Even before the February election, there had been some criticism within the party about the economic policies pursued by the Conservative government. It was argued that it had paid too little attention to monetary policy, had become too dirigiste, and in particular had got entangled in the statutory control of prices and incomes at a considerable economic and political cost. This criticism became more open and widespread after the election defeat. It initiated a debate about the whole balance of the party's economic policy between those who wanted a more market-orientated approach and those who thought that the previous government's intervention in the economy was inevitable and justified. The argument was pursued with great vigour and differences were often exaggerated by the enthusiasm for controversy of the protagonists. The manifesto in October obviously had to be broadly acceptable to both sides, and to that extent may be thought to represent—like later documents—a treaty between those with different points of view.

Between February and the October election, there was no time for the sort of broad, elaborate and detailed policy-making that had taken place in earlier periods. But it is not true, as the *Economist* has argued,[20] that there were no formal policy groups. A small number (like those on housing and local government finance) was in fact set up on much the same model as 1964–70 and serviced by the Research Department. The manifesto, published in September, was based on the work of those groups and on some of the policy speeches made by shadow ministers, particularly the then shadow chancellor, Mr Robert Carr.

The next stage of policy work followed the October defeat and the election of Mrs Thatcher as the new party leader in 1975. She appointed Sir Keith Joseph as chairman of the Advisory Committee on Policy with overall responsibility for policy work. Sir Ian Gilmour left his post as chairman of the Research Department and was replaced by Mr Angus Maude. Mrs Thatcher's election and Sir Keith Joseph's appointment were seen as shifts towards the market wing of the party.

Many of the principal features of the organisation of policy work in this period were similar to those of 1964–70. Most policy groups were chaired by a shadow minister, or by a backbencher nominated by him. Membership of groups was drawn from the parliamentary party and from a number of outside experts. The shadow cabinet was the focus of the policy work and decided collectively which recommendations of policy groups could be accepted as party policy. The chairman of the Advisory Committee on Policy and the chairman of the Research Department determined the direction of the work and its coordination and the whole exercise was serviced by the Research Department. The Advisory Committee on Policy acted as a sounding board; an early draft of the party's 1976 review of policy, *The Right Approach*, was, for example, considered in detail by this committee at about the same time as it was discussed by the shadow cabinet.

There were, however, some differences. First, since 1975 the party was more concerned with its philosophy and its general approach than it was in the 1960s. This owes something to the change in the style of leadership. It is also partly the result of scepticism about the 'problem-solving' attitude to policy work, a deep awareness of the constraints within which any British government today has to operate, a caution about promising too much or attempting too many changes in government too rapidly, and a growing opposition to the notion that a detailed manifesto should be regarded by the nation as holy writ for a five-year parliament. These attitudes were not solely or mainly a reaction to the party's record in the decade 1965–75. They stemmed much more from a view of Britain's problems and of the role of government in trying to solve them.

Another major difference is that the policy work was less tightly controlled than in 1964–70. All policy work had to be funnelled eventually through the Research Department, the Advisory Committee on Policy, the shadow cabinet, and the 'inner' shadow cabinet—known as the Steering Committee and made up of the leader's most senior colleagues—before it received official endorsement. But there were more policy groups, running on an initially lighter rein, than before. Again, this owed something to the change. More backbenchers wanted to be involved in policy work and the shadow cabinet was wisely disposed to let a hundred flowers bloom. In order to ensure that they could be picked without placing too large a burden on the shadow cabinet itself, which must necessarily spend quite a lot of its time determining parliamentary tactics week by week, a policy sub-committee under Sir Keith Joseph's chairmanship was established to vet policy proposals before their submission to the shadow cabinet. This sub-committee, all of whose members were in the shadow cabinet, met from time to time over lunch in the Research Department.

The principal documents produced during this period have been *The Right Approach* and *The Right Approach to the Economy* (1977). A Scottish policy document, *Onward to Victory*, was published for the Scottish party conference in 1978. *The Right Approach* was based on an exhaustive and exhausting shadow cabinet review of the first year's policy work. It showed the party's concern for setting out coherent general principles of action rather than a detailed blueprint for office. It is significant that it was always referred to initially as a *strategy* rather than a *policy* document. Publication of *The Right Approach* brought the first phase of work to a conclusion, so that many policy groups finished the main part of their work at the same time. A rather tighter grip was subsequently imposed on policy work. *The Right Approach to the Economy* brought together the main policy work undertaken in the fields of public expenditure, taxation, industrial policy and industrial relations. It set out once more the party's general approach, but also presented an intellectually rigorous argument on the problems of economic reform. The fact that the document was signed by Sir Keith Joseph, Sir Geoffrey Howe and Mr James Prior—who had been associated from time to time with different shades of the economic argument— led some commentators to see it as another example of the policy document as treaty. The manifesto for the next election was based on these documents, just as the 1950 and 1951 manifestos were based on the *Charters*.

It was intended that policy work after the publication of *The Right Approach to the Economy* should be completed by the late summer of 1978 before the election campaign widely expected in the autumn. A manifesto was actually completed and approved by the shadow cabinet, and discussed by the Advisory Committee on Policy, before the Prime Minister's announcement that he intended to carry on into the winter and perhaps beyond. This work was not wasted, however. It brought to attention a few areas where more work needed to be done, and the last stage of policy work in the parliament was directed towards them.

Policy making throughout this period consciously drew on the experiences of 1945–51 and 1964–70. Before work began, the Research Department undertook a review of the earlier periods and some of the findings of this review are included in this chapter. As things have turned out, the exercise this time clearly reflects some of the different strengths of the earlier periods. Much detailed work of a technically proficient nature was done, but the party was more concerned to convey a broad approach rather than to scatter public commitments over a wide area. *The Right Approach*, for example, owes much of its style and sweep to the *Charters*. Whether the work since 1975 also repeats earlier mistakes, or has managed to produce new ones, will be for others in time to argue.

V CONCLUSION

Four rather obvious questions emerge from any study of policy-making. First, does all the policy work matter? As King points out,[21] a party today cannot campaign on 'men not measures', and when it is out of power, policy making gives its MPs and leading party activists 'a sense of purpose and something to do'. It may be fair to question whether all this work, however skilfully planned and efficiently carried out, actually makes much difference to voting behaviour. King seems to be arguing that even the Conservative party conceded this in 1970 when, though its policy-making exercise may have been sophisticated, 'its electoral appeal was pretty primitive'.[22]

But showing that it is prepared for government is an important, if small, weapon in an opposition's armoury. Of all the factors that affect voting, the performance of the government of the day is one of the most significant. In a real sense a general election is an opportunity for the electorate to give or withhold a vote of confidence in the government and to that extent it is true that governments do lose elections rather than oppositions winning them. This is not, however, the whole truth. The opposition has to be a credible alternative government in order to pick up support, and because policy making contributes to or detracts from its credibility it can be very important indeed.

The second question is how detailed policy has to be. I have already quoted Churchill's reply to this and, as Punnett notes, he was only repeating what others (including Disraeli) had said before. But in the event, Churchill went along, albeit reluctantly, with the policy-making work master-minded by Lord Butler. This work succeeded in the vote-maximising task of balancing credibility as an alternative government against the political embarrassment of taking too many commitments publicly on board.

There are four main potential embarrassments. First, there is always a danger that opponents will steal some of the more attractive policies produced. This is sometimes seen by commentators as an attempt in the run-up to an election to capture the middle ground of politics. A wise party does not allow itself to be provoked, as a result, into changing its policies to ones that are less attractive—and appear less moderate—just in order to look different. Imitation is flattering, and not unhelpful, in politics as in the rest of life.

Secondly, an opposition may incur electoral unpopularity by setting out policies which appeal more to its activists, who had a say in producing them, than to anyone else. Labour does this periodically with proposals for enlarging the public sector, raising taxation and extending socialism in ways which may enthuse the constituency workers but not its private pollsters.

Thirdly, it may be only too obvious when a policy is scrutinised by the experts that it cannot easily be implemented.

Fourthly, circumstances can change so much as to make commitments undertaken sometime previously look impractical or harmful as time passes.

A party in opposition has to surmount these difficulties as well as it can, and it may not always have a totally free hand in determining where to place the balance between the general and the particular. In 1964, as we noted, the Conservative party was obliged by the public mood to demonstrate intellectual vigour across the whole field. In 1974-5, there was a greater demand to know what the party stood for in general before specific policy questions were tackled. A party's own supporters in parliament and in the country can shift the balance, and the same can be true of its political leaders' inclinations. They may well conclude that turning out the vote by a lowest common denominator approach should not be their main preoccupation, that they know what is good for the country, and that they will not be able to do what they want unless they are fully prepared for office and have worked out their policies in sufficient detail to answer the questions that civil servants will raise. Even if this work can be done behind the scenes, there is always the danger of leaks, with work that was never meant for public consumption appearing indigestibly with the daily papers on everyone's breakfast table. Preoccupation with detailed policy work can also obscure the main message that a party is trying to communicate; it may finish up with a lot of cleverly conceived items of policy but no comprehensible message at all.

A successful opposition will seek to strike a balance which ensures that its general message is clear and is presented with sufficient supporting evidence to be credible. The quantity of the evidence which is necessary has probably increased with the growth in sophistication of political commentary and interrogation. Mr Heath has put this point: 'There is probably a place for both the main themes and for detailed policies. The argument for detail is this: people today are so cynical and sceptical about the whole machinery of government that detail is needed to convince them that you really intend to carry out your promises.'[23]

Political craft will always be needed in opposition policy making to counter the 'heads I win, tails you lose' attack that every government will make on its opponents—claiming both that they have no policies and are therefore unfit to govern, and that they do have policies which would lead to instant disaster if they were ever given the chance to carry them out.

The third question, which was referred to earlier, is who makes policy in the Conservative party? The theoretical model that the leader alone is responsible for policy, and the 'presidential model' school of political scientists, both underestimate the extent to which decisions are collective.

Since the Conservative party does not suffer from the 'general will' notion of political authority which afflicts the Labour party, the role of the party conference is not so decisive in policy making, though its influence is not negligible and no party leadership could afford to ride roughshod year after year over its fixed and prevailing opinions. The celebrated '300,000 houses' amendment at Blackpool in 1950 illustrates what a Conservative party conference can achieve if it gets the bit between its teeth. Furthermore, as the textbooks have all pointed out since R. T. McKenzie's classic study *British Political Parties* first published in 1955, though the party is authoritarian in theory, its whole structure in practice provides for a constant process of consultation and two-way flow of ideas within its rank and file. The process ensures that in the measures they advocate, leaders and MPs have the views of their rank and file well to the fore of their minds. The Conservative party is a mass party.

But the really effective policy-making college is the shadow cabinet, and within that body the views of those who have been irreverently called 'the big beasts in the jungle'—the senior political figures—obviously matter most. The leader can and should point the direction in which policies will develop. She (or he) can make the running on policy both publicly and privately to an extent and with an authority denied to colleagues. The leader can decide which colleagues are in the most influential positions to shape policy and indeed (within certain obvious constraints) who should have a seat in the college of cardinals. Yet there is no papal throne. The shadow cabinet is in effect the collective policy-making body in opposition, and because of the additional strength which this gives to any policy statement, no sensible leader would have it otherwise.

The last question—and most important—is how good are the policies that emerge? Performance is both uneven, as I suggested earlier, and more untidy than this sort of review might suggest. This is inevitable in any exercise which depends on voluntary effort by busy and sometimes temperamental people. The absence of the resources of government also affects quality of work, and its relevance can be limited by the fact that planning in opposition tends to concentrate on policies that touch on more or less permanent features of government. Responding to transient features is bound to be less planned, and yet dealing with the passing scene is what government is about for much of the time.

Even allowing for all that, a fair-minded critic of, say, the policies produced in the 1964–70 period would surely conclude that technically many of them would have done credit to a Brookings Institute or some other school of public policy. Major reforms of structures that had been left untouched for decades were carried out in ingenious and sometimes administratively elegant ways.

Nevertheless, the resources for policy work in Britain are decidedly meagre and the technical loads placed on a party in opposition are immense. More work on policy by long-term policy units attached to the political parties as in Germany, by schools of public policy, and by strengthened select committees, would help to eliminate those policy options which are unlikely to work in practice and to ensure more careful study of the practical operation and effect of those options which have more to recommend them.

This should also have the advantage of raising the level of informed political debate. Policy-making in opposition is not just a matter of finding sophisticated solutions to the problems that are faced by governments; it is also a question of mobilising consent for those policies. Most of the Conservative party's failures of the recent past can be found in this area of political persuasion and education. Conservative politicians in the last fifteen years have failed more as persuaders than as policy innovators. The result has not been conspicuously good for the country.

NOTES

1. In writing this paper, I have drawn extensively on the unpublished work of my predecessor as director of the Conservative Research Department, Mr James Douglas, and have been assisted on the history of the Conservative party and the Research Department by my colleague Mr Geoffrey Block.

2. J. D. Hoffman, *The Conservative Party in Opposition 1945–51* (London: MacGibbon and Kee, 1964).

3. R. M. Punnett, *Front-Bench Opposition* (London: Heinemann, 1973).

4. Studies of British general elections since 1945 carried out by David Butler and associates, e.g. D. Butler and D. Kavanagh, *The British General Election of October 1974* (London: Macmillan, 1975).

5. A. King, 'How the Conservatives Evolve Policies', *New Society*, 20 July 1972, pp. 122–4.
   There are also a number of unpublished monographs on various aspects of policy in the form of higher degree theses deposited at British and American universities, and which deserve more attention than they perhaps get.

6. Lord Butler, *The Art of the Possible* (London: Hamish Hamilton, 1971), especially Chapter 7.

7. John Ramsden's history of the Conservative Research Department, commissioned to mark its 50th birthday in 1979–80, should do much to fill this gap.

8. Lord Fraser was director of the Conservative Research Department from 1951–64, and chairman of the Department from 1970–74. He was deputy chairman of the Conservative party from 1964–75.

9. J. D. Hoffman, op. cit.

10. A. King, op. cit.

11. There is one full-length study of the Research Department in the form of a PhD thesis: Arnold Beichman, *The Conservative Research Department: how an elite subsystem within the British Conservative Party participates in the policy-making process* (Colombia University Thesis, 1973), obtainable from Xerox University Microfilms.

12. R. Rose, *The Problem of Party Government* (London: Macmillan, 1974), p. 186.

13. Lord Butler, op. cit., p. 135.

14. Ibid.

15. Lord Woolton, *Memoirs* (London: Cassell, 1959), p. 347.

16. Lord Butler, op. cit.

17. R. M. Punnett, op. cit., p. 264.

18. Political education involved local study-groups, political education officers in every area, a 'two-way movement of ideas' on pre-determined themes, area and national seminars, and Swinton college courses. All these built up the education movement in the late forties and fifties and did much to transform opinion in the country.

19. D. Butler and M. Pinto-Duschinsky, *The British General Election of 1970* (London: Macmillan, 1971), p. 89.

20. The *Economist*, 15th April 1978, pp. 37–42.

21. A. King, op. cit.

22. Ibid.

23. Quoted in D. Butler and M. Pinto-Duschinsky, op. cit., p. 66.

2 Economic Policy

Andrew Gamble

We were returned to office to change the course of history of this nation—nothing less. It is this course—the new course—which the Government—your Government—is now shaping.

Edward Heath, Conservative Party Conference 1970

We believe that Government knows less about business than businessmen, less about investment than investors, and less about pay bargaining than trade union negotiators and employers. We think we understand the limitations on what a government alone can do. This is surely the beginning of wisdom and common sense.

The Right Approach to the Economy (1977) p. 53

I INTRODUCTION

In framing their economic policy since the war, Conservative leaders have stressed individual responsibility and freedom, opposing the disciplines of the market to the interference of the state, urging reductions in taxation and public expenditure, and fighting the extension of state ownership and state intervention. The most recent expression of these ideas has been the doctrine of the social market economy,[1] pioneered initially by Enoch Powell and the Institute for Economic Affairs, and promulgated since 1974 by the Centre for Policy Studies (founded by Sir Keith Joseph and Margaret Thatcher), the Selsdon Group, and the National Association for Freedom, as well as the leader writers of the *Daily Telegraph* and *The Times*, and economic commentators such as Samuel Brittan and Peter Jay.

The chief impulse behind the spread of social market thinking has been the reaction against the policy of Keynesian demand management[2] and the associated policies of high public expenditure and intervention in the markets for labour and products, which have been pursued by all governments since the war, and with extra effort since 1960. This reaction in turn reflects the growing problems that have beset economic policy-making in Britain in the 1970s; among them, the acceleration of inflation, the rise in unemployment, the commodity price boom, the undermining of the stability of the international monetary system and the difficulty of financing public expenditure. Underlying those symptoms of disorder has been a crisis of profitability which led to the first major recession in the world economy since the war in 1974–5, ending a period of unprecedented expansion. The very Keynesian techniques which, at the height of the boom, had been praised as the means whereby the performance of capitalist economies had been so much improved were now seen to be frail instruments indeed, unable to cope with many of the new problems, particularly inflation. Social market thinking went one stage further, however, in arguing that Keynesian and interventionist policies were not just disarmed in the face of the new slump but were the chief reasons for it.

Four main strands in social market thinking mark it out from the orthodoxy that has ruled economic policy since the war:

(i) Economic management: monetarist ideas replace Keynesian; the control of the money supply becomes the most important target for policy in place of full employment and economic growth. Intervention to fix or control either prices or incomes is ruled out.

(ii) Taxation and public expenditure: levels of both are considered far too high and drastic changes in policy are proposed to permit a reduction to around 25 per cent of GNP in order to create real personal incentives and restore individual responsibility.

(iii) Industrial policies: all forms of intervention in industry— national and regional subsidies, public ownership, price control, support for bankrupt and declining concerns—would be phased out on the grounds that the market is distorted by such policies and that the state is a much less efficient entrepreneur than private firms, and a much less efficient allocator of credit than the City of London.

(iv) Trade unions: the union problem would be dealt with partly by legislation, to withdraw many legal privileges the unions currently enjoy, partly by administrative means to reduce the effectiveness of strikes. In addition, government avoidance of pay policies and return to responsible free collective bargaining would end the 'politicisation' of industrial relations and restore the disciplines of the market in pay determination.

At first glance the doctrine of the social market economy might seem to be only a more radical version of the programmes for government developed by the Conservative party during their last two spells in opposition—the call in 1951 to 'set the people free' and the plans in 1970 for a 'quiet revolution' to 'change the course of history of this nation'. It seems surprising, therefore, that the social market doctrine has created a deep division on economic policy within the leadership, a division which is more than just a matter of emphasis or personal rivalry and can be seen in retrospect to have been developing since 1960.[3] Within the common ideology of the free market there is now a much sharper ideological divide than ever before over the question of how far the party should go in framing its policies in accordance with those beliefs when it is in office. The dispute is not simply over techniques for controlling inflation or restraining the growth of public expenditure; it is about whether the Conservatives can and should govern within the institutional constraints of social democracy, or whether it should seek to alter those constraints by changing the balance of forces on which they ultimately rest. The dispute thus concerns the fundamental question of the role of the Conservative party in British politics and its relation to the state. The 'Tory' wing of the leadership, which is opposed to social market doctrine, argues that the Conservatives have always governed according to circumstances rather than according to principles;[4] they have conceived their political task to be directing the affairs of the state by being flexible and making concessions when circumstances suggested they were necessary or desirable. This Tory view of government is explicitly countered by 'social market' Conservatives who are convinced that such a policy leads to a steady retreat before the advance of collectivism and that what is required is not pragmatism in government but a set of clearly defined principles which can help Conservative ministers resist the short-term pressures they will face in government and reverse the 'ratchet' of socialism.[5]

To understand the forces that shape Conservative economic policy in office and in opposition it is first necessary to grasp why it is that the doctrine of the social market economy, although intellectually highly fashionable, espoused by the party leader and some of her principal lieutenants, and promulgated by numerous groups and institutes, and so much in tune with one of the fundamental strands of the party's ideology, has yet occasioned so much hostility within the party and was resisted by a majority of the shadow cabinet. The question might be put another way. What is there in the experience of government that persistently separates the outlook of the majority of the party leaders from that of many of their supporters and gives the Tory perspective within the party such resilience whatever may be its shortcomings in intellectual coherence? This chapter intends to explore these questions by looking firstly at the context of policy making in government, and secondly at how Conservative economic policy has evolved since 1960.

II THE POLITICAL ECONOMY OF SOCIAL DEMOCRACY

In matters of economic policy the Conservative party was traditionally the party of the national economy and the party of protection, opposed to the doctrines of free trade and economic liberalism.[6] Its leaders were strong defenders of the rights of property but not of the idea of the free market. The party of the land and of the institutions of the state proved itself at times a vigorous champion of particular business interests but its political and ideological links with industry, and particularly finance, remained weak until the 1920s, when it became the umbrella party for the protection of all property in the face of the apparent threat of confiscation posed by the Labour movement. The party's ideological rhetoric at this time became noticeably more liberal in economic terms and the party's financial policy more orthodox, but it did not rule out policies in the 1930s that protected the national economy by reinforcing economic ties with the Empire and restricting domestic competition by encouraging cartels and price agreements.

Conservative economic policy has developed since the war within the limits set by the external relations of the British economy and the organisation of the social democratic state. For more than one hundred years Britain has been dependent upon its political and trading relationships with other territories in the world economy for the food and raw materials necessary to support its specialised industries and urban population. Britain's industrial and commercial superiority permitted the development of an international financial centre in the City of London as well as great export industries. The international perspectives and activities of these interests, now reinforced by the largest group of multinationals outside the United States, have exerted enormous direct and indirect pressures on British governments to maintain and, where they can, increase the openness of the British economy to the free flow of goods and capital. Relinquishing the Empire meant relinquishing also the prospect of any viable alternative to linking British prosperity to the prosperity of the world economy and accepting the severe disciplines of the world market and world division of labour which make cost competitiveness and comparative advantage the criteria for determining the survival of economic activities. The economic rationale for more ambitious protectionist policies which the existence of the Empire provided, as well as the limited protection it gave to British trade and living standards, has been removed. This made the balance of payments a much more direct concern of policy and led to the major policy initiative undertaken by the Conservatives since the war—the application to join the EEC.

Since 1940 the establishment of a social democratic state by the wartime Coalition and the succeeding Labour administration created a significantly different context for internal economic policy. The main changes were firstly the considerable enlargement of the public sector in terms of employment and expenditure and the financial implications of this for levels of taxation; and secondly the acceptance by government of a much greater responsibility for economic outcomes, particularly in four areas: prices, employment, the balance of payments and living standards. The techniques for governments' new role were supplied by Keynesian economics, and the rationale by the size of the existing public sector, but the pressure for it came largely from the long-standing demands of the Labour movement for policies that promoted social justice and economic welfare, demands whose legitimacy were recognised in the New Conservatism that arose under Mr Butler's careful cultivation after 1945.

The social democratic state brought with it a new political economy, in the sense of a new set of constraints, techniques and principles for economic policy, and established an important degree of consensus between the parties on how the economy should be handled, based on the acceptance of a 'mixed economy', the idea of an economy that remained capitalist in ownership and organisation but which contained a large public sector enabling public agencies to oversee and influence its development and realise wider social purposes. Such economic management has been guided by three main objectives. Governments have sought to use Keynesian monetary and fiscal measures to 'fine tune' the level of aggregate demand, so as to minimise fluctuations in output and maintain full employment without inflation, by making investment and expansion profitable. Secondly, governments have accepted an obligation to promote investment in the infrastructure of the economy— particularly in energy and transport and in high technology sectors such as aircraft, and to bear many other costs, such as research and education. Thirdly, governments have accepted the desirability of high levels of government spending to provide welfare for and promote equality between all members of the community and all regions of the economy.

Certain political trends have developed as a result. The state itself has had to be funded increasingly by taxation levied on the great majority of the population (the overall balance of the tax system is slightly regressive,[7] and as the tax has risen so public expenditure has appeared to be directly financed out of wage packets); unions and employers have become involved more and more in the formulation and implementation of economic policy; and the leaderships of the two main parties have become used to competing for the prize of taking office and directing the great administrative apparatus, through a process of competitive bidding for votes and the raising of expectations about government performance that has helped to make the state of the economy the single most important issue in determining how people vote.[8]

These three aspects of the political economy of the social democratic state reflect and are limited by the balance of forces in the major political and economic markets. These forces include the powerful financial sector, independent of the state and industry; an industrial sector split between internationally-oriented, capital-intensive firms and declining heavy and basic industries; a highly efficient capital-intensive agriculture; a unified Labour movement, containing approximately 50 per cent of the labour force, and organised both industrially and politically; and an electoral market lacking major regional, religious, or racial divisions and in which manual workers predominate.

The constraints on economic policy-making may therefore be

summarised in terms of the four main markets that policy makers
have to reckon with and which supply the short-term pressures
which are generally much more powerful than the most pressing of
pressure groups in concentrating the minds of ministers.

	Supply	major conditions for supply	failure to maintain conditions	main sanction
Financial Markets	credit, foreign exchange	stable money values	sterling crisis; public expenditure crisis	withholding of credit
Product Markets	consumer & capital goods	profit-ability	unemploy-ment crisis	cutbacks in output and investment
Labour Markets	labour power	real wages	pay crisis	strikes
Political Markets	votes	standard of living	electoral defeats	withdrawal of support

An economic policy that fails to maintain the confidence and
consent of the agents in each of these markets can swiftly multiply
the pressures for a change of policy. Economic management
becomes a matter of navigating between these rival perils, and
accounts for many of the dramatic conversions and 'U-turns' of
policy which recent British political history displays. The constraints are tight and have grown tighter as external economic
relations have worsened, so that managing to keep the confidence of
all four markets and avoiding a crisis in any one of them is an art no
government since 1960 can claim to have mastered, and explains
the frequency of the attempts to intervene directly in one or more of
these markets so as to smother their pressures and create greater
freedom for the implementation of government policy. In opposition, however, parties are subjected to direct pressures only from
the political market. The tendency has been for each set of leaders to
condemn the form of intervention practised by their opponents, and
promise greater 'freedom'. The serpentine trails left by the

economic policies of the two main parties owe much to the adversary style of British politics and the frequent changes of government.[9]

III MANAGING SOCIAL DEMOCRACY

> Ever since the end of the war the British economy has suffered from stop go . . . I knew there was only one way to create the prosperity which our people rightly demanded . . . That was a faster rate of expansion. So I determined that whatever the immediate problems which inevitably beset a government from time to time during any Parliament, I would not be deflected from that strategy.
>
> Anthony Barber, Conservative Conference, 1973

Once returned to office in 1951 the Conservatives were anxious to demonstrate that setting the people free stopped short of dismantling the social democratic state and that they could govern successfully within its constraints. The government continued the relaxation of controls, reduced public expenditure and taxation by modest amounts, and revived monetary policy as a major instrument of economic management. It was fortunate enough to preside over the surge of prosperity in the 1950s which was part of the great expansion in the world economy, and won two further elections by being identified with it. It was in this period that electoral and trade union expectations about steadily improving living standards were created and the state of the economy became the decisive factor in the electoral popularity of governments.

Conservative priorities in the 1950s were to maintain the strength of sterling by aiming for a balance of payments surplus; to maintain full employment by manipulating aggregate demand; and to satisfy expectations about living standards by adopting a conciliatory approach to pay negotiations. In this way pressures were warded off, the most difficult proving to be keeping the confidence of the financial markets. Though there was a trading surplus on the balance of payments it was frequently insufficient to support the scale of overseas military spending and capital export that was desired by British military, diplomatic, and financial interests, and maintain the position of sterling as an international currency given its weak reserve position.[10] To maintain financial confidence in

sterling the government was forced to deflate the economy periodically to reduce imports and create a temporary balance of
payments surplus at considerable cost to industrial investment and
economic growth. These checks to the growth of output and
productivity made the containment of costs more difficult and
produced the first clashes on pay. They also helped ensure that
although the rise in living standards in the 1950s was faster than at
any time since 1870, it was much slower than the average for
Western Europe.

This awareness of relative economic decline and its long-term
implications caused mounting impatience with the policy of
deflation to protect the balance of payments and the exchange rate,
and produced a marked change of emphasis in the party's economic
policy after their third election victory in 1959, and their third
sterling crisis in 1961. The Conservatives now became the party of
Europe and the party of growth. To remedy the evident shortcomings
of British industrial performance, indicative planning measures
were introduced, institutionalised in bodies like the NEDC, and
aimed at securing agreement between industry, labour, and
government on a strategy for the growth of production and incomes
and the containment of costs. The government also launched major
new public spending plans to modernise the transport system,
hospitals and education, and in 1963 embarked on a reflation of the
economy which was planned to be self-sustaining and which the
government pledged would not be cut short by deflationary
measures to ward off a sterling crisis. Making growth the priority
instead of the balance of payments was made possible firstly by the
political decision to complete the withdrawal from Empire and seek
entry to the EEC, which recognised Britain's reduced status as a
world power and so brought into question the wisdom and
feasibility of maintaining sterling as a reserve currency; and
secondly by the growing pressures that the policy of 'stop-go' was
creating in other markets.[11]

Maudling's belief that Britain could break out of the 'stop-go'
cycle and enjoy its own belated 'economic miracle' was based on a
plan to borrow overseas to cover the temporary deficit which was
expected on the balance of payments and so maintain the expansion
of demand.[12] Whether the policy could have prevented a further
crisis in the financial markets, and how the Conservatives would
have reacted, was never tested because Labour won the election in
1964, inherited the deficit, precipitated the crisis, and were soon

busy sacrificing their own plans for growth to protect the exchange rate.

Though the Conservatives in opposition criticised Labour's interventionist policies which for the most part were continuations of Conservative initiatives, the building of a strong, expanding national economy able to compete within the EEC remained the central priority of their economic policy. But in reaction to Labour's failures to build such an economy, despite the battery of interventionist measures employed, the Conservatives began to stress the need for greater market disciplines, lower public expenditure, more incentives and trade union reform, and launched a detailed policy-making exercise based on their 1965 policy document *Putting Britain Right Ahead*. As a result, the preparation for government between 1964 and 1970 was the most thorough ever undertaken by an opposition in Britain. The 'competition' policy that emerged was certainly liberal in inspiration and devoted to shaking up the British economy by injecting more dynamism, speeding change, and enforcing greater efficiency, particularly through the reform of tax and industrial relations. Heath has sometimes been accused of not being a Conservative at all, and it is true that economic liberalism is a radical rather than a conservative doctrine in its implications for the pace and desirability of social change. But Heath was never an economic liberal like Powell or the later social market Conservatives. His conception of government remained Tory and the purpose behind the competition policy was to find a better set of instruments for forcing unwelcome change on the British economy in the belief that only industrial strength would allow Britain to play a leading political role in the EEC.[13]

Against the background, however, of the tensions, frustrations and failures of the Labour government's policies and the industrial and social turmoil of the late-1960s, the Conservative leadership was subjected to intense pressure from its own supporters and from the increasing number of economic liberals in the party to promise a major change of direction in economic policy that would overturn many of the policies that had not been challenged since the war. This process reached a climax at the Selsdon Park Conference[14] at the beginning of 1970, which was planned to co-ordinate the work of the various policy committees and finalise the details of the competition policy ready for the election. But with the assistance of the Conservative press, and Harold Wilson, the conference was publicised as committing the party to radical policies aimed at restoring order, discipline and individual responsibility in both economy and society by introducing tough new laws against strikers, demonstrators and prospective immigrants, and allowing the free play of market forces in welfare, housing and the distribution of income.

This impression was confirmed by the first two years of the new government which saw so many of the policies discussed in opposition put into practice with a determination that marked a significant rupture with the established policies of the welfare consensus and made the Heath government the only radical government in actions as well as rhetoric since the war-time Coalition. But it is important to grasp the nature of this radicalism in order to understand the reason for the several 'U-turns' in policy in 1972 that were so criticised in the party, particularly after the election defeats in 1974. Such criticisms are often based on the mistaken notion that the Heath government was attempting to establish a social market economy in its first two years of office— reducing public expenditure and taxation, abolishing the agencies and instruments of government intervention in the economy, reforming trade union law, allowing market forces to determine pay and prices—an attempt which was then recklessly abandoned in 1972 because the government 'panicked' in the face of industrial militancy, the steep rise in unemployment, and the fear that inflation would accelerate following the successful miners' strike.[15]

In many respects, however, the government's new course fell far short of a coherent social market strategy, one bent not just on giving a different emphasis to economic policy but on changing the framework that determines which economic policies are politically possible. The purpose of the competition policy, including its Selsdon version, was to give the highest priority to economic growth (despite the manifesto commitment to halting inflation), because it was held that only a rapidly expanding economy could reverse Britain's relative economic decline, overcome the economic failures of the 1960s and defuse the social tensions they were creating. Free market policies were the favoured instrument but were applied selectively to force changes in the attitudes and behaviour which were thought to be obstacles to creating a dynamic and efficient economy. Such economic shock treatment made the quiet revolution a very noisy one, as subsidies were withdrawn from lame ducks, some trade unions were fined, a few trade unionists were jailed and charges imposed on many public services from school milk to museum admissions. Whilst such policies and the manner of their introduction stirred up considerable political and industrial conflict (five states of emergency had to be declared between 1970 and 1974), they did not represent an adherence to social market principles by the Conservative leadership. The priority remained improving the relatively slow rate of growth of the British economy rather than restoring the conditions for a free market economy as the economic liberals conceived them, and implied a particular strategy for handling the pressures from the economic markets.

Like its Conservative predecessor in 1963–4, the Heath government was determined not to permit the balance of payments to obstruct economic growth, although it, too, was inconsistently committed at first to fixed exchange rates. The large balance of payments surplus inherited from Labour, however, defused any immediate pressure from the financial markets. By the time the Conservatives began reflating the economy they had also been forced to float the pound, which removed (briefly) a fundamental obstacle to an expansionist policy.

The government attempted to cope with labour market pressures by reforming trade union law and renouncing a formal incomes policy as it had pledged itself to do in the 1970 manifesto, hoping that the new laws and market pressures would contain wage costs. The Industrial Relations Act,[16] however, was not a credible social market measure and reflected the ambiguity in Conservative party attitudes to trade unions that had existed since the war, the problem of whether Conservative policy should aim at increasing or reducing union power: creating strong, centralised industrial unions which have control over their members and can bargain 'responsibly', trading higher productivity for higher wages; or weak, decentralised unions that are incapable of resisting supply and demand pressures in the labour market, mounting effective strikes and 'coercing' private employers, that is, interfering with managers' freedom to direct production. The 1971 Act contained some clauses, such as outlawing the closed shop, that favoured the latter, but more, such as increasing the power of union officials over shop stewards, which favoured the former. Containing both, the Act helped to unite most sections of the Labour movement against it, failing to achieve its main objectives, increasing industrial conflict in the process, and damaging the prospects for co-operation with the Labour movement when the government actively began to seek it in

1972 for its counter-inflation policy. Governing with rather than against the trade unions had been a fundamental axiom of policy since the war, expressed most clearly in the commitment to full employment. Relaxing the constraint of the trade unions on policy would have required a much more far-reaching measure than the Industrial Relations Act. By February 1974 the Act had been effectively crippled and the Conservative manifesto was promising substantial amendments.

On pay the Conservatives abolished all Labour's incomes policy machinery and professed to rely on market forces and free collective bargaining to control inflation, but quickly encountered the problem of pay determination in the public sector. The attempt to set an example to the private sector and gradually lower pay settlements in the public sector, the 'N minus 1' policy, led to a series of strikes and courts of enquiry which resulted in some victories and some defeats for the government. The explanation, however, of the government's sudden abandonment of this policy and conversion to the need for a statutory incomes policy was not only due to the fear of accelerating inflation following the 1972 miners' strike, [17] but also because ministers had become convinced that, given the priority of raising the rate of growth, the best means of containing rising costs in the labour markets was a formal prices and incomes policy.

In the product markets, government policy was aimed, firstly, at reducing public expenditure so as to permit large tax reductions that would restore the incentives for risk-taking and effort; secondly, at withdrawing most subsidies and other forms of government interference to force industry to solve its own problems and become more efficient and competitive (and more eager to resist excessive pay claims). The overriding aim was to restore profitability, boost investment and so pave the way for a rapid expansion of output and productivity. The outcome in both cases, however, fell short of a social market policy, and both were reversed in the face of the pressures they generated.

Barber's package of measures in October 1970 followed a familiar Conservative logic by reducing the planned *rate* of growth of public expenditure (though by less than 1 per cent), and cutting direct taxes. In subsequent years direct taxes were reduced further, particularly on high incomes, and major tax reforms were introduced, (like VAT) or foreshadowed (like the tax credit scheme). After 1971, however, public expenditure was expanded again to play its part in the growth strategy. At no time were changes in policy contemplated of the kind advocated by Enoch Powell before the election in his 'Morecambe budget',[18] which alone could have provided the scope for really substantial cuts in direct taxation. The tax incentives that were provided after 1971 were not financed by cuts in public expenditure but by an increase in the budget deficit designed to help expand the economy, and more effort went into reforming taxes than into reducing them. In the face of the sluggish response of industry to the quiet revolution, the government came to consider that boosting the demand for the products of industry by maintaining and increasing public expenditure was more important in encouraging growth than boosting individual incentives by cutting public expenditure further.

A similar pattern was evident in industrial policy. The policy of withdrawing subsidies from 'lame ducks' was selective and ambiguous from the start, as was apparent when John Davies tried to explain it at the 1970 Conference:

> I believe that simply to abandon great sectors of our productive community at their moment of maximum weakness would be folly indeed . . . But I will not bolster up or bail out companies where I can see no end to the process of propping them up.[19]

The government made no move to end the public funding of major technological projects in aerospace and heavy engineering like Concorde, nor did it try to sell off or break up those industries already publicly owned, apart from hiving off profitable subsidiaries which made little difference to the monopoly status of these industries or the constraint they placed on government policy in the fields of pay and finance. Apart from the well-publicised decisions like the refusal of further aid to Upper Clyde Shipbuilders in 1971, the new policy made little progress in raising investment to the levels required for the growth strategy, so when the government decided to meet what it took to be a rising trend of unemployment in 1971–2 by reflating the economy, it also revised its industrial policies and began providing large sums for firms in difficulties and for firms that would expand in regions where unemployment was high. These policies seemed more sure of success than the ones they replaced, and the 1972 Industry Act, whilst not re-establishing the Industrial Reorganisation Corporation, gave new and far-reaching powers of intervention to the Secretary of State for Industry, powers which were to prove sufficient for most of the subsequent interventionist forays undertaken by Labour. The Conservatives had decided that a close partnership between state and industry was necessary to raise the rate of growth, and except in the field of finance, they did not shrink from equipping the state with the powers of intervention they thought necessary.

Pressures from the economic markets thus prevented the new government from wandering too far from social democratic orthodoxy and prompted in 1972 the adoption of a more familiar set of policies for achieving growth. The apparent 'U-turns'—the reversal of the industrial policy, the increases in public spending, the counter-inflation policy—were dictated by the change of emphasis in the growth strategy, and have been criticised as betrayals of the 1970 Manifesto, but the aspect of policy which attracted least criticism (at the time, although most since), was the handling of the money supply.

It is a curious feature of post-war economic policy that the Conservatives have generally proved far more financially irresponsible than Labour, which may reflect the greater political necessity for the Conservatives to preside over an expanding economy, and the greater fear Labour ministers have of the financial markets. Social market Conservatives now argue that the acceleration of inflation to 26 per cent in 1974/5 was directly caused by the monetary expansion of 1972/3. The government and most observers were only dimly aware of the scale of this monetary growth,[20] and Keynesian theory held in any case that the growth in the money supply was less important than the growth in the economy it might stimulate. The Barber boom was in many respects a re-run of the Maudling plan of 1963/4. Heath had inherited Macmillan's political perspective that Britain's full participation in the EEC was necessary and desirable, that the shortcomings in British economic performance had to be remedied to make this possible, and that the Conservative party could not afford to be identified electorally with a negative deflationary policy but must actively encourage faster rates of economic growth, if necessary by using state agencies to prod private capital into more efficient and ambitious levels of production. In 1972/3 the Heath government showed it was prepared to risk inflation in order to achieve growth, but it believed in any case that the upward spiral of costs and prices could be controlled in the short term by the counter-inflation policy and that if the policy of reflation succeeded in raising profitability, investment and output, the increase in demand would not prove inflationary in the long run.[21]

This belief was never tested because although a 5 per cent growth rate was achieved in 1973 and the counter-inflation policy proved very successful in its first two stages, the whole policy suffered spectacular shipwreck at the end of 1973 with the quadrupling of oil prices (the final phase of the great commodity price boom) with its implications for the balance of payments, already in severe deficit, and by the eruption of a pay crisis caused by the miners' refusal to settle within the Stage Three guidelines which led to the dramatic decision to put industry on a three-day week and the holding of an early general election. This failure and the subsequent onset of recession in the world economy was greatly to discredit Keynesian demand management as a means for maintaining prosperity and speeding growth, and led to inflation becoming for the first time since the war the major priority of government policy. But it is also important to remember that the monetary boom and the subsequent inflation would have been much smaller if the increase in public spending and the reduction of interest rates to stimulate industrial investment had not sparked off an explosion of bank lending, the proliferation of secondary banks and an unprecedented boom in property values and other non-industrial investment—which was made possible by the adoption in 1971 of *Competition and Credit Control*—a new freedom for the banking system much applauded by economic liberals and monetarists at the time. This was one aspect of the new course which could well have done with a 'U-turn', but none was forthcoming.[22]

IV THE SEARCH FOR THE RIGHT APPROACH

The highest national interest, overtopping all others in the economic sphere, is honest money—money that holds its value. Growth, full employment, expanding public services—all these are worth nothing unless that first and great condition is fulfilled.
Enoch Powell, Conservative Party Conference, 1973.

After 1974 the Conservatives found themselves once more in opposition facing a serious task of rebuilding their electoral support and restoring the confidence of their party rank and file, encumbered by a record in government which had certainly not enhanced the party's reputation as the party that could best handle national affairs. A major debate began on economic policy and the party's aims since the war and, following the change of the leadership in 1975 and the removal of some of Heath's closest supporters from the shadow cabinet,[23] the impression was given that a major break with previous Conservative policy was contemplated and that a future Conservative government would be committed to the establishment of a social market economy. But although the social market Conservatives filled the major economic ministries after the election, and Mrs Thatcher's speeches in opposition gave the party's economic policy a more thorough-going liberal image, social market doctrine has remained a minority viewpoint in the leadership as a whole. The 'Tory' majority in the leadership has fought back with such success that if an election had been held in October 1978 the Conservatives would have fought it on a programme less radical in several important respects than its programme in 1970.

The two main policy documents, *The Right Approach* and *The Right Approach to the Economy*, are fairly vague, consensual documents which commit the party to extremely little in detail and keep all policy options open. It is a technique known in the party as 'positive ambiguity'.[24] The main change that can be observed is that the party leadership as a whole has become very much less ambitious. In the new world economic climate managing the economy means managing the recession and, like the government, the Conservative party has made the control of inflation its central priority. As *The Right Approach to the Economy* puts it: 'If the management of money is handled wrongly everything goes wrong'.[25] The document lists a number of guidelines for policy, among them:

a. The provision of 'a more stable economic climate';
b. strict control of the rate of growth of money supply;
c. 'firm management' of government expenditure, (the idea being that it should drop as a percentage of GNP each year);
d. lower taxes (a number of specific proposals are made, involving a further switch from the principle of pay as you earn to pay as you spend);
e. the removal of 'unnecessary restrictions' on business expansion;
f. the encouragement of 'better methods of collective bargaining' (but legislation explicitly ruled out) and

g. the education of the public about the 'inescapable financial constraints'.[26]

Amidst these vague and hardly radical proposals the main sign of the influence of social market doctrine is the attempt to signal a phased withdrawal of government from the responsibility it hitherto accepted for economic outcomes. The monetarist ideal of the neutral policy stance is a restatement of pre-war financial orthodoxy. The government's job is envisaged once again as enforcing the laws on property and contract and maintaining the value of the currency, creating a framework in which whether the economy grows or not depends on decisions of individual workers, consumers, savers and employers, and whether unemployment is high or not depends on the real wage trade unions insist on.

Relinquishing responsibility for what happens in the economy, however, does not immediately bring relief from the pressures which the economic and political markets continually generate. Monetary restraint and monetarist logic can easily produce a spiral of deflation and industrial unrest of the kind experienced by the French government in 1979. The Tory wing of the leadership seems well aware of this, and on the evidence of the policy statements issued in 1976 and 1977 it seems unlikely that a future Conservative government will go through a phase of refusing to bail out companies on the grounds of social market principles, or suddenly to cease support for the large number of companies, including British Leyland, [27] that are currently receiving state aid. The result will be less than a social market economy, though it may well produce a stagnant market economy, since the commitment on inflation will rule out a major new expansionist policy.

Such cautious policies may well offer the best hope of holding the party together in government. The social market faction would be satisfied that the government was not pursuing interventionist policies, imposing statutory controls on incomes and prices, or increasing public expenditure. The Tory faction would welcome both the pragmatic response to specific problems faced by firms and regions, and also the maintenance of high levels of public spending and public involvement. Whether it will prove viable in a wider political sense is more doubtful. The policy of monetary targets will reassure the City of London and keep sterling strong; the CBI will welcome a reduction in some kinds of government intervention. But the central question which has dominated British economic policy since 1960—how to reverse the relative decline—will not be resolved. Since it is the inability of successive British governments to improve the poor performance of the national economy that caused the substantial loss of support for the two main parties in 1974 and the increasing readiness of voters to change their party, any party that returns to government without an effective policy for national revival is likely to find its support hard to maintain.[28]

Within the social market group in the leadership two views on decline may be seen. There are those like John Biffen who support social market policies on libertarian grounds and who advocate them whether or not they assist a revival of British national economic fortunes and Conservative political fortunes (though they believe they can do both).[29] But there are many others like Keith Joseph who believe social market policies to be the only means for national economic recovery. They see the social market policy as far more than just a déflationary, defensive policy, imposed by the economic failures of recent governments and the unfavourable world economy. It is rather an ambitious attempt to change the balance of political forces, preventing governments from using the public sector to manage the economy, in order to restore the foundations for expansion and prosperity.

The key policy associated with the social market group is monetarism, but as the Labour government showed between 1976 and 1979, monetarism as a technique can be employed to reassure the financial markets without making any fundamental changes or abandoning budget deficits, incomes policies, or industrial strategies. The social market persuasion in the party has, to some extent, been sheltering behind monetarism in the past few years, often giving the impression that monetarism offers a painless way of managing the economy and avoiding the kind of crisis in the labour markets over pay which incomes policies have regularly provoked in their later stages. Until the events of the winter of 1978/79 the Conservatives were strong supporters of 'responsible' collective bargaining.[30] The only reason offered as to why it should be responsible was contained in the proposal for a national economic forum which would spread 'understanding' about the economic facts of life.

Monetary guidelines can indeed only be the beginning for a social market policy. What would also be needed are policies that reduce the pressures governments face in their management of the economy—in the markets for products, for labour, and for votes.[31]

One priority would therefore be a major and irreversible dismantling of the public sector—the phasing out of all subsidies and interventionist agencies including the NEB and BNOC (both reprieved in the party's latest plans), the repeal of the 1972 Industry Act, a commitment to denationalisation and major changes in the financing of major services like road construction and health to shift them out of the public sector altogether. Only in this way can the mixed economy be unmixed and the size of public sector employment and expenditure, and hence the resulting pressure for the government to intervene to control pay and prices and to promote economic growth, be significantly reduced, and the opportunity for tax changes created on a scale that would make a noticeable difference to net incomes.

In isolation, however, a policy that dismantled the institutional reasons for government intervention might only intensify the slump that monetary policies were already creating. So the second priority would be to reduce trade union 'monopoly' power in the labour markets so as to restore the opportunity for profitable investment throughout industry to compensate for losing the cushioning of profits by government subsidies and the management of demand. Any social market policy that did not attempt to transform the labour market would merely be inviting deflation and stagnation, not a promising platform for Conservatives on which to appeal for support, however adept at it Labour governments may have become. From the social market perspective the problem of union power was set out very clearly by Enoch Powell in the 1960s when he argued[32] that the 'private coercion' of the trade unions rested on three legal privileges: the freedom to intimidate (peaceful picketing), the freedom to impose costs on others with impunity and the immunity of trade unions from action of tort. These legal privileges, he claimed, were enhanced by the closed shop but not caused by it. From this viewpoint trade unions have no economic merits and impose severe economic costs on a capitalist economy—overmanning, restrictions on productivity and the distortion of pay relativities. To redress the balance, measures to curb the ability to strike have been canvassed.[33] As Sir Keith Joseph has declared on many occasions, 'Monetarism is not enough', and where it most obviously is not enough is in its ability to reduce the power of organised labour.

V CONCLUSION

The theme of this chapter has been that all Conservatives since the war have drawn on the liberal ideology of individual responsibility and the free market to differentiate their economic policy from that of their opponents by identifying themselves as the party of lower taxes, reduced public expenditure and less government intervention. Nevertheless they have accepted the political economy of postwar social democracy—Keynesian demand management, to promote full employment and rising living standards, and high public spending on welfare. Such a stance has guaranteed the party regular spells in office, but it has failed to produce policies that could stem the accumulation of problems arising from the relatively poor performance of the British economy. Two distinct responses have emerged in the party in the last twenty years to this dilemma. The party under Macmillan, Home and Heath committed itself to the EEC and a strategy of growth and a readiness to use the spending, administrative and legal powers of the state as levers to create the right framework for expansion, when market policies appeared to be failing. This policy meant trying to solve the problems of the social democratic state within the institutional constraints of that state—that is, without challenging fundamentally the size of the public sector, the bargaining strength of the unions, or the expectations of the electorate. The social market approach of Powell and Joseph by contrast seeks to restore the foundations of a market economy—a 'flexible' labour market, the rule of law, minimal government (with a consequent reduction in electoral expectations), monetary disciplines, low taxes and low public expenditure. The best chance of achieving such an economy was in the 1950s when internal and external conditions were most propitious, but the government at that time was preoccupied with protecting sterling and Britain's world role, showing it could avoid conflict with the unions and maintain high levels of public spending. Social market medicine may now seem too harsh for the patient, but the social market case is that no other medicine will effect a cure.

Both positions lay claim to the Conservative tradition of One Nation and the Middle Way because both are seeking a viable political strategy for the party, an economic policy that will win support for the defence of capitalist institutions. Any such policy must in a representative democratic state seek co-operation between capital and labour, but whereas Tories believe this is best secured through the state, using public agencies where necessary to remedy deficiencies and injustices in the private sector, social market Conservatives believe it can only be achieved through the market by winning popular support for its operation. The progress of the dispute is to some extent obscured because under Margaret Thatcher the party has often identified itself with populist responses to economic issues—the burden of taxation, the inefficiency of bureaucracy and nationalised industries, the abuses of welfare, the injustices of pay policy and, in 1979, the power of the unions, and may in the process have raised expectations about what a Conservative government can achieve that the party will find difficult to fulfil with its stated policies, particularly as it inherited a sizeable budget deficit (unlike 1970) and is pledged to increase defence spending (unlike 1951). Amidst the smoke and turmoil of its early days, it will be surprising if, in the end, the new administration does not become another exercise in Tory government which will disappoint many of the hopes that have been raised, shorn as it will be of the ambitious programme of national revival proposed by either Peter Walker[34], or Keith Joseph. But the reality of relative economic decline remains, ameliorated but not averted by income from oil in the North Sea and overseas investments, and it is by its ability or good fortune in halting it that the economic policy of the Conservative government will be judged, and on which the political future of the Conservative party may come to rest.

NOTES

1. Social market thinking may be sampled by looking at the publications of the Institute for Economic Affairs and the Centre for Policy Studies; especially, *Why Britain needs a Social Market Economy* (London: CPS, 1975); S. Brittan, *Government and the Market Economy* (London: IEA, 1971); Sir Keith Joseph, *Reversing the Trend* (London: CPS, 1975); Sir Keith Joseph, *Stranded on the Middle Ground* (London: CPS, 1976); J. E. Powell, *Freedom and Reality* (London: Batsford, 1969). The theoretical underpinnings for the doctrine can be found in the writings of F. A. Hayek and Milton Friedman.

2. The theoretical principles and practical consequences of Keynesian demand management can be found in the following: A. Shonfield, *Modern Capitalism* (London: Oxford University Press, 1965); M. Stewart, *Keynes and After* (London: Penguin Books, 1972); and S. Brittan, *Steering the Economy* (London: Penguin Books, 1971).

3. For recent accounts of this split see T. Russel, *The Tory Party* (London: Penguin Books, 1978) and T. E. Utley, 'The Significance of Mrs Thatcher' in M. Cowling (ed.) *Conservative Essays* (London: Cassell, 1978).

4. I. Gilmour, *Inside Right* (London: Hutchinson, 1977).

5. *Inter alia*, Sir Keith Joseph, *Reversing the Trend*, and R. Boyson, *Centre Forward* (London: Temple Smith, 1978).

6. The best account of protectionism in the Conservative party before 1914 is contained in B. Semmel, *Imperialism and Social Reform* (London: Allen & Unwin, 1960).

7. F. Field *et al.*, *To Him Who Hath* (London: Penguin, 1977).

8. D. Butler & D. Stokes, *Political Change in Britain* (London: Macmillan, 1974) ch. 18.

9. M. Stewart, *The Jekyll and Hyde Years* (London: Dent, 1977).

10. S. Strange, *Sterling and British Policy* (London: Oxford University Press, 1971).

11. Particularly the rising unemployment which peaked at 878,000 in February 1963, and the battles over the government's Pay Pause.

12. For Maudling's own account as well as some interesting memoranda by him on incomes policy see his *Memoirs* (London: Sidwick & Jackson, 1978).

13. See the important account of the formulation of the new policies and their implementation by B. Sewill, the former head of the Conservative Research Dept., 'In Place of Strikes' in R. Harris (ed.) *British economic policy 1970–74* (London: IEA, 1975).

14. D. Butler & M. Pinto-Duschinsky, *The British General Election of 1970* (London: Macmillan, 1971) ch. 6.

15. A point of view presented by R. Harris 'A Self-Confessed Monetarist . . . ?' in Harris, op. cit. For an assessment of the meagre size of the tax cuts see P. Hutber, *The Decline and Fall of the Middle Classes* (London: Penguin Books, 1977) ch. 5.

16. The provisions and the passage of the Act are described by M. Moran, *The Politics of Industrial Relations* (London: Macmillan, 1977). See also C. Crouch, *Class conflict and the Industrial Relations Crisis* (London: Heinemann, 1977).

17. S. Brittan, *The Economic Consequences of Democracy* (London: Temple Smith, 1977) ch. 7.

18. E. Powell, *Income Tax at 4/3 in the £* (London: Stacey, 1970).

19. J. Davies, quoted in *Notes on Current Politics*, no. 15, Conservative Research Dept. (1970) p. 334.

20. Indeed, Anthony Barber claimed at the party conference in 1973 that the M1 measure of money supply was under tight control. For a discussion of both sides of the question see Harris, op. cit. In 1972 M1 rose 14 per cent and M3 28 per cent; in 1973 M1 rose 7 per cent and M3 29 per cent.

21. See Barber's speech at the party conference, October 1973. The scale and structure of the boom can be seen from the following figures cited in M. Stewart (1977) op. cit.

1971–3 (constant prices)	
consumers expenditure	+ 11 per cent
public consumption	+ 8 per cent
GDP	+ 7 per cent
investment	+ 5 per cent
imports	+ 27 per cent
exports	+ 14 per cent

22. Until the secondary bank collapse in 1974 after the Conservatives had left office. Bank lending to the private sector rose by 48 per cent in 1972 and 43 per cent in 1973.

23. See the account by R. Behrens, *The Conservative Party in Opposition 1974–1977*, Department of Applied Social Studies, Lanchester Polytechnic, Coventry (1977).

24. Peter Jay began his review of *The Right Approach* in the *Times*, headed 'All Things to all Tories', as follows: 'The spectacle of a political party coming down resoundingly on both sides of an issue, more particularly when a sharp fence divides the rival points of view, can be distressing or hilarious according to one's sensibilities' (7 October 1976).

25. *The Right Approach to the Economy* (London: Conservative Central Office, 1977) p. 14.

26. Ibid., p. 7.

27. Although 50 Conservative MPs voted against the granting of further subsidies to British Leyland in 1975. In an unpublished paper 'The Price for Conservatism: the Conservative party and the economy since 1974', delivered to the PSA Contemporary British Politics Workshop in January 1978, Michael Moran concludes that there are few differences of substance between the policies the Conservatives followed in government and the policies they have become committed to in opposition.

28. In 1970 the Conservatives lost popularity faster than any government since the war, and the parliament saw major shifts of electoral opinion to third parties.

29. See J. Biffen, *Political Office or Political Power?* (London: CPS, 1977).

30. See the two policy documents and the Conference debates on industrial relations and economic policy in 1976 and 1977.

31. Despite the hostility of the social market wing to electoral reform it may prove that only after the adversary two-party system has been reformed will a sustained, long-term experiment with social market policies become possible.

32. E. Powell, *Freedom and Reality*, op. cit., ch. 10.

33. The general problems which the public sector and union power create for a social market strategy have been recognised by Sir Keith Joseph in two important speeches. *Monetarism is Not Enough* (London: CPS, 1976), and *Solving the Union Problem is The Key to Britain's Recovery* (London: CPS, 1979). During the winter of 1978/79 the Conservative party moved towards a new commitment to introduce legislation on industrial relations, concentrating on picketing, the closed shop and welfare benefits for strikers. But any proposals seemed likely to fall far short of the concentrated assault on the right and the ability to strike thought necessary by many economic liberals.

34. Peter Walker's views are contained in *The Ascent of Britain* (London: Sidgwick & Jackson, 1977). He is a modern representative of the Chamberlain tradition within the party.

3 Immigration

Zig Layton-Henry

I INTRODUCTION

At the end of the Second World War the Conservative party still regarded the Empire and the Commonwealth as the supreme achievement of the British people and as the most successful experiment in international relations that the world has ever known.[1] Many Conservatives felt that Britain's role in the world as a great power depended in large measure upon the Empire which was still an institution worth preserving, and both the Empire and Commonwealth had contributed mightily to the war effort. One of the major factors maintaining the unity of Empire and Commonwealth, and especially the links with Britain, was the common citizenship and allegiance that all British subjects owed to the Crown. While many of the King's subjects were also British by birth or descent, the vast majority were neither born in Britain nor did they have any family ties with the mother country, but they were all British subjects.

In 1948 the Labour government introduced a British Nationality Bill. This was partly in response to the Canadian Citizenship Act of 1946 and partly in anticipation of similar legislation being enacted in newly independent Commonwealth countries, notably India. The Nationality Act divided British citizens into two classes: citizens of independent Commonwealth countries, and the remainder who were classified as citizens of the United Kingdom and Colonies. The bill was opposed by the Conservative opposition who felt it was unnecessary and that by giving primacy to local citizenship the derivative British nationality would gradually decline in importance and eventually lapse altogether thus weakening the unity of the Commonwealth.

Sir David Maxwell-Fyfe, who led Conservative opposition to the bill, was also concerned lest its provisions might be used to discriminate against Commonwealth citizens. He argued that there would be no point in these new categories unless to drop the idea of the common status and our proud boast of the open door. 'We are proud,' he stated, 'that we impose no colour bar restrictions making it difficult for them when they come here'.[2] The opposition was so concerned with the implications of the bill that they reserved the right to revert to the old common citizenship if this should be the wish of the other Dominions and member states of the Commonwealth.

It was a considerable source of pride among many Conservatives that a British subject from any part of the Empire (and Commonwealth), no matter what his colour or creed, could come to the mother country, serve in the armed forces or public service, stand for parliament, and enjoy the same rights and obligations as any other British citizen. *Civis Britannicus sum* was not an empty phrase but a statement of considerable substance, part of the ideology which legitimised British rule in the Empire. 'In a world in which restrictions on personal movement and immigration have increased we still take pride in the fact that a man can say *civis Britannicus sum* whatever his colour may be, and we take pride in the fact that he wants and can come to the Mother Country.'[3]

It is worth emphasising the importance of Britain's imperial past not only because it was the legacy of common citizenship which facilitated migration from the West Indies and South Asia to Britain but also because it contributed substantially to the reluctance of Conservative governments to initiate immigration controls before 1962. Many Conservative ministers, members of parliament and leading party officers had served in the Empire or had relatives who had done so, for example as governors, administrators or soldiers. Many more had relatives who had emigrated to the Old Dominions or parts of Africa. These Conservatives were reluctant to allow any weakening of imperial ties, including both the granting of independence to the colonies and the weakening of the obligations of the mother country.

The Conservative party was therefore committed to common citizenship for all British subjects in the Empire and Commonwealth, and to complete freedom of migration between Britain and the Empire. 'There must be freedom of movement among its members within the British Empire and Commonwealth. New opportunities will present themselves not only in the countries overseas but in the Mother Country and must be open to all citizens.'[4] It was assumed that the movement of population was likely to continue to be an outflow from Britain to the older Dominions and to the climatically suitable parts of Africa but it was emphasised that a welcome should be extended to all those who came from the Dominions and colonies to live and work in Britain.

After the war, the government found that the economy was being seriously held back by an acute shortage of labour. A number of schemes were initiated by the government to resolve the problem, such as the Polish Resettlement Act and the European Voluntary Workers Scheme, but these did little to meet the crisis. When traditional migration to the Old Dominions resumed, the government became seriously concerned. This was the situation facing the Conservatives who assumed office in 1951. However, by then the migration from the West Indies had begun, encouraged both by the availability of work in Britain and, after 1952, by the blocking of traditional West Indian migration to the United States due to the passing by Congress of the McCarran-Walter Immigration Act. At this time there were no readily available sources of labour in Europe, apart from Eire, as the expanding European economies were absorbing millions of workers from eastern Europe and southern Italy.

The practical implications of migration from the West Indies were raised in the House of Commons at the very start of the migration by a Labour member, James Harrison. He was concerned at the problems of accommodation and integration that the new immigrants on the SS Windrush, which docked in June 1948, would face. He even raised the possibility of the need to control such immigration. However, his concern went unheeded and almost unnoticed. Gradually immigration from the West Indies grew as the early migrants quickly found employment in the expanding British economy. It was shortly followed by immigration from India and Pakistan.

The reaction to the immigration of black and brown Commonwealth citizens was initially subdued. Certain industries welcomed them eagerly due to the serious problems of obtaining skilled and unskilled labour. In 1956 the London Transport Executive established liaison with the Barbados Immigrant Service so that migrants would have a job waiting as soon as they arrived. The most serious initial problems of helping the immigrants fell on the local authorities and few additional resources were made

TABLE 3.1 Estimated net immigration from the New Commonwealth 1953–62[5]

	West Indies	India	Pakistan	Others	Total
1953	2,000	–	–	–	2,000
1954	11,000	–	–	–	11,000
1955	27,500	5,800	1,850	7,500	42,650
1956	29,800	5,600	2,050	9,350	46,800
1957	23,000	6,600	5,200	7,600	42,400
1958	15,000	6,200	4,700	3,950	29,850
1959	16,400	2,950	850	1,400	21,600
1960	49,650	5,900	2,500	−350	57,700
1961	66,300	23,750	25,100	21,250	136,400
1962 (First 6 months)	31,800	19,050	25,080	18,970	94,900

available to those local authorities with special problems caused by the concentration of immigrant settlement in particular areas.

II THE CAMPAIGN AGAINST IMMIGRATION

A campaign against coloured immigration from the new Commonwealth was initiated early in the period of migration by Cyril Osborne, Conservative MP for Louth. His campaign was conducted largely in the House of Commons and the press. In the period 1952–7 Osborne's campaign had little success. His questions in the House on disease and crime among immigrants received little consideration from Sir Anthony Eden, Harold Macmillan and the other ministers who had to deal with them.[6] Frequently, in reply, ministers paid tribute to the contribution of West Indian nurses to the hospital service and other West Indians to public transport. The cabinet gave every appearance of being determined not to interfere with the free movement of Commonwealth citizens.

The ministers in charge of Commonwealth relations and the colonies tended to be strongly opposed to control and there were important reasons for this. The progress of the West Indian colonies towards independence was proving difficult as the British government attempted to create and sustain the ill-fated Federation of the West Indies. There were also the complicated negotiations which preceded the granting of independence to the colonies in east and central Africa. The imposition of immigration controls, it was felt, would make relations with Commonwealth countries and colonial governments much more difficult and jeopardise the transition from Empire to Commonwealth.

Surprisingly, Harold Macmillan reveals in his memoirs that the problem of coloured immigration was brought to the attention of the cabinet in 1954 and that early in 1955, after some rather desultory discussions, it was agreed that a bill should be tentatively drafted. 'I remember,' he writes, 'that Churchill, rather maliciously, observed that perhaps the cry of "Keep Britain White" might be a good slogan for the election which we should soon have to fight without the benefit of his leadership'.[7] Macmillan notes that the matter was shelved and no action was taken until the racial disturbances in Nottingham and Notting Hill brought the issue forcibly to public attention. However, this incident suggests that many members of the cabinet shared popular concern about coloured immigration and were not in principle opposed to the introduction of controls. It was not, however, a high priority.

Pressures on the cabinet continued to increase. Some local authorities were lobbying the government for help in housing, educating and integrating the immigrants. After 1955 Cyril Osborne was joined in his campaign by Norman Pannell (Kirkdale) and Martin Lindsey (Solihull), and the number of questions and adjournment motions demanding control increased. Opposition to coloured immigration was also gaining support among the Conservative rank and file. In 1955 the Central Council passed a resolution, by a small majority, proposing that the laws against aliens should be applied against Commonwealth citizens and at the party conference in October there were five resolutions demanding health checks on immigrants. Gradually resolutions on immigration favouring control appeared on the agendas of annual party conferences.[8]

The campaign for control gained considerable impetus in the latter half of 1958. The racial attacks in Nottingham and Notting Hill in August and September dramatically publicised the problems of integration and growing public hostility to continuing coloured immigration. In October Sir Alec Douglas Home, Minister of State for Commonwealth Relations, speaking in Vancouver, said that 'curbs will have to be put on the unrestricted flow of immigrants from the West Indies'.[9] Later that same month the Conservative party conference, despite Butler's opposition, passed a resolution favouring immigration control.

Cyril Osborne immediately stepped up his campaign, raising the issue in the debate on the Queen's speech and again in a private member's motion on 5 December, but David Renton, replying for the government, stated that this country was proud to be the centre of an inter-racial Commonwealth, and denied that there was any need for control.[10] However, the *Economist* reported that in many government departments the view was that controls could not be long postponed.[11]

Immigration was not an issue in the general election of 1959, except in one or two local contests like North Kensington where Sir Oswald Mosley stood as the candidate of his own Union Movement. Mosley came bottom of the poll and lost his deposit despite a well-publicised campaign. However, the general election had greatly strengthened the position of those favouring control in the House of Commons, as a strong contingent of Birmingham MPs who favoured immigration control was returned.[12]

Despite the growth in pressure for control, the government remained reluctant to take action. Most ministers still regarded the Commonwealth as a major asset to British standing and diplomacy in the world although doubts as to the value to Britain of the new Commonwealth members had grown after India's strong condemnation of British action over Suez in 1956. The civil service was also divided as the treasury could see strong economic reasons for supporting free entry while other home departments favoured control. In the cabinet Boyle and Macleod were the leading opponents of control and the cabinet appeared unwilling to override their opposition. In July 1960 Butler told the House that 'It is very unlikely that this country will turn away from her traditional policy of free entry'.[13]

In October no provision was made for a debate on immigration at the annual party conference, although there were seven resolutions sent in from constituency associations. On 13 October the Birmingham Immigration Control Association was established and this strengthened the position of those Birmingham MPs who were pressing for control. In December and again in January Harold Gurden organised a series of meetings of backbench MPs to discuss control and lobby the Home Secretary. In February Butler told Gurden he was prepared to consider controls but there was still no agreement in cabinet on the need for positive action and David Renton, again replying to a private member's bill introduced by Cyril Osborne, told the House that the government refused to contemplate legislation which might restrict the historic right of every British subject regardless of race or colour, freely to enter and stay in the United Kingdom.[14]

However, by the summer it was clear that the numbers of immigrants entering Britain had risen dramatically, partly in response to the growing campaign in Britain to restrict entry, and popular concern was reflected in the lobbying of MPs, the resolutions to the Conservative annual conference, and in the opinion polls. In May 1961 the Gallup Poll found 73 per cent in favour of control (6 per cent wanted a total ban on all immigration) and 21 per cent in favour of free entry, with 6 per cent undecided.[15] There were 39 resolutions at the annual conference demanding control, and while Butler made no positive commitment to introduce a bill in reply to the debate, the strength of feeling at the conference and the dramatic rise in numbers convinced the cabinet that action was urgently needed. A bill was hurriedly prepared, the decision to legislate was announced in the Queen's speech on 31 October and the bill was published the following day.

Since control had been considered by the cabinet as early as 1954 and as the Home Office had been asked to prepare legislation in 1955, it is remarkable that the bill presented in 1962 was so rushed and poorly prepared. The government felt the legislation would command general support and were amazed by the opposition the bill received from the Labour and Liberal parties and in the press. Macmillan and Butler were shocked by Gaitskell's furious on-slaught on the bill and found it difficult to counter his arguments. Gaitskell argued that immigration was self-regulating and that the substantial increase in immigration had been caused by the wholly artificial conditions created by the growing campaign to introduce controls. Gaitskell also exploited the ambiguities in the bill and the mishandling of the Irish provisions by Macmillan. Despite this opposition to the bill there is no doubt that it commanded widespread support among the electorate.

The conversion of the Conservative party from free entry for all Commonwealth citizens thus coincided with the decline of Britain from a great power with world-wide territories and commitments to a European power which was making more and more insistent attempts to join the EEC, of which full membership was finally achieved on 1 January 1973. Some Conservatives who still believed in the importance of the Empire and of its successor, the Commonwealth, were reluctant to see any weakening of

Commonwealth unity which might result from legislation against Commonwealth citizens. Lady Huggins, the wife of a former governor of Jamaica, gave expression to this view when she said, 'The increase in West Indian immigration in recent years has created domestic difficulties in this country. But what is the Commonwealth worth? Is domestic difficulty here an adequate reason for abandoning the whole concept of the Commonwealth? If we are not prepared to pay that price we shall imperil our whole colonial policy and our whole Commonwealth ideal.'[16] The commitment to the Commonwealth made many of these Conservatives opposed to moves to join the EEC. However, during the 1960s these Conservatives had become increasingly disillusioned with the Commonwealth as the new Commonwealth members refused to show the loyalty and support which Britain had received in the past from the Old Dominions. The Suez crisis in 1956, when Britain was strongly condemned by India in the United Nations for the invasion, and the withdrawal of South Africa from the Commonwealth in 1961 were two important factors contributing to this disillusionment.

Conservatives on the progressive wing of the party had also opposed immigration controls but for rather different reasons from those who wished to maintain imperial traditions. They favoured the transformation of the Empire into the Commonwealth and hoped that a multi-racial Commonwealth would be an important influence in the world and give Britain greater moral authority in world councils. They were opposed to controls because they suggested racial discrimination and colour prejudice. Those Conservatives who most strongly supported controls appeared to be the self-made Conservatives, small businessmen and working-class Conservatives with popular authoritarian views, who belonged to the 'radical right' of the party. These Conservatives were stronger in the constituencies and the electorate than in parliament or the executive committee of the National Union. In parliament their views were supported by MPs usually representing constituencies with substantial numbers of working-class Conservatives, often in areas 'threatened' by an influx of immigrants. The newly-elected MPs for Birmingham could be said to represent this section of the party.

The major factors contributing to the change in Conservative policy were firstly the growing feeling among many ministers that increasing racial tension could only be avoided if controls were introduced. The substantial increase in coloured immigration after

1959 raised more acutely the problems facing local authorities but it was the possible reaction of the indigenous population against coloured immigration, if immigration remained uncontrolled, which concerned members of the government. Secondly, the pressure for control was building up strongly in the National Union to such an extent that party leaders felt concessions had to be made. Thirdly, it also appeared that electorally such legislation would be very popular and although the party leadership was reluctant to make much of this it clearly was an important consideration.

The Commonwealth Immigration Act of 1962 does not seem to have allayed public concern for long. In September 1963 the Southall Residents Association was formed to protest against the increasing numbers of Indians settling in the borough and the growing proportion of immigrant children in Southall schools. In the 1964 general election campaign, immigration control was not an issue in the national campaigns of the parties, although Sir Alec Douglas Home, one of the early converts to control in the cabinet, raised the issue in speeches at Bradford and Birmingham, claiming credit for excluding a million coloured immigrants who would have come to Britain but for the Act.[17] The dramatic importance of the election was, of course, the impact of Peter Griffiths' victory at Smethwick after an anti-immigrant campaign. Griffiths captured the seat with a 7.5 per cent swing to the Conservatives in the face of a national swing of 3.2 per cent to Labour. The Labour party's cautious move away from Gaitskell's total opposition to controls was accelerated by the Smethwick result and completed by Gordon Walker's further defeat at Leyton, where race was thought to be an unspoken issue.[18] The Labour party's about-turn on this issue was dramatic. In less than three years the Labour party had moved from furious opposition to any controls, to acceptance of controls and by 1965 to proposing even tougher controls. Moreover, the Conservatives were criticised for introducing weak and ineffective controls and some Labour candidates were reported to be blaming them for allowing coloured immigration to occur at all![19]

The explanation for Labour's change was largely the fear of electoral disaster. Crossman has argued in his Diaries that 'ever since the Smethwick election it has been quite clear that immigration can be the greatest potential vote loser for the Labour party' and 'We felt we had to out-trump the Tories by doing what they would have done and so transforming their policy into a bipartisan policy'.[20] The smallness of Labour's majority and the likelihood of an early election made Labour leaders determined to remove race as an issue dividing the parties. Labour MPs were also coming under increasing pressure from their own constituents and party members to support immigration control.

There were also signs that the Conservative party, having accepted the need for control, would propose tougher and more effective measures. This was the implication of Sir Alec's speech in Hampstead on 3 February and also of his replacement of Edward Boyle by Peter Thorneycroft as party spokesman on race and immigration, later in the month. Edward Boyle no longer represented party opinion on immigration control and his replacement was probably precipitated by Cyril Osborne's success in the ballot for private members bills—the second consecutive time! Osborne, continuing his campaign as vigorously as ever, announced yet another bill to control immigration, proposing to ban all immigrants except those whose parents or grandparents were born in the United Kingdom. Such a bill would have been anathema to Edward Boyle. Thorneycroft persuaded Osborne to modify the provisions of his bill which was then supported by Sir Alec and many members of the shadow cabinet. On 6 March, shortly after his bill had been defeated by 99 votes, the Central Council passed a resolution in support of further legislation to control immigration. The motion had the support of the shadow cabinet.[21] Cyril Osborne must have felt that his long campaign had finally triumphed in the party!

Since 1962 the Conservative party has adopted a dual approach to the problems of immigration and race relations. The first part of this approach has been an emphasis on firm controls to limit the entry of new immigrants and the conditions under which they were allowed to enter. The second part of the policy was a commitment to positive steps to 'fit into our country those immigrants already here who wish to remain'. 'We are determined', said Sir Alec, 'that every immigrant who comes here is treated like any other British citizen'.[22] However, the Conservative party has given most priority to the first part of the dual policy and tended to ignore the second. The pressures within the party and policy preferences of the electorate have contributed to this bias. Perhaps a prime reason has been the continuing campaign of those opposed to coloured immigration which has increased rather than subsided as tougher controls have been introduced and has also found an oratorical champion in the person of Enoch Powell.

III THE RE-ESTABLISHMENT OF CONSENSUS

This dual approach to immigration and race relations was also adopted by the Labour party. However, Labour appeared to place more emphasis on both sides of the policy equation. The Labour government came to office committed to a Race Relations Bill to outlaw racial discrimination and this was published in April 1965. However, this more even-handed approach went together with a determination not to be outbid by Conservative calls for tougher controls on immigration and a bipartisan policy on immigration and race relations appears to have been established by the end of March. The Commons debate on race and immigration, which was held on 25 March, saw a great deal of unanimity in the speeches on both sides of the House and much self-congratulation on the bipartisanship shown in the debate. The government reaffirmed its commitment to effective control of immigration.

Labour's commitment to the bipartisan approach was endorsed by the white paper entitled 'Immigration from the Commonwealth' published in August, which reduced the quotas of vouchers in a period of acute labour shortage, and strengthened deportation provisions.[23] It confirmed that further substantial immigration from the new Commonwealth was over. Further evidence of the government's determination to remove immigration and race relations as an issue dividing the parties occurred in the autumn when the Race Relations Bill was passed after the government had accepted Conservative proposals to substitute conciliation for criminal sanctions. It was clear that the Labour government was more concerned to impress public opinion with its tough policies on immigration control than it was to outlaw racial discrimination and support those bodies it had created to promote good race relations, like the National Council for Commonwealth Immigrants and the Race Relations Board.

The success of Labour's policy can be seen in the general election of 1966 when Conservative claims that the Labour party had adopted their policies were endorsed by the electorate, at least to the extent that 61 per cent could see no appreciable difference between the parties on the issue.[24] The fact that immigration played such a small part in the general election was also due to Mr Heath's insistence that the issue should not be exploited by Conservative parliamentary candidates. The recapture of Smethwick and other seats where racism was thought to have played a role in the previous general election caused considerable relief and a widespread feeling that the exploitation of race had been eliminated as an election-winning issue.

IV ENOCH POWELL'S CAMPAIGN

Before the general election of 1964 Enoch Powell does not appear to have been active in attacking Commonwealth immigration. As a minister he defended government policy and when Cyril Osborne approached him in 1958 to support his campaign he refused.[25] After rejoining the government in 1960 he became a firm advocate of control within the cabinet but he did not break collective cabinet responsibility and campaign publicly. In the House of Commons, as Minister of Health, he paid tribute to the work of overseas doctors in British hospitals. It was not until the series of anonymous articles in *The Times* in April 1964 that Powell was to state categorically his disenchantment with the Commonwealth and his opposition to coloured immigration.[26] From 1964 Powell gradually developed his campaign which was to become a major challenge to the party leadership.

The bipartisan approach continued after the election although some Conservatives were concerned at the Home Secretary's plans to extend the Race Relations Act and introduce further anti-discrimination legislation. However, by 1968 immigration and race relations had once again become central issues in British politics. In February, after a campaign by Duncan Sandys and Enoch Powell, the government rushed through legislation restricting the entry of British Asians from Kenya. Although the opposition did not formally oppose the bill, many Conservatives were outraged at the betrayal of promises made by a previous Conservative administration and every previous Colonial Office minister in both Houses, except Sandys, opposed the legislation.[27] Iain Macleod strongly attacked Sandys' campaign as it was Sandys himself who had been instrumental in providing the loophole for non-African Kenyans to retain British citizenship; although the main aim of the arrangement was to safeguard the position of white settlers who might not wish to remain under an African government, it was realised and accepted that the commitment extended to the Asian community as well.[28]

The Conservative opposition was also deeply divided on how to react to the Race Relations Bill which was published by the government at the beginning of April. The bill had enthusiastic supporters on the progressive wing of the party, including some support in the shadow cabinet, but the bulk of party opinion on the back benches and in the constituencies was opposed to the bill. The compromise which was agreed—a reasoned amendment approving the principles of the bill but deploring the measures themselves—was a victory for the anti-immigration Conservatives and a defeat for the liberal progressives, one of whom resigned from the party in protest.[29]

It was in the middle of these deep emotional divisions within the party that Powell made his apocalyptical speech on immigration and race relations which so outraged his colleagues in the shadow cabinet. Heath's immediate dismissal of Powell prevented the disintegration of the shadow cabinet but the enormous publicity that Powell's speech obtained and the widespread popular support it evoked made Powell a major political figure overnight and even a threat to the leader. The popular support for Powell could be measured in the polls, the deluge of letters he received, and the public demonstrations of support. It was clear that Powell's views and Powell himself commanded much wider support in the constituency associations and among the electorate than they did on the Conservative benches in the House of Commons. He had become a factor that the party leader could not ignore. Powell's speech tapped the widespread popular frustration with the bipartisan approach to immigration and race relations which had existed since 1965. There was dissatisfaction with the anti-discrimination legislation which many people did not understand or support. Some felt it gave coloured immigrants a privileged position. Moreover, the growing support for the Monday Club suggested there might be an organised section within the Conservative party which could turn to Powell for leadership.

There was substantial evidence to suggest that Powell's views had considerable support within the party and this was confirmed by the agenda for the annual party conference which included 80 resolutions on immigration and race relations, most of which demanded further controls. In September Mr Heath announced that Commonwealth immigrants should only enter Britain under the same conditions as aliens and that dependants would also be subject to controls. Even this was not enough for Powell who argued at the conference that immigration control was not enough, and he had considerable support, as the official Conservative policy was only narrowly endorsed. He spelt out his views in more detail at Eastbourne in November when he emphasised the importance of re-emigration or repatriation. In January 1969 Mr Heath called for legislation to prevent further settlement by Commonwealth immigrants so that new immigrants would not automatically have the right to bring their dependants with them. This speech anticipated the Conservative government's immigration bill of 1971 and represented the complete abandonment of the ideal of Commonwealth citizenship. Henceforth the citizens of independent Commonwealth countries, unless they were patrials, would be treated as aliens. This was a far cry from the common citizenship which the party had supported twenty years earlier.

The pressures within the party, which had forced the leadership to abandon Commonwealth citizenship and impose tighter and tighter controls, had been considerable. Nevertheless the policies which Mr Heath proposed in 1969 appeared to contradict the fundamental beliefs of many prominent Conservatives, like Lord Hailsham. Every compromise was not enough to satisfy the 'radical right' of the party who felt they had widespread support both within the party and among the electorate. The reasoned amendment to the 1968 Race Relations Bill, which had been adopted to appease the right wing, was not sufficient to prevent 45 Conservative MPs voting against the bill on the third reading. The support for Powell and his views among constituency associations was so substantial that the shadow cabinet made concessions again and again.[30]

V THE GENERAL ELECTION OF 1970

The party leaders did not exploit the race issue in the general election despite the fact that opinion polls suggested that the Conservative move towards tougher controls was preferred by most electors and that the issue was considered to be the fourth most important in the campaign. Only 26 per cent of Conservative candidates mentioned immigration in their election addresses and only 2 per cent of Labour candidates.[31] The reticence on the Conservative side was largely due to central disapproval of using the issue. Crossman even suggested there was a tacit understanding by the party leaders not to raise the issue in the campaign.[32] The

Conservative manifesto reflected Mr Heath's more recent policy statements. It reaffirmed the commitment to existing Commonwealth immigrants that they could bring in their wives and young children but confirmed Conservative intentions to end further large-scale immigration by ensuring that work permits in the future would not carry the right of permanent settlement for the holder or his dependants and that they would normally only be issued for twelve months.

The most extraordinary feature of the 1970 election campaign was the role of Mr Powell who, though a Conservative candidate, acted as though he were a political force in his own right. His election address, issued early in the campaign, was treated by the press as a manifesto and on the issues of immigration and the Common Market was a direct challenge to the party leadership. It was widely believed that if the Tories lost the election Mr Powell would attempt to gain the leadership for himself. Powell's impact was increased by the virulent attack on him by Wedgwood Benn and in the closing stages of the campaign by Mr Powell's dramatic accusations that there were traitors in the civil service who were concealing from a worried public the true extent of coloured immigration. Mr Heath refused to disown Powell as a Conservative candidate and contented himself with saying that 'I will never use words or support actions which exploit or intensify divisions within our society'.[33] The violence of the language used by Mr Benn against Powell distracted attention from the Conservative leader's embarrassment with his maverick colleague. Powell realised that he would have no chance of serving in a Conservative administration if Mr Heath won the election, but perhaps hoping to succeed the Conservative leader after the likely defeat, he called on his supporters to vote Conservative.

The unexpected Conservative victory enormously strengthened Mr Heath's position in the party and led to Powell's increasing isolation and finally his departure to the Ulster Unionists. However, his role and impact on the result of the election remains difficult to assess. Initial analyses concentrated on Powell's role in mobilising the immigrant vote for Labour and contributing to their substantially higher turnout than in previous general elections.[34] However, the very high swings to the Conservative party in parts of the West Midlands suggested that Mr Powell's campaign had an important local effect in Birmingham and parts of the Black Country. In constituencies in Birmingham with substantial numbers of immigrant voters the effect was beneficial to the Labour party but in other constituencies there were some dramatic swings to the Conservatives, although not consistently in seats where Mr Powell's supporters were candidates.[35] It is extremely difficult to assess the national impact of Mr Powell's campaign. Certainly after his 'rivers of blood' speech in April 1968 the opinion polls showed that the public perceived the Conservative party as being much more restrictive in their immigration policies than the Labour party and these policies were preferred by most of the electorate. One recent analysis of the 1970 election suggests that the national impact of the immigration issue was very substantial and made a considerable contribution to the Conservative victory, but the author admits there may have been other factors contributing to this result.[36]

VI THE CONSERVATIVE GOVERNMENT 1970–4

The new Conservative administration proceeded to fulfil its policy commitments by introducing the Immigration Act of 1971, which came into force on 1 January 1973. The main provisions of the bill were that employment vouchers would be replaced by work permits which would not carry the right of permanent residence or the right of entry for dependants; secondly, that patrials, that is, people with close connections with the United Kingdom through birth or descent, would be free from all controls. There were also provisions to strengthen the powers to prevent illegal immigration and finally voluntary repatriation was to receive some financial assistance. This legislation appeared to fulfil the Conservative manifesto promise that 'there will be no further large-scale permanent immigration'.

The hope that this legislation would defuse the race issue was brutally shattered on 4 August when General Amin, the President of Uganda, announced the expulsion of Asians from his country. The Ugandan Asian crisis, which received considerable publicity in the press, was a boon to the anti-immigrant organisations within the Conservative party and on the far right. The Monday Club, which had a growing membership and was very hostile to many of Mr Heath's policies, started a 'Halt Immigration Now' campaign and the National Front, exploiting the issue for all it was worth, began a period of growth and electoral advance that continued until 1976. There was considerable lobbying of Conservative MPs by their associations and constituents but the government remained firm and insisted that British commitments should be honoured. The majority of the Ugandan Asians were admitted to Britain although substantial numbers were accepted by India, Canada and other countries.

At the annual party conference in October immigration was not chosen for debate but a resolution on this issue from Hackney South and Shoreditch was placed on the agenda by ballot; it was to be moved by the president of the association, Mr Enoch Powell. Fortunately for the party leaders, the Young Conservatives and Conservative students—who are allowed generous representation at party conferences—determined to mobilise the progressives in the party to defend the government's actions. David Hunt, chairman of the Young Conservatives, moved an amendment to Powell's motion 'congratulating the government on its swift action to accept responsibility for the Asian refugees from Uganda'. The amended motion was carried by a substantial majority.[37] It was a rare victory for progressive Conservatism. However, the defeat infuriated some Conservatives who felt that the Young Conservatives had fixed the result.[38]

Meanwhile there appeared to be increasing cooperation between members of the Monday Club and the National Front, and it appeared that in some cases this was due to National Front infiltration of Club branches. At the Monday Club rally on 16 September in the Central Hall, Westminster, there was ample evidence of National Front participation. At the Uxbridge by-election in December the West Middlesex branch of the Monday Club was dissolved for endorsing the National Front candidate. There also appeared to be support by members of the Club for the anti-Common Market candidate at the Sutton and Cheam by-election.[39] These activities discredited the Monday Club as an influential group within the Conservative party and most of its prominent members quickly resigned. The Club then became increasingly involved in an internal struggle over the leadership which was to leave it a spent force by 1974.

VII DEVELOPMENTS SINCE 1974

Immigration and race relations were overwhelmed by other issues in the general elections of 1974. In February the constitutional crisis between the government and the miners, the three-day week and the defection of Enoch Powell focused public attention on constitutional and economic issues. However, in the analyses of the results the growing importance of Asian and West Indian voters became apparent to both the major parties and this led to a reappraisal of party policy towards these minorities. There had already been requests from constituency associations with significant numbers of immigrant voters for help from Central Office and suggestions from prominent immigrants for the Conservative party to make more positive efforts to appeal to and recruit Asians and West Indians. These factors led to the establishment of an ethnic minorities unit in Central Office. The establishment of the Anglo-Asian and Anglo-West Indian Conservative Societies were early initiatives of the new unit. The Conservative party thus appeared to be moving towards a more positive approach. There were now too many Asian and West Indian voters for the party to ignore and leave to Labour by default.

However, in February 1976 the arrival of Asians from Malawi raised the salience of the immigration issue once more and inspired many of the 140 resolutions on the issue which appeared on the agenda of the annual party conference. Both Mr Whitelaw's speech to the conference and the section on immigration in *The Right Approach* suggested a further hardening of Conservative party policy in order to reduce immigration which had 'increased by a very substantial amount under this government'.[40] Mr Whitelaw did go out of his way to emphasise the commitment of the party to equality of treatment for all immigrants now settled here but argued that a harmonious and multi-racial society could only be promoted if a policy were followed, which was clearly designed to work towards an end of immigration as we have seen it in the post-war years.[41]

In the autumn the Conservative party's policies on immigration and race relations became increasingly confused. On immigration control the party was committed to even tougher policies than those envisaged in the 1971 Act and also to a tighter definition of UK citizenship. On race relations, which had before 1976 been a matter of empty rhetoric, the party appeared to be moving in a positive direction. The decision by the shadow cabinet not to oppose the Race Relations Act (1976), which greatly strengthened previous legislation, suggested that the party leadership wished to support efforts to encourage harmonious race relations and oppose incitement to racial hatred. Mr Whitelaw also gave strong support to the

Federation of Conservative Students' campaign against racialism which was launched in November 1977. However, the efforts to involve the Conservative party in the Joint Committee Against Racialism led to confusion and embarrassment for the party, especially the unprecedented decision by the executive committee of the National Union to overrule Mrs Thatcher and participate against her wishes. It suggested that there was a serious division within the party on the extent to which it should be identified with public campaigns against racialism in cooperation with other political groups.

The controversy over the leaks concerning the Speed proposals and Mrs Thatcher's subsequent statements on immigration have emphasised the divisions within the party and the problems facing party leaders in developing a coherent policy. Mrs Thatcher was clearly under pressure from members of the shadow cabinet, backbenchers and constituency associations who wished her to commit the party to end coloured immigration as quickly as possible and also to exploit the issue for electoral advantage. She was clearly tempted to follow this strategy. However, there were others in the shadow cabinet, in Central Office, and in parliament, who would have preferred priority to be given to solving the problems of racial integration and especially unemployment among coloured youth which they saw as major future sources of division and conflict within society.[42] Many Conservative MPs would welcome a more positive approach as they are aware of the growing numbers of their constituents who are of Asian or West Indian ethnic origin. It is uncertain, at the present time, how these conflicting pressures will be resolved.

VIII CONCLUSION

The contention by some observers that public hostility to immigration has been created by party politicians in order to achieve electoral advantage is hard to sustain.[43] Certainly some politicians were opposed to coloured immigration almost from its beginning and attempted to mobilise support against it. However, these politicians carried little weight in the highest councils of the Conservative party and had little support among the general body of MPs. Their efforts to influence party policy were unsuccessful for a number of years. The government was more concerned with maintaining a strong economy at home, which would have been held back by an acute shortage of labour without immigration; and it was also determined to create a multi-racial Commonwealth to ease the process of decolonialisation and mitigate the effects of imperial decline.

The government was supported in this policy by two currents of opinion in the Conservative party. Many Conservatives on the right of the party still felt, in the 1950s, that the Empire was an important expression of Britain's greatness and believed, paternalistically, that the mother country had the duty to protect and support, as well as exploit, the various parts of the Empire. While many Conservatives in this tradition were reluctant to accept the 'wind of change' and independence for the colonies, some of them saw the Commonwealth as a continuation of the Empire through which British influence could be maintained. Part of their belief was the ideal of common citizenship throughout the Empire (and Commonwealth)—*civis Britannicus sum*—and to many of these Conservatives the obligations of the mother country outweighed the problems created in Britain by the arrival of relatively small numbers of Commonwealth immigrants. This view was also held by the ministers in charge of the colonies and Commonwealth relations. If the Commonwealth were to be a success, Britain should be seen to take the lead in maintaining Commonwealth ties and obligations. During the early period of migration the immigrants were from colonies in the West Indies and not from independent Commonwealth countries, so legislation barring them from entry would have been unthinkable.

It was only during the 1960s that it became clear that the relationship between Britain and the Old Dominions could not be sustained with the new Commonwealth countries. The Suez crisis, the withdrawal of South Africa from the Commonwealth and the collapse of the Central African Federation showed that the vision of maintaining a dominant role for Britain through the Commonwealth could not be maintained as new Commonwealth countries became the largest group in the Commonwealth. It became clear that many new Commonwealth countries felt they had more in common with the newly independent countries of the Third World than with their old imperial power, and in fact were anxious to prove their independence by criticising British policy. By the middle-sixties many imperial Conservatives were reconciling themselves to a Britain which was increasingly a European power and not a world power. They increasingly came to favour strict immigration controls.

The second body of opinion in the party which opposed immigration controls can be described as liberal progressive. The Conservatives associated with this tradition had a different vision of the Commonwealth from those influenced by the imperial tradition. They supported independence for the colonies as progressive and inevitable and felt that the colonies would only become responsible nations if they were given responsibility. This was also the best way for Britain to maintain good relations with her former colonies. They saw the Commonwealth as a multi-racial forum in a world in danger of serious divisions between rich, white nations and poor, black or brown nations. They were therefore opposed to immigration controls which they saw as racialist and as a danger to their ideal of a multi-racial Commonwealth. Many of them also realised the valuable contribution immigration was making to the British economy and standard of living.

Those Conservatives who campaigned for immigration controls and who were eventually successful in determining party policy belonged to a tradition that was narrowly chauvinistic, and which saw immigration as an invasion of foreigners entering the country and taking the jobs, housing and welfare benefits which belonged to British citizens. They were in the same tradition as those who had opposed Jewish immigration at the turn of the century. They would agree with Powell in his view that 'The West Indian or Asian does not, by being born in England, become an Englishman. In law he is a United Kingdom citizen by birth; in fact he is a West Indian or Asian still'.[44] Cyril Osborne, Norman Pannel and Peter Griffiths represented this view in the Conservative party.

The campaign by Osborne and Pannel initially had very little support in parliament where their efforts to obtain immigration controls met with constant rebuffs. Macmillan's revelations show, however, that their views had more support in the cabinet than was publicly admitted. It was the racial clashes in 1958 which gave considerable impetus to the campaign for control and this campaign stimulated immigration, which added fuel to the campaign. After 1959 the small group of MPs promoting the campaign in parliament were supported by considerable numbers of activists in local Conservative parties and growing support in the opinion polls. The growing campaign in the party and the rise in immigration figures caused the party leaders to introduce the first bill to control

Commonwealth immigration in 1961. Since then the level of immigration control and its administration have become political issues of some electoral importance and the Conservative party has led the way towards accepting populist demands to end coloured immigration as far as possible. The Conservative party has justified the policy of strict controls on the grounds that these are needed to preserve racial harmony and to encourage integration within Britain. But the party has not developed a positive strategy to foster integration or eliminated the discrimination from which the members of the new ethnic minorities suffer. The one advantage Commonwealth immigrants have compared with immigrants from the EEC or southern Europe is that they are British citizens and their growing electoral importance may encourage the Conservative party to develop a more positive approach to the problems facing Britons belonging to the new ethnic minorities.

NOTES

1. *Imperial Policy* (Conservative and Unionist Central Office [CUCO], June 1949) p. 1.
2. *Hansard*, 453, col. 405 (7 July 1948). N. Deakin, 'The British Nationality Act of 1948', *Race* (July 1969) p. 81.
3. Henry Hopkinson, Minister of State for the Colonies, *Hansard*, 532, col. 827 (5 November 1954).
4. *The Right Road for Britain* (CUCO, July 1949) p. 58.
5. House of Commons Library Research Paper no. 56, *Commonwealth Immigration into the UK from the 1950s to 1975—a survey of statistical sources*.
6. e.g. *Hansard*, 563, col. 392 (24 January 1957).
7. H. Macmillan, *At the End of the Day* (Macmillan, 1973) p. 73.
8. The number of resolutions demanding immigration control 1957–61 were:

1957	– 3	1960	– 7
1958	– 6	1961	– 39

Agendas and Reports of Conservative Party Conferences 1957–61 (CUCO).
9. P. Foot, *Immigration and Race in Britain Politics* (Harmondsworth: Penguin Books, 1965) pp. 154–5.
10. *Hansard*, 596, col. 1579–80 (5 December 1958). Also cited in Ira Katznelson, *Black Men, White Cities* (Oxford, 1973) p. 127.
11. The *Economist* (29 November 1958).
12. Among newly-elected members who supported control were Leonard Seymour (Yardley), Leslie Cleaver (Sparkbrook), John Hollingsworth (All Saints). Other MPs who supported control were Harold Gurden (Selly Oak), Geoffrey Lloyd (Sutton Coldfield), Martin Lindsey (Solihull), Edith Pitt

(Edgbaston). Two Birmingham MPs strongly opposed to controls were Sir Edward Boyle (Handsworth), Aubrey Jones (Hall Green).

13. *Hansard*, 626, col. 689 (7 July 1960).
14. *Hansard*, 634, col. 2009–19 (17 February 1961).
15. H. Macmillan, op. cit., p. 73.
16. Lady Molly Huggins, 28 April 1959, cited in P. Foot, *The Rise of Enoch Powell* (Cornmarket, 1969) p. 155.
17. D. Butler and A. King, *The British General Election of 1964* (London: Macmillan, 1965) p. 363.
18. L. A. Teear, *Colour and Immigration in British Politics*, M.A. Thesis (unpublished), University of Sussex (1966).
19. P. Foot, *Immigration and Race*, op. cit., pp. 180–1.
20. R. Crossman, *Diaries of a Cabinet Minister* (Hamish Hamilton and Jonathan Cape, 1975) p. 149.
21. P. Foot, *Immigration and Race*, op. cit., pp. 150–2.
22. *The Campaign Guide 1966* (CUCO, 1966) p. 245.
23. *Immigration from the Commonwealth*, Cmnd. 2739 (HMSO 1965).
24. D. Studlar, 'Policy Voting in Britain: The Coloured Immigration Issue in the 1964, 1966 and 1970 General Elections', *American Political Science Review*, 72 (1978) pp. 46–64.
25. P. Foot, *Enoch Powell*, op. cit., p. 35.
26. *The Times*, 1, 2, 3 April. There appears to be wide agreement that the author was Powell. See Foot, *Enoch Powell*, op. cit., p. 29.
27. N. Fisher, *Iain Macleod* (Andre Deutsch, 1973) p. 296.
28. Iain Macleod, 'A Shameful and Unnecessary Act', *Spectator*, 1 March 1963.
29. R. R. James, *Ambitions and Realities, British Politics 1964–70* (Weidenfeld and Nicolson, 1972), part III, p. 180. H. Berkeley, *Crossing the Floor* (London: Allen & Unwin, 1972) pp. 36–7.
30. M. Walker, *The National Front* (Glasgow: Fontana, 1977) p. 111. In December 1968 the Conservative Political Centre conducted a survey to establish the views of their 412 constituency groups. 327 wanted all immigration stopped indefinitely and a further 55 wanted strictly limited quotas of dependants combined with a five-year halt on immigration.
31. D. Butler, M. Pinto-Duschinsky, *The British General Election of 1970* (Macmillan, 1971), pp. 439–40.
32. N. Deakin, J. Bourne, 'Powell, the Minorities and the 1970 Election', *Political Quarterly*, 41 (1970) pp. 399–415.
33. D. Butler, M. Pinto-Duschinsky, op. cit., p. 163.
34. Ibid.
35. Z. Layton-Henry, 'Race, Electoral Strategy and the Major Parties', *Parliamentary Affairs*, XXXI, 3, (1978) pp. 268–81.
36. D. Studlar, op. cit.
37. Conservative Party Conference Report 1972.
38. Interview with Anthony Reed-Herbert, who resigned from the Conservative party after this conference and joined the National Front.
39. M. Walker, op. cit., Ch. 5. D. Humphrey and M. Ward, *Passports and Politics* (Harmondsworth: Penguin Books, 1974), pp. 129–31.
40. *The Right Approach* (CUCO, 1976), pp. 47–8.
41. Conservative Party Conference Report (1976) pp. 40–7.

42. e.g. P. Walker, 'Race the Real Divide', *Guardian*, 4 February 1978; 'The Road of the Crowd', *Spectator*, 15 April 1978.
43. P. Foot, *Immigration and Race*, op. cit., pp. 233–4.
44. Speech to the London Rotary Club, Eastbourne, 16 November 1968.

Appendixes

1   Net immigration to UK from the New Commonwealth and Pakistan 1962–77[a]

1962 (2nd half)	16,453	1970	37,893
1963	56,071	1971	44,261
1964	52,840	1972	68,519
1965	53,887	1973	32,247
1966	48,104	1974	42,531
1967	60,633	1975	53,265
1968	60,620	1976	55,013
1969	44,503	1977	44,155

NOTE
[a] Control of Immigration statistics 1977, Cmnd. 7160 (HMSO 1978).

2   Resolutions to the Conservative Party Conference on immigration and race relations

1957	3	1968	80
1958	6	1969	31
1959	a	1970	19
1960	7	1971	30
1961	40	1972	30
1962	1	1973	54
1963	2	1974	a
1964	a	1975	17
1965	31	1976	140
1966	5	1977	60
1967	0	1978	31

[a] This indicates no conference.

4 Devolution

Vernon Bogdanor

> Never have the servants of the state looked at the whole of your complicated interests in one connected view. They have taken things by bits and scraps, some at one time and one pretence, and some at another, just as they pressed, without any sort of regard to their relations or dependencies.
>
> (Burke: Speech on American Taxation)

I INTRODUCTION—TORY ATTITUDES

The Conservative party is once again the Unionist party in Scotland. Yet its defence of the Scottish Union has not been marked by that unswerving consistency which characterised the struggle against Irish Home Rule before the First World War. In 1950, Winston Churchill flirted with the Scottish nationalists; and in 1968, Edward Heath promised devolution in opposition only to ignore it in office. It took the Conservatives fully ten years from the time of the SNP challenge to become unambiguous Scottish Unionists. This uncertainty of touch can be traced back not only to a basic lack of awareness of Scottish conditions by a predominantly English leadership, but also to the failure to articulate clearly a principle of dispersal of power which ought to be fundamental to Conservatives.

For devolution poses two fundamental questions: the first is whether national unity is best secured by centralised government, or by distributing power between the centre and the component parts of a country; and the second is whether the recognition of a sense of nationality in one of the component parts of a country is compatible with the maintenance of the state itself. These questions, however, are not to be answered by *a priori* reasoning but through a consideration of the circumstances surrounding particular claims.

The Conservative party became Unionist not to defend the 1707 settlement with Scotland which was, after all, a triumph of Whig statesmanship, and therefore not an object of Tory veneration, but to defend Pitt's Union with Ireland. The difference between Tory attitudes to the Union with Scotland and the Union with Ireland can be ascribed surely to factors of national psychology, to the attraction or dislike which the English feel for the other component nations of the United Kingdom. For political attitudes towards these nations have always been indelibly coloured by cultural images; and the Conservative party has always been better disposed to the claims of Scotland than to the demands of Parnell or De Valera. In this, Conservatives were doing no more than reflecting wider English cultural attitudes, for what killed Irish Home Rule in the nineteenth century was less the force of constitutional argument than anti-Irish and anti-Roman Catholic prejudice—'the Anglo-Saxon stereotype of the Irish Celt'[1]—who has always occupied a peculiarly disreputable position in the catalogue of English demonology.

About the Irish Nationalist movement, Conservatives had no doubts—Irish Home Rule was 'repulsive to them because they regard it as the triumph of a movement deeply tainted with Jacobinism'.[2] They could not, therefore, accept Gladstone's contention that Home Rule was itself a policy of conservative character, based upon securing a community of interest between an Irish upper class led by Parnell and the rulers of the Empire. For Conservatives, the Parnellites were men motivated by a deep-rooted antagonism to England, and that antagonism could be assuaged only by separation.

But Scottish nationalism could not be disposed of so easily. For the Scots were not as hostile to the English connection as the Irish seemed to be, and after the failure of the '45, most Scots were willing to accept the Union. But this acceptance was conditional upon the preservation of Scottish institutions, and Scottish Tories, in particular, saw themselves as guardians of the sense of Scottish identity which these institutions sustained. In Scotland it was the Tories who were the nationalists:

For the Tory noble houses and the landed gentry, with their memories of the role their ancestors had played on the stage of history when Scotland was a Stewart Kingdom, it was a matter of family pride to exalt the past, to cling to tradition, to seek to save what remained of Scottish ways of life and speech from the insidious pressure of English influence. It was the Whigs the Hanoverians, the party led by the professional middle class who were the anglicisers, the assimilationists in Scotland.[3]

If the Union was an accomplished fact, a solid part of the established order, and therefore sanctified for the Conservative by history, how much older were the national traditions of Scotland which could at any time be endangered by the insensitivity of London politicians. Contemplating the Union, Sir Walter Scott, 'the outstanding example of what Scottish nationalism meant both in its depth of feeling and in its practical good sense',[4] found welling up within him a 'mixture of feelings which I do not attempt to describe'.[5] In 1808, after a debate in which he had fiercely opposed alterations in the procedure of the Scottish judicial system, his companions began to joke about it:

'No, no' cried Scott, ' 'tis no laughing matter; little by little, whatever your wishes may be, you will destroy and undermine until nothing of what makes Scotland Scotland shall remain'. And so saying, he turned round to conceal his agitation—but not until Mr Jeffrey saw tears gushing down his cheek.[6]

Conservatives then could respect the feelings which animated Scottish nationalism, and they were therefore able to support reforms designed to decentralise administration in Scotland. The creation of the office of Secretary for Scotland in 1885 resulted from a bipartisan policy; the first holder of the post, the Duke of Richmond, was a Conservative; and under Conservative administrations, the holder of the office was made a Secretary of State in 1926 and the Scottish Office was moved to Edinburgh in 1939.

But clearly the Conservative party could not support a policy of Home Rule for Scotland at a time when the *raison d'être* of the Unionist coalition created in 1886 was opposition to Irish Home Rule; and so until the Second World War, Scottish nationalism appeared to be a left-wing cause. The first secretary of the Scottish Home Rule Association established in May 1886—the date is significant in relation to Gladstone's espousal of Irish Home Rule— was Ramsay MacDonald, and its president was Dr G. P. Clark, the member for Caithness, and the crofters' champion. Later in the

1920s, Scottish nationalism was associated with red Clydeside, with near-Communists such as John Maclean; and Conservative newspapers of the 1920s attempted to discredit nationalism by associating it with 'Bolshevism' and 'Papists'.

II SCOTTISH NATIONALISM AND ANTI-SOCIALISM

Nevertheless, during all these years, the bulk of the nationalist movement remained moderate, and contented itself with demanding devolution rather than separation. After 1945, the main vehicle for Scottish nationalism came to be the Scottish Convention, an all-party movement for devolution led by John MacCormick. For a brief period, Conservatives and Nationalists became allies in their complaints against the depredations of 'London government'. The Attlee administration adopted an unimaginative attitude towards Scottish claims, and its nationalisation programmes transformed industries hitherto managed in Scotland into branches of London-based public corporations. 'For Scotland', claimed Walter Elliot, a former Secretary of State, 'nationalisation means de-nationalisation'.[7]

Scottish nationalism could thus be harnessed to the anti-socialist chariot. When MacCormick stood in the Paisley by-election in February 1948, he found himself supported not only by Walter Elliot, but by such unlikely figures as Peter Thorneycroft, Reginald Manningham-Buller (later Lord Dilhorne), and Lady Grant (later Lady Tweedsmuir). And, in the election campaign of 1950, Winston Churchill, speaking in Edinburgh, explicitly bid for the nationalist vote.

> If England became an absolute Socialist state, owning all the means of production, distribution and exchange, ruled only by politicians and their officials in the London offices, I personally cannot feel that Scotland would be bound to accept such a dispensation. I do not therefore wonder that the question of Scottish home rule and all this movement of Scottish nationalism has gained in strength with the growth of Socialist authority and ambitions in England. I would never adopt the view that Scotland should be forced into the serfdom of Socialism as the result of a vote in the House of Commons. It is an alteration so fundamental in our way of life that it would require a searching review of our historical relations.

But here I speak to the Scottish Nationalists in words, as diplomatic language puts it, of great truth and respect, and I say this position has not yet been reached. If we act together with our united strength it may never arise.

Scotsmen would make a wrong decision if they tried to separate their fortunes from ours at a moment when together we may lift them all to a higher plane of freedom and security. It would indeed be foolish to cast splitting votes or support splitting candidates, the result of which might be to bring about that evil Whitehall tyranny and centralisation, when by one broad heave of the British national shoulders the whole gimcrack structure of Socialist jargon and malice may be cast in splinters to the ground.[8]

Churchill was not in favour of legislative devolution; but he appointed his close friend, James Stuart, as Secretary of State, and Lord Home as Minister of State at the Scottish Office was given instructions to 'quell those turbulent Scots'.[9] A Royal Commission was set up to consider the structure of government in Scotland. Its terms of reference precluded it from advocating devolution, but it recommended further administrative decentralisation to Edinburgh, and this was accepted by the Churchill government.

III THE COMMITMENT TO DEVOLUTION AND ITS ABANDONMENT

The Conservatives reached their post-war peak in Scotland in 1955 when they secured both a majority of the Scottish seats and a majority of the Scottish vote—the only time that this has been achieved by any party since 1945. By 1966, however, the Scottish Conservatives were in sharp decline, and they had lost within eleven years sixteen seats and 12.4 per cent of their vote in Scotland. At a time when Scotland's economic problems seemed more serious than those of England, the traditionalist attitudes of Scottish Conservatives seemed to have little to offer that was specifically Scottish. Christopher Harvie has suggested that during the period of the Macmillan government, the appearance of the Prime Minister north of the Border 'suggested that the Tories still viewed Scotland as a huge sporting estate, and were only doing their best to keep it that way. Their perception of English politics seemed to be that of the custodians of the picturesque political museum whose exhibits—Clydeside reds and Grousemoor lairds alike—were to be cherished rather than challenged.'[10]

The response of the Scottish Conservatives was to set up a committee under the chairmanship of Sir William McEwan Younger to consider how governmental arrangements in Scotland could be improved. At the same time, a parallel investigation into Scottish government was being carried out by a new Conservative 'ginger group' called the Thistle Group and founded in the summer of 1967. The stated purpose of the Thistle Group was to reintroduce into the Conservative party an element of Scottish awareness which seemed to be lacking, and it issued its first publication a few days after the Hamilton by-election, in which Winifred Ewing succeeded in capturing one of Labour's safest strongholds for the SNP. It received, therefore, a degree of publicity which surprised even its most optimistic members. This pamphlet took the form of a general critique of the Conservative party in Scotland and emphasised the need for a greater awareness of Scottish political identity both in the Conservative party and in British politics generally. Although the pamphlet did not specifically mention devolution, the group came to be regarded as a pressure group for devolution, and just before the Scottish Conservatives' conference at Perth in 1968, the group issued a second pamphlet which contained an article arguing for a Scottish parliament.

It should be emphasised that both the McEwan Younger committee and the Thistle Group began their work well before the Hamilton by-election, and were motivated by a concern for the structure of Scottish government and the fortunes of the Conservative party in Scotland, rather than by the rise of the SNP. Although there were no direct consultations between the two groups, they came to strikingly similar conclusions. They both claimed that the existing structure of government in Scotland was inefficient, because the range of functions for which the Scottish Office was responsible was too wide to be scrutinised properly either by parliament or by ministers, and the system therefore allowed too much power to rest in the hands of civil servants. The Conservative case for devolution, then, was based not upon 'exploitation' of Scotland by England, as claimed by the nationalists, but upon the unsatisfactory nature of governmental arrangements in Scotland.

The party leadership could, of course, have ignored these grassroots attitudes, especially since there was still considerable hostility to devolution in the Scottish party. But Mr Heath was himself deeply worried by the decline of the Conservative party in Scotland and he told Richard Crossman a week before the Hamilton by-election that 'nationalism is the biggest single factor in our politics today'.[11] If the Conservatives were to regain lost ground, they badly needed a distinctive policy to differentiate themselves from the centralising Socialists and the separatist SNP. In the 'Declaration of Perth' made to the Scottish Conservative conference in 1968, therefore, Mr Heath committed the Conservative party to the principle of a directly elected assembly in Scotland. But this declaration seems to have been made after only perfunctory consultation with the shadow cabinet, and none at all with the parliamentary party. This was to cause serious difficulties later, when English members came to appreciate the nature and extent of the commitment.

Mr Heath's speech at the Perth conference was remarkable in that, coming from a leader thought at that time to be stolid and unimaginative, it contained many of the themes which were to animate British politics in the 1970s. It displayed a far-sightedness which, if circumstances had been more fortunate, could have gone a long way towards dealing with the new issues posed by the nationalists.

Mr Heath began by contrasting the Conservative party's stand for diversity with the pressures in 'a world of mass industrialisation, mass communications and increasingly complex organisation' towards 'uniformity and centralisation'. He instanced the United States where power was seeping away from the states towards the federal government; and Europe, where countries were being asked to merge their sovereignty into a larger unit.

But large institutions caused political alienation, a feeling on the part of many individuals that they were losing control over the shaping of their lives: this led to frustration and resentment towards government. Members of the Labour party, according to Heath, were natural centralisers, and unable to understand the nature of this discontent; the SNP understood it, but proposed an unrealistic remedy which involved sacrificing the gains of centralised economic management together with the losses. 'The art of government', however, was 'to reconcile these divergent needs: the need to modernise our institutions so as to cope with our complex changing society; and the need to give each citizen a greater opportunity to participate in the decisions that affect him, his family, and the community in which he lives'.

If these needs were to be reconciled, a balance had to be found between two fundamental principles. The first was the unity of the United Kingdom which the very name of the Scottish Conservatives—Unionists—showed that they existed to defend; but the second was 'our belief in the devolution of power'. And Mr Heath concluded his analysis by quoting from Quintin Hogg's *Case for Conservatism*:[12] 'Political liberty is nothing else but the diffusion of power. If power is not to be abused, it must be spread as widely as possible throughout the community'.

Mr Heath then proposed that a small constitutional committee be established—'not a Royal Commission, which is too large, too slow, and too cumbersome'—to consider whether an elected Scottish assembly was constitutionally viable, and what form it should take.

When the Labour government rejected this suggestion, Mr Heath himself set up a committee under the chairmanship of Sir Alec Douglas-Home with an impressive membership including Sir David Milne, the vice-chairman, a former permanent under-secretary of state at the Scottish Office; Sir Arthur Goodhart, formerly Professor of Jurisprudence at Oxford; J. D. B. Mitchell, Professor of Law at Edinburgh; and Sir Charles Wilson, Principal of Glasgow University. The two constitutional advisers to the committee were Sir Robert Menzies, the former Prime Minister of Australia, and Sir Kenneth Wheare, then Rector of Exeter College, Oxford, and a leading authority on federal government.

The committee's terms of reference were not, however, wholly clear: was it to consider the case for devolution, or to consider how devolution might be implemented? Mr Heath's declaration would seem to indicate that the latter was the purpose which he had in mind; yet two members of the committee, Professor Mitchell and Sir Charles Wilson, were hostile to the principle of devolution, and unable to accept the committee's report, published in March 1970.

The committee asked itself whether it were possible, while preserving 'the essential principle of the sovereignty of parliament'[13] to meet the 'very reasonable desire of the majority of the people of Scotland to have a greater say in the conduct of their own affairs'.[14] These considerations could, it appeared, be reconciled, but only if the proposed Scottish assembly were 'to be a natural evolution and extension of parliamentary practice as we know it'.[15] It should therefore be a part of the Westminster machinery—the equivalent of a third chamber of parliament dealing with the second reading, committee and report stages of Scottish bills, thus taking over much of the work done by the Scottish standing committees and the Scottish Grand Committee. Parliamentary sovereignty would, according to the committee, be preserved, since the third reading of Scottish bills and the legislative stages in the Lords would still remain at Westminster.

If the proposed assembly, or convention, were to yield a genuine improvement in the machinery of government in Scotland, and act as a focus for Scottish opinion, it had to be directly elected. Otherwise it would be dominated by the local authorities and, according to Sir William McEwan Younger, the reorganisation of local government in Scotland would not itself lead to decentralisation. 'The effect could, in practice, very well be the opposite. If no other body is interposed, these much larger units could easily become an instrument of greater, even of much greater, centralisation'.[16]

The central advantage of the proposed reform was that it did not make too great a breach with existing constitutional practice. The unitary system of government could continue unchallenged, and there would be no case for reducing Scotland's representation in the Commons. A critic, however, might complain that the proposed remedy was hardly proportionate to the serious weaknesses in the government of Scotland which the committee itself had diagnosed. For example, the committee showed itself anxious that decision-making on Scottish industrial matters should be speeded up. 'Long delays in deciding on matters which seriously affect the level of Scottish employment and generally influence the Scottish standard of living cannot be tolerated.' And the committee found itself 'particularly impressed by evidence of the operations of the Northern Ireland Ministry of Commerce—and especially by the speed of its decision-making'.[17] Yet what was proposed fell far short of the Stormont model. The Scottish convention would have little power to prevent delays in decision-making; for it would be a purely legislative body without any executive powers. It is not indeed wholly clear from the arguments presented by the committee why it did not proceed to recommend full-scale legislative devolution.

It could also be argued that the committee placed rather too much emphasis upon legislative activity as an influence upon government; for parliamentary activity is a far less important vehicle of political influence than the gaining of a share in the formation of public policy. By the time a bill is presented before parliament, its main outlines have usually been agreed after consultations between government departments and the relevant interest groups, and governments will generally be unwilling to re-open the package at the request of parliament. Yet the Scottish convention proposal did not offer Scotland an improved role in the process of policy formation, since Scotland's executive would remain responsible to parliament and not to the convention. Moreover, any legislative proposals made by the convention could be overturned at Westminster, and this might exacerbate conflict and cause yet further disillusionment with London governments.

The viability of the proposal depended upon a presumption of goodwill and consensus in Scotland. 'Our proposal', the committee stated, 'does involve an act of faith in the commonsense, objectivity, and tolerance of Scottish people'.[18] But would such 'commonsense, objectivity, and tolerance' be able to sustain a directly-elected convention whose majority was different from that at Westminster, especially when it was in the interest of one of the parties which would be represented at the convention—the SNP—so to exacerbate conflict as to secure political pressure for separation?

The committee, however, argued that conflict would be lessened, because Scottish legislation 'in the main consists of legislation which is not unduly controversial'.[19] But this meant that the Scottish convention would not be given the powers to deal with the issues that really worried Scots voters and had tempted them to turn to the SNP; for such issues were, almost by definition, controversial in their nature. If the convention was to be restricted to bills of a merely technical kind, it would hardly be likely to attract the interest of the general public, or to assuage Scottish discontent. It would, therefore, either be revealed as a talking-shop, or it would intensify bitterness in Scotland.

Nevertheless, these objections to the scheme need not have been fatal. For the establishing of the convention would itself be in the nature of a symbolic act, signalling to the Scottish electorate that Westminster would take more notice of the Scottish point of view. Once the principle of a directly-elected assembly was accepted, perhaps the particular kind of assembly that was actually estab-lished was an issue of smaller importance; and perhaps the setting up of an assembly might have succeeded in pre-empting the rise of the SNP.

It is difficult to estimate the extent of the support amongst Scottish Conservatives for the Douglas-Home proposals. They certainly secured some surprising adherents: Mr Alex Fletcher, later a fervent anti-devolutionist, had come out in favour of an elected assembly as early as November 1968, and Mr Teddy Taylor welcomed the Douglas-Home committee's report as offering 'an exciting new prospect for the nation's administration and economic future'.[20] But many observers believed that grass-roots opinion was hostile. Mr Charles Graham, the chief leader writer of the *Scottish Daily Express*, complained that the Scottish Tories 'even reject, in large numbers, Ted Heath's very moderate plan for a Scottish assembly'[21]; and Mr Robert Black, at the time prospective parliamentary candidate for North Lanark, complained: 'It is a comment on Scottish Conservatives' political awareness that they have been offered something of a political gift horse and can't even recognise it as such'.[22] Nevertheless, the Conservative election manifesto of 1970 promised that the Douglas-Home report, including the 'Scottish convention sitting in Edinburgh, will form a basis for the proposals we will place before parliament, taking account of the impending re-organisation of local government', and the Queen's Speech in July 1970 promised that plans would be produced 'for giving the Scottish people a greater say in their own affairs'.

But the Conservative government of 1970–4 made no move to establish the Scottish assembly, since it felt itself compelled to wait for the report of the Royal Commission on the Constitution set up by the Wilson government in 1969; for, if the Conservatives had proceeded with legislation on devolution, the Commission intended to resign, and this would have caused the government considerable embarrassment. In 1970, the Commission's report was expected to appear within the year. In the event, it was delayed until October 1973, by which time Britain was in the grip of the rise in oil prices following the Yom Kippur war, and governments had other things to think about.

Instead of devolution, the Conservatives decided to proceed with local government reform in Scotland along lines advocated by the Wheatley committee which reported in 1969. Local government reform in itself need not have precluded devolution, but the particular reform proposed by Wheatley involved a two-tier system of local government in Scotland, the upper tier consisting of regions, the largest of which, Strathclyde, would contain nearly half of the population of Scotland. Such a local government structure would almost certainly not have been adopted if local government reform had been seen in the context of devolution. Indeed, on 13 October

1975 Mr Malcolm Rifkind, then a front-bench spokesman, claimed: 'We find it inconceivable that Strathclyde could long survive the assembly. It cannot be desirable that the assembly should operate alongside a local authority that covers a massive geographical area and over half the population of Scotland.[23]

As we have seen, the Conservative commitment had been to establish a Scottish assembly, *taking account of the impending re-organisation of local government* and, since Wheatley reported in 1969, it cannot be said that local government reform was a new issue, or one that confronted the Conservative government unexpectedly. Indeed, the committee chaired by Sir William McEwan Younger had written to Sir Alec Douglas-Home when the constitutional committee was established, saying:

> We feel most strongly that whilst any proposals for the reform of the central government mechanism must be seen in the context of a reformed local government structure, they must not be subordinated to it. The mechanism of government in Scotland must be settled first, and the local government structure must then be designed as a coordinated component of that mechanism.[24]

For the most natural way to reform Scottish local government, if devolution were seriously intended, would be to allow a Scottish assembly, as the representative body of Scotland, to put forward and discuss its own proposals, rather than presenting it with a *fait accompli*.

Mr Geoffrey Smith has argued that the failure of the Heath government to implement its promise of a directly-elected assembly was due 'like so much else in that government's record, to three factors: an imperfectly considered promise, bad timing, and bad luck'.[25] The probability is that at no time during the government's period of office did devolution seem an urgent priority. The SNP had failed to make gains in the general election of 1970; and until late 1973, it did not seem a serious threat in Scotland. Perhaps if the Secretary of State for Scotland had been a strong political personality, the issue would have been pressed in cabinet, but Mr Gordon Campbell, who held the office, lacked the weight, and also the political backing, as the representative of a minority party in Scotland, to press such proposals, and his permanent under-secretary of state, Sir Douglas Haddow, was widely thought to favour local government reform as an alternative to devolution. Moreover, Conservative opinion in Scotland was becoming markedly hostile to devolution, and in 1973 the Scottish Conservative conference turned down by a large majority a proposal to establish a directly-elected assembly.

In the February 1974 general election, the Scottish Conservatives lost four seats to the SNP, and Mr Campbell himself was defeated by Mrs Winifred Ewing. The Conservative share of the vote in Scotland slumped from 38 per cent to 32.9 per cent, and was lower than it had been even in 1966. The new shadow secretary of state for Scotland, Mr Alick Buchanan-Smith, was, however, a confirmed devolutionist, and he proceeded to set up a devolution committee to rethink the party's commitment. But the 1974 Scottish Conservative conference at Ayr marked a further retreat in that the party now committed itself only to an indirectly elected assembly, and in the Conservative party's Scottish manifesto for the October election, it was stated that 'Initially the assembly's membership will be drawn from the elected members of the new local authorities though direct elections could evolve in the future'.

The October election, however, marked a further decline in the fortunes of the Scottish Conservatives. They lost five more seats in Scotland, four more to the SNP and one to Labour and now held only 16 of the 71 Scottish seats. The Conservative percentage of the vote in Scotland fell by a further 8.2 per cent to 24.7 per cent, nearly 6 per cent behind the support for the SNP. After this election Mr Buchanan-Smith immediately proposed a directly-elected assembly for Scotland although, in contrast to the Labour proposals, the assembly would lack a separate executive, and it would approximate to the local government style of organisation. Yet another committee, chaired by Malcolm Rifkind, MP for Edinburgh Pentlands, was set up to work out precise proposals. But Conservative plans were again put in the melting pot when, in February 1975, Mrs Thatcher became leader of the party.

It is generally assumed that Mrs Thatcher's succession to the leadership was the crucial factor leading to the abandonment of the Conservative commitment to devolution. But that is only a partial explanation. For both the change of leadership and the abandoning of the commitment were themselves consequences of back-bench dissatisfaction with the personality and style of leadership offered by Mr Heath. Not only had he lost two elections in rapid succession, but in the later phase of his administration he had, in the view of many back-benchers, strayed far from the tenets of traditional Conservatism.

It is obviously impossible to know whether, if Mr Heath had retained the leadership, the commitment to devolution would also have been retained. It had always sat lightly upon the shoulders of Conservative MPs; it had 'never really entered the party's bloodstream. It did not become part of the essential being of a Conservative.'[26]

On 19 January 1976 Mr Whitelaw, then the party's spokesman on devolution, argued that English Conservatives, who comprised 253 out of the 277 Conservative MPs, 'have only now started to give their minds to the problem. It is as if English members—and certainly our constituents—have awoken to the cold realities of a morning which many find extremely unwelcome. This is irritating the Scottish and Welsh members, who have been living with the problem for many years.'[37]

Mr Heath had done little to prepare English Conservatives for devolution, and this was partly because, until he lost the leadership, he was offering only devolution of a very limited kind; but it was a result also of his high-handed methods with back-benchers. Ronald Bell was surely speaking for many when he said of Mr Heath, 'He thinks that if something is discussed in the policy committee of the Conservative party, which is a very small body, it is somehow percolated and permeated through the whole party, and we all know about it. That is a lot of rubbish.'[28]

A major difficulty—perhaps *the* major difficulty—in securing a satisfactory constitutional settlement in Scotland has always been the difference in time-scale between Scotland and England. A reform which then seemed to many Scots to be one of some urgency was seen by English members as calling for leisurely and prolonged consideration before action could be taken. When English members came to be aware of the implications of devolution they were almost unanimously hostile, as were the Welsh Conservatives. Even the sixteen Scottish Conservative MPs were deeply divided on the issue, and little love was lost between the factions.

It could, however, be argued that skilful leadership might have helped persuade English and Welsh MPs not to oppose Scottish devolution but to allow a free vote on the issue. But under Mrs Thatcher's leadership the opposition of English MPs to devolution hardened, because of her known attitude, to hostility. Nevertheless Mrs Thatcher was very loth during the early months of her leadership to overthrow any of Mr Heath's commitments. Realising that many of the senior members of the party had been opposed to her campaign for the leadership, she was determined to tread cautiously, even though her basic instincts were hostile to devolution. At the Scottish Conservative conference in 1976, both she and Mr Whitelaw, the deputy leader of the party, reaffirmed their support for a directly-elected Scottish assembly; and consequently the pro-devolutionists were able to beat off a strong challenge from a 'Scotland is British' committee set up by Mr Iain Sproat, the member for South Aberdeen, Mr Michael Clark Hutchison, the member for Edinburgh South, and Miss Betty Harvie Anderson, the member for East Renfrewshire and a respected senior backbencher.

In December 1976, however, the shadow cabinet had to determine its attitude to the Labour government's Scotland and Wales bill. After a very long argument, the shadow cabinet decided to issue a three-line whip opposing the bill, although it was prepared to conciliate Mr Buchanan-Smith by first putting forward a reasoned amendment to it. For it sought desperately to preserve unity in the party by reaffirming its general commitment to devolution, while rejecting the Labour government's proposals.

This attempt at compromise did not work, however, since Mr Buchanan-Smith refused to vote against the Scotland and Wales bill on second reading on the grounds that, however defective the bill itself might be, a second reading vote was a vote on the principle of devolution, and therefore a vote against would be interpreted in Scotland as a vote against devolution. He resigned from the shadow cabinet, and was replaced by Mr Teddy Taylor, now a fervent unionist, and representing a know-nothing populist version of Conservatism whose connection with any of the historic tenets of the party remains obscure. After the defeat of the guillotine motion on the Scotland and Wales bill, abortive all-party talks on devolution were begun, and in May 1977 Mr Pym announced that the Conservative commitment to devolution was now 'inoperative' although he also indicated that the party would be prepared to examine various other forms of devolution, varying from a mild tinkering with the Grand Committee system to a full-scale federal structure. Mr Pym called for all-party talks to examine the various options and, in December 1978, in a pamphlet published shortly before the beginning of the referendum campaign, he insisted that

. . . the people of Scotland should be aware that the Scotland Act is not the only possible form of devolution . . . Other viable schemes are available, and if the Scotland Act is rejected the Conservative party will ensure that these are considered and that the changes that are made as a result will actually overcome existing defects in the government of Scotland without creating a whole new range of problems for its relationship with the rest of the UK.[29]

During the referendum campaign, Lord Home, the Conservative who, in the eyes of many, had done the most to educate the party to the need for devolution in Scotland, advised rejection of the Scotland Act, on the grounds that it did not secure proportional representation in the elections to the proposed Assembly, and that it did not give the Assembly revenue-raising powers. It would be better, in his view, for the proposals to be returned to parliament for further consideration rather than endorse legislation so fundamentally flawed as the Scotland Act. Mrs Thatcher also opted for this approach, and ensured Scottish electors that a 'No' majority in the referendum would not be interpreted to mean a rejection of devolution.

The result of the referendum—a narrow 'Yes' majority, 32.85 per cent compared with a 'No' vote of 30.78 per cent, and falling far short of the 40 per cent requirement laid down by parliament— would seem to indicate that most Conservatives followed Mrs Thatcher's advice. For there were 'Yes'· majorities only in the central belt of Labour–controlled regional authorities, and in the Highlands and the Western Isles. The issue of devolution had become intertwined with the survival of the Labour government, and the collapse of Labour popularity in Scotland following a winter of industrial disruption put paid to chances of implementing the Scotland Act. There was, moreover, a deep public scepticism as to the value of further institutional change, and a yearning for stability and the retention of familiar landmarks. Mrs Thatcher shared this feeling, and identified herself with it, sensing accurately the public mood of disenchantment. To that extent, the referendum result confirmed her political judgment that the Scotland Act could be defeated and Mr Callaghan's government humiliated, through determined Conservative opposition.

Yet the verdict of the electorate in Scotland can be seen as a Unionist triumph only in a very superficial sense. The Conservative

Party may find itself embarrassed by its commitment to consider alternative forms of devolution following the repeal of the Scotland Act, since many Conservatives remain opposed to devolution in any shape or form. Moreover, Parliament may be unwilling to give detailed consideration to further devolution legislation, having already spent two years on the subject; nor can there be any guarantee that an improved version of devolution can be found, eliminating the flaws of the Scotland Act while still capable of securing a majority in the Commons.

More fundamentally, the Conservative government has to confront a situation in which a Scottish majority, however narrow, has voted for devolution while Westminster is unprepared to grant it. Such a polarisation of opinion between England and Scotland might well benefit the SNP, rather than the Conservative party, and the Conservatives may find it difficult to govern a Scotland in which they continue to hold only a minority of seats— 22 out of 71 in the general election of 1979. It cannot be said, therefore, that the repeal of the Scotland Act offers a final settlement of the constitutional issue raised by devolution.

IV THE ROLE OF THE LEADER

The course of events just described well illustrates McKenzie's dictum that in the Conservative party, 'when appointed, the leader leads and the party follows, except when the party decides not to follow—then the leader ceases to be leader'.[30] The leader of the Conservative party is given what amounts to very nearly a *carte blanche* to make policy, so long as his authority is accepted. In 1968, Mr Heath was perfectly at liberty to decide whether he would or would not respond to the pressures for devolution in Scotland. In deciding to do so, there is no evidence that he was in any way influenced by back-benchers, by the party machinery, or by outside pressures. Yet always in the background of Conservative politics there lies the implicit threat of veto on the part of back-benchers when the leader's electoral prowess is seen to be failing, or when the traditional sentiments of Conservatives are outraged. The switch in the party's policy in 1976–7 owes just as much to the force of English back-bench opinion as to the change of leadership, and if Mrs Thatcher's instincts had not been in tune with that opinion, she would have found it a difficult task to win the support of English

MPs for devolution. The back-bench power of veto is something that generally lies dormant in the Conservative party, a reason why it often goes unnoticed by political commentators—but a wise Conservative leader will take good care to ensure that it is never exercised.

After losing the leadership, Mr Heath showed a more powerful commitment to devolution than many had suspected; he has committed himself to a federal solution for Scotland, and argued in favour of an assembly for Wales, although in 1969 he had forbidden Mr Gibson-Watt, then shadow Welsh secretary, from giving evidence to the Royal Commission on the Constitution, something which the Labour party has continually cited to support its claim that the Conservatives do not care about government in Wales.

Thus the issue of devolution became entangled in the dispute over the leadership, and it could be argued that Mr Heath's support for devolution has been a mixed blessing to other Conservative devolutionists. In these events, one can perhaps see a new pattern in Conservative politics, a pattern hitherto confined to the Labour party, whereby personal differences become transmuted into ideological disputes through a process which makes compromise and the recovery of party unity exceedingly difficult to attain.

V DEVOLUTION AND CONSTITUTIONAL CHANGE

Much of the literature on devolution has been concerned with the shortcomings of the Scotland and Wales Acts, and the process of political expediency through which the Labour party became the party of devolution, although its instincts told it that the success of social democracy rested upon centralisation; since only a powerful central government could ensure that the distribution of economic resources between different regions of the United Kingdom was based upon considerations of need, rather than upon regional political pressures.

Yet if the Labour party's record is a chequered one, it is doubtful if many Conservatives are proud of their own party's record on devolution. For the Conservative party seems to have been unable to pursue any consistent policy for very long; and the basic principles which should animate Conservative policy toward Scotland and Wales have never been clearly defined. The Conservatives might have adopted either of two alternative strategies: they could have offered a full-blooded defence of the Union, stressing the benefits to be obtained from a revival of British patriotism; or they might have welcomed devolution as an aid to the dispersal of power which, by removing decisions on matters such as pay beds and comprehensive schools away from central government entirely, would prevent the imposition of socialist policies at national level. But the party preferred to adopt a policy of ambiguity, supporting devolution in theory while opposing it in practice. It has been unwilling to lay before the electorate any constructive picture of the kind of society it seeks to create. Instead of grappling with the complex problems raised by the advance of the SNP, and the need to combat over-centralised government, the Conservative party preferred to adopt a policy which, by clouding the issue, could secure the support both of devolutionists and anti-devolutionists. The success of such a tactic must depend upon the future course of events in Scotland. If the SNP disappears, it will be said that the party kept its head, while all around them panicked; but if Scottish devolution returns to haunt British politics as Irish Home Rule tormented an earlier generation, then the Conservatives will stand exposed to the accusation drawn up two hundred years ago by Edmund Burke against a Tory government unwilling to devolve power to the American colonies, the accusation 'of not having large and liberal ideas in the management of great affairs'.[31]

NOTES

1. L. P. Curtis Jnr, *Anglo-Saxons and Celts* (Bridgeport, Conn., 1964) p. 103.
2. Lord Hugh Cecil, *Conservatism* (London: Williams and Norgate, 1912) p. 241.
3. Sir Reginald Coupland, *Welsh and Scottish Nationalism* (London: Collins, 1954) p. 246.
4. Ibid.
5. Scott's phrase in the introduction to his *Minstrelsy of the Scottish Border*, (London: Harrap, 1971) p. 70.
6. J. G. Lockhart, *Life of Sir Walter Scott*, vol. i (Paris: C. A. & W. Galignani & Co., 1838) p. 299.
7. Quoted in William Ferguson, *Scotland: 1689 to the Present*, (London: Oliver and Boyd, 1968) p. 388.
8. R. Rhodes James (ed.), *Winston S. Churchill: His Complete Speeches, 1897–1963*, vol. viii, 1950–63 (New York: Chelsea House, 1974) pp. 7937–8, Election Address, February 14, 1950.
9. Lord Home, *The Way the Wind Blows*, (London: Collins, 1976) p. 103.
10. C. Harvie, *Scotland and Nationalism*, (London: Allen & Unwin, 1977) pp. 182, 184.

11. R. Crossman, *Diaries of a Cabinet Minister*, vol. ii (London: Hamish Hamilton and Jonathan Cape) pp. 550–1.
12. Quintin Hogg, *The Case for Conservatism*, (London: Penguin Books, 1947, rev. ed. 1959).
13. *Scotland's Government*: The Report of the Scottish Constitutional. Committee, (Edinburgh, 1970) p. 62.
14. Sir William McEwan Younger, in *New Scotland*, no. 15, (Summer 1970).
15. *Scotland's Government*, preface, p. v.
16. *New Scotland*, op. cit.
17. *Scotland's Government*, op. cit., p. 41.
18. Ibid., p. vi.
19. Ibid., p. 65.
20. Quoted in *New Scotland*, op. cit., no. 15 (Summer 1970).
21. Ibid., no. 8 (April 1969).
22. Ibid., no. 11 (July 1969).
23. Press release by the Scottish Conservative party.
24. Quoted in G. Smith, 'Devolution and not saying what you mean', *Spectator* (26 February 1977).
25. Ibid.
26. G. Smith, 'The Conservative Commitment to Devolution', *Spectator* (19 February 1977).
27. *Hansard*, vol. 1046 (House of Commons) col. 903.
28. Ibid., vol. 903, col. 623, 15 January 1976.
29. Francis Pym, MP, and Leon Brittan, MP, *The Conservative Party and Devolution*, (Scottish Conservative Party December 1978) pp. 1–2.
30. R. T. McKenzie, *British Political Parties*, (London: Mercury Books, 1970) p. 145.
31. E. Burke, *Speeches and Letters on American Affairs*, (London: Everyman, 1961) p. 8, Speech on American Taxation.

5 The European Economic Community

Nigel Ashford

I CONSERVATIVES AND EUROPE 1945-75

'With Europe but not of Europe' 1945-61

In the immediate post-war period the Conservatives were seen on the Continent as the great hope for the idea of European unity in Great Britain. The Labour government of Attlee appeared ignorant, uninterested and sometimes even hostile to the European movement. In contrast, Winston Churchill gave the movement great impetus with his Zurich speech of September 1946, when he called for the creation of 'a kind of United States of Europe'.[1] The United Europe Movement was launched in 1947, largely at the instigation of Conservatives, especially Duncan Sandys, Churchill's son-in-law, who persuaded him to become chairman. A strong Conservative delegation attended the Congress of the Hague in 1948, which launched the Council of Europe. At the Council's Parliamentary Assembly, the Conservatives played an active role, nicknamed 'the Tory Strasbourgers'. In 1948 a motion in favour of federalism was signed by 60 Conservative MPs. When the Schuman Plan was launched for the European Coal and Steel Community, the Conservatives urged participation in the discussions, and attacked the Labour government for their hostility.

Many Europeans, both in Britain and abroad, were thus very disappointed when the new Conservative government, elected in 1951, failed to participate in the European initiatives. Churchill's attitudes had been widely misunderstood. In his Zurich speech he had talked of Britain as one of 'the friends and sponsors' of a united Europe, not as a member. His participation in European affairs had been at the encouragement of others, such as Sandys, although he soon appreciated that this was an arena where he could act as an international statesman. His attitude was clearly expressed in 1953 when he told the House of Commons that Britain was with Europe but not of Europe. Conservative policy was based on the concept of Britain at the centre of three interlocking circles: the USA, the Commonwealth and Europe. For Conservatives Europe was one of the circles, with a certain degree of importance, in contrast to the attitude of the Labour party, and there was an active body of Conservative MPs including Sir David Maxwell-Fyfe and Harold Macmillan in the Cabinet who sought to place greater emphasis on the European circle. However, both Churchill and his Foreign Secretary, Anthony Eden, who together dominated Conservative foreign policy for most of the 1950s, viewed Britain as still a great world power. Eden, in particular, was very unsympathetic to the idea of European unity, failing to participate in the United Europe Movement and coming out against a European Army.

Conservative policy until 1961 was to support European co-operation at an intergovernmental level, while resisting any moves towards supranational structures. The 1950s were marked by a series of Conservative attempts to prevent a divided Europe, as federalist forces on the Continent gained strength. In 1954 Eden proposed that the Coal and Steel Community should be within the auspices of the Council of Europe; in 1956 the Grand Design proposed that the institution of the Six should be incorporated with the intergovernmental institutions such as the Council of Europe and the Western European Union; in 1956 the government wanted a free trade area (FTA) for the whole of Western Europe, to avoid the more far-reaching integration of the Treaty of Rome; and the European Free Trade Area (EFTA) was created as a block to build a bridge with the EEC. Many Conservative MPs, through their participation in the Council of Europe and the Western European Union, came to understand and share the impulses for European unity, but Eden failed to understand these forces and continued to look warily on European developments.

The First Application 1961–63

The decision for Britain to join the European Economic Community was the personal decision of Harold Macmillan. This is not the appropriate place to discuss the reasons for his decision but they included the decline of Britain as a world power; the declining value, both politically and economically, of the Commonwealth; the weak economic situation marked by 'stop-go'; the unexpected success of the EEC; and the shift of opinion in informed circles of Whitehall, business and the media. Another element in the decision was the need to provide new inspiration and energy to the Conservative government, and give the party an exciting and progressive policy to win votes, especially of the young, in the next election.

The problem was to win the support of all sections of the Conservative party for the new policy of membership. For years the Conservative leaders had argued that British vital interests conflicted with full participation in European integration. The major difficulties hindering membership were four: EFTA, the Commonwealth, agriculture and sovereignty. None of these difficulties were as great as they seemed: some members of EFTA would join the EEC if Britain joined, and agreements could be made to protect the interests of others; the Commonwealth was no longer so dependent on trade with Britain and special conditions could be achieved for the developing nations as existed for the former French colonies; a common agricultural policy had not yet been adopted by the EEC although the principle to have a common policy had been accepted; and the EEC had been less supranational in practice than British governments had feared. The problem was that this was not the situation that the party leadership had been presenting to the party membership. Macmillan decided on a strategy of 'softly, softly', or as Neustadt aptly puts it, he acted 'by disguising his strategic choice as a commercial deal'.[2] The decision to apply was sold in stages, firstly just as discussions about whether to begin negotiations, then negotiations just to discover the conditions, and then discussions on improving the conditions, and only then would a decision to apply actually be made. Of course, Macmillan knew that the credibility of the government would become dependent on the success of the application, and thus the pressures for acceptance by the cabinet would be very great.

The second element of his strategy was to lay down certain conditions of membership, based on the four problem areas. Macmillan knew that the spirit of these conditions was in contradiction to membership of the Community. Gradually these conditions became weaker and less specific, until they became little more than a request for confidence. Thus Macmillan was able to obtain the acquiescence of the Commonwealth and the National Farmers' Union, even if not their support. Edward Heath, the negotiator in Brussels, was able to demonstrate a genuine attempt to protect their interests.

The third element was to ensure that no major figure in the party would publicly oppose his policy. A cabinet reshuffle in July 1960 had placed pro-Europeans in certain key positions: Lord Home as Foreign Secretary, Edward Heath, Lord Privy Seal, as Minister for Europe, Duncan Sandys as Commonwealth Secretary, Christopher Soames as Minister for Agriculture and Peter Thorneycroft as Minister of Aviation. There were three potential sources of opposition within the cabinet. Rab Butler was unsympathetic to Europe (his autobiography does not even mention the European Community), so Macmillan appointed him chairman of the committee to oversee the negotiations where he was able to express his concern about the situation of his agricultural and horticultural constituents in Saffron Walden. By co-opting Butler into the negotiations, Macmillan added to Butler's natural sense of the importance of unity in the party together, perhaps, with his natural ambition to follow Macmillan as party leader. Butler gradually became committed to the policy. Lord Hailsham, Lord Chancellor, was the second possible source of opposition, but he was attracted to European unity as the defence of Western Christian values, even if uncomfortable with the technicalities of economic cooperation. Perhaps a simple lack of interest in the question prevented him from playing any role, either for or against. The third possible source was Reginald Maudling, who favoured the free trade area, but as he doubted that the negotiations would succeed he concentrated on his portfolio as Colonial Secretary. So no major cabinet figure strongly opposed the step-by-step decisions, even though several were markedly unenthusiastic. The consequence was that no member of the government, not even a parliamentary private secretary, resigned over the final decision to apply for membership.

The final element of Macmillan's strategy was an active campaign to convert the party activists, through a series of publications and meetings. The 1961 party conference in Brighton, which immediately followed the start of the negotiations in Brussels, endorsed the policy as a question of confidence in the government. The real campaign was concentrated on ensuring overwhelming support at the 1962 conference in Llandudno. Exceptionally, Macmillan published a pamphlet, called *Britain, the Commonwealth and Europe*,[3] designed to influence the conference vote (as the party leader traditionally spoke only at the end). An excellent speech by Butler attacking Labour led to an overwhelming vote in favour of Britain's membership, with only 50 delegates voting against. Thus Macmillan obtained the endorsement of the party that he wanted.

The traditional interpretation of the change of policy in favour of Community membership by the Conservative party is that it was a demonstration of the tremendous power of the Conservative leader to determine his party's policy. This interpretation, however, ignores important factors. Firstly the existence of a strong European lobby within the party has not been given the importance that it deserves. In the cabinet there was a group of ministers who were far more enthusiastic Europeans than either Macmillan or Heath. Duncan Sandys, Lord Kilmuir, Christopher Soames and Peter Thorneycroft had long been publicly committed Europeans. In the parliamentary party there was an active group of Europeans, many of whom had been on parliamentary delegations to the Council of Europe or Western European Union, and throughout the fifties there had been motions and amendments from Conservative MPs urging greater participation in Europe. Three prominent Europeans in the parliamentary party were Geoffrey Rippon, Peter Kirk and Maurice Macmillan. There was thus already a substantial body of support in the parliamentary party.

The second factor favouring membership of the EEC was the changing mood of the business community. This was due to the EEC becoming the major growth area for exports, the desire for competitive stimulus and the advantages of economies of scale. Large firms had become firmly in favour, together with leading industrial spokesmen such as Lord Chandos, head of the Institute of Directors. The Federation of British Industries, due to its consensual nature, failed actively to promote membership, but the major industrial leaders made their position clear.

The third factor was the declaration of support for membership of most of the Conservative-oriented press. The *Observer*, the *Economist* and the *Financial Times* came out in favour of membership in 1960, followed in early 1961 by the *Sunday Times*, *Daily Telegraph*, *Daily Mail* and *The Times*. The only Tory newspaper in opposition, and in violent opposition, was the *Daily Express*. Macmillan thus had the support, even before his announcement, of most of the Conservative press.

Fourthly, the depth of attachment to the Commonwealth in the party was exaggerated. The Commonwealth was no longer the Empire. South Africa had been excluded, Imperial Preference had increasingly worked against British products, the increasingly poor image of the Commonwealth served to undermine feelings of kinship, and the younger generation lacked the emotional attachment toward the former Empire. These factors, together with the behaviour of some Commonwealth leaders towards Britain, served to undermine possible opposition based on the Commonwealth. There was probably one Commonwealth figure with enough respect in the Conservative party to have had a substantial impact—Sir Robert Menzies, Prime Minister of Australia—but he kept his substantial fears largely to himself, and placed his confidence in the Macmillan government.

Another substantial body normally viewed as in opposition was the agricultural interest in the Conservative party. However, the political importance of the farmers' vote has been exaggerated.[4] More significantly, agriculture was by no means united in its opposition. There were expected real benefits for certain sections of British agriculture as a result of membership, and those sections, particularly among large farmers, favoured membership. One survey in the East Midlands showed 42 per cent of the farmers interviewed in favour.[5] Lord Netherthorpe, NFU President 1946– 60, favoured membership, together with many agricultural economists. Much of the agricultural debate was not in terms of opposition to entry, but in terms of obtaining entry on the best possible conditions for British agriculture.

The main focus of criticism by the parliamentary anti-marketeers was the question of sovereignty. Why did this issue not gain more attention? The situation can better be understood when it is remembered that the Conservative party had already accepted the surrender of sovereignty in the field of defence in its support for NATO. For many Conservatives, British membership was part of the increasing need for Western democratic nations to combine together against the Soviet threat. The 1961 party conference was held after the building of the Berlin Wall and the failure of Macmillan's attempts at détente. Macmillan appealed to this sense of threat in his speech. 'We must now accept the fact that the bleak ideological struggle may last for another generation, perhaps even longer. We cannot retire from this contest, but we cannot wage it alone. It is with this in mind that we have approached the question of Europe and of the Common Market.'[6] While the question of the

EEC entering the field of defence was never raised, the need for European cooperation against the Communist threat established a good reason for the supposed loss of sovereignty. The effect of economic weakness on defence was established with the cancellation of the Blue Streak missiles. Thus sovereignty failed to establish itself as a major issue.

The weakness of the Conservative anti-marketeers was not only due to the appeal for loyalty. They failed to win the support of any leading Conservative. Lord Avon was much courted by Beaverbrook, who offered finance and publicity if he would lead the opposition, but his health was too poor. They were led by men of moderate stature, former ministers such as Derek Walker-Smith and Robin Turton, but they were elderly men out of touch with the younger members of the parliamentary party. The Anti-Common Market League was founded in August 1961 to rally anti-market Conservatives but it never established substantial support. An expected source of support, among the Suez diehards, proved to be disappointing, with one of its leading figures, Julian Amery, a fervent European. The anti-marketeers were vocal but never secured a strong base in the party.

In fact, British membership was popular with some segments of the party. The 1962 conference showed a degree of enthusiasm that conflicts with the image of a party being dragged into membership only out of loyalty to its leadership. The Young Conservatives, who account for up to one quarter of the conference representatives, enthusiastically wore 'Yes' buttons, together with many other representatives. Many Conservatives felt that this was an issue which was an election-winner.

Labour opposition had been expected, indeed perhaps hoped for, by Macmillan. When it came with a speech by Hugh Gaitskell accusing the Government of turning their backs on 'a thousand years of history' just before the 1962 Conservative conference the issue became a partisan one, and this enabled partisan rhetoric to be used in favour of membership, as it was, effectively, by Rab Butler when he said, 'For the Labour party a thousand years of history. For us, the future.' The issue gave the Conservatives a progressive and internationalist image, which contrasted with a reactionary and inward-looking image of the Labour party over this issue.

A major element in the Conservative conversion to the EEC was the belief that Europe would win the party the next election. The government had appeared tired and lacking in ideas. The EEC gave the government new inspiration, as Macmillan had intended. Macleod, the party chairman, and Conservative Central Office believed that Europe should be the main platform in the election campaign, where it should be presented 'with trumpets'. The young and opinion-formers were the key to success and they were strongly pro-European. One Central Office worker described Europe as the 'deus ex machina'[7] of the Conservative election campaign. Opinion polls showed that more people favoured membership than favoured the Conservatives, and these were a potential source of support. Above all, Europe gave the Conservatives a new image as a forward-looking party that could compete for the new technocratic middle class votes.

Macmillan's personal decision, and the appeal to party loyalty, obviously played an important role in the decision to apply for membership, but Macmillan would never have taken that decision unless there had existed a substantial body of party opinion in favour of membership. Macmillan took a risk but not as large as it has usually been portrayed.

From Disillusion to Renewed Support 1963–70

De Gaulle's veto stunned the party, and the country, and the ability of the party to recover as much as it did in the 1964 election was astounding. Everyone accepted that British membership was not a realistic possibility. The 1964 election manifesto called for a strong Atlantic partnership and for the closest cooperation with the Six. However, an important decision with regard to the Conservative party and Europe was made with the election of Edward Heath as leader against Reginald Maudling in 1965. While Heath was not as committed a European as some other Conservatives before the decision to apply in 1961, he had developed a strong commitment during the negotiations. He established, in the 1966 manifesto, the policy of working energetically for entry at the first favourable opportunity. It is noticeable that there was no mention of protecting the Commonwealth's interests as a condition of entry.

The most important new development in European policy under Heath was that new policies were designed with British member-ship in mind, such as the reform of agriculture towards levies, and the introduction of value added tax. These policies were presented as valid in themselves but they were clearly meant to ease British membership.

At the 1966 conference a ballot was held on British membership, with 1452 votes in favour and 475 against. This was a large increase in opposition, due to disillusion over the de Gaulle veto, the fact that the Labour government had decided to seek entry, and that the party leadership usually has less influence in opposition.

Europe did not play a major role in the Conservative party in opposition. The party loyally supported attempts at entry by the Labour government, despite criticism that the opposition should oppose, and their own commitment remained firm. However, by 1969 there were a number of disturbing trends. Firstly, Europe was unpopular in the opinion polls. Secondly, the Conservative anti-marketeers had found a leader in Enoch Powell, who had already established strong support over his immigration policies. Thirdly, there was a danger that the Labour government would obtain entry and thus 'dish the Tories'. Finally, there was strong criticism of a certain inflexibility by Heath in the face of party criticism. These factors led to the decision not to emphasise Europe at the party conference in 1969. Home, speaking on Europe, 'deliberately drained his speech of all emotion',[8] emphasising that a final decision could only be taken after negotiations. The vote in favour of membership was only two to one.

Thus Europe did not play a primary role in the election campaign. The manifesto emphasised that 'Obviously there is a price we would not be prepared to pay', that only after negotiations could the price be known, and that 'Our sole commitment is to negotiate; no more, no less'. Only 3 per cent of Heath's speeches during the campaign were on Europe, and there was little mention in the candidates' election addresses.

Campaign for Entry 1970–3

However, after the surprise election victory in June 1970, Heath established membership as a major priority of the new government, beginning negotiations only twelve days after the election, and appointing his close friend, Anthony Barber, to be in charge of the negotiations. Heath seemed confident that, having established a good relationship with President Pompidou, the negotiations would be successful. The major problem was to ensure that entry would achieve the support of a Conservative majority in the Commons, without reliance on other parties. This was necessary, firstly, to relieve the pressure on Labour marketeers to vote against in order to

bring down the government; secondly, to maintain the credibility of
the government that one of its major policies did not depend upon
opposition votes; and thirdly, to establish Heath's mastery over the
party.

The problem in the party was greater than with the first
application. Firstly, the party no longer saw Europe as an election
winner, and it was widely perceived as an election liability.
Secondly, the anti-marketeers now had an articulate and well-
known leader in Enoch Powell, who had belonged to the Macmillan
government which applied for entry but who now felt that the
political arguments against membership were too strong. Powell
was strong enough to create real divisions in the party, far deeper
than just on the question of Europe, which could leave deep
wounds. Thirdly, some MPs felt that their local Conservative
associations were uncertain on the EEC, and they were reluctant to
offend them. Central Office judged the feeling in the constituencies
to be pro-market, but there was concern over specific questions,
such as sovereignty and the Common Agricultural Policy, and the
party workers felt that they were not well-informed, and that they
had not been adequately consulted.

Thus the strategy was to create strong enthusiasm and support for
British entry, which would both enable the more insecure MPs to
vote in favour and place the maximum pressure on those liable to
vote against. The main thrust of the campaign was to deal with the
fears expressed, to calm fears rather than make converts; special
pamphlets were produced dealing with sovereignty, food prices, the
regions and industry.

There followed the largest internal education campaign that has
ever been undertaken inside the Conservative party. The party
machine supported the government through a massive campaign of
leaflets, pamphlets, discussion groups, speakers, conferences and
meetings. An advisory service to answer questions from MPs was set
up, and special briefs were written by the Conservative Research
Department for MPs. After a year's campaign, a large meeting of up
to 3000 leading Conservative activists (officially called the Central
Council) met at Central Hall, Westminster, on 14 July 1971 to listen
to Heath and ask questions. The massive support there demonstrated that the party activists were now firmly in favour.

Inside the parliamentary party, the Conservative Group for
Europe, an unofficial party pressure group associated with the

European Movement, with membership of over half the parliamentary party, appointed Norman St John Stevas as an unofficial whip. It also provided parliamentary questions sympathetic to Europe to balance those of the anti-marketeers, organised parliamentary delegations to Brussels, held briefing sessions in the House, sustained marketeers under pressure from their local parties, exercised informal 'family-type' pressure on doubters and provided a useful and amazingly accurate estimate of feeling inside the party.

The anti-marketeers organised themselves into the '1970 Group', more popularly known as 'Derek's Diner', as they regularly met for dinner under the auspices of Sir Derek Walker-Smith. They cooperated on party and parliamentary committees, asked hostile questions and cooperated with anti-marketeers in the country. The anti-marketeers were clearly identifiable at an early stage. They were the traditional opposition from the first application: Walker-Smith, Turton, Marten and Fell, five Ulster Unionists who had now broken off relations with the Conservatives, ten of the new MPs, some fishing MPs and Powell and his close supporter, John Biffen. The Anti-Common Market League reorganised itself, although it never became as strong as in 1961–3. The doubters in parliament were Du Cann, Goodhart, some MPs from the Celtic fringe and a few with specific interests such as horticulture or New Zealand.

Heath's original timetable was for a parliamentary vote in July 1971, but he was strongly advised against this, because MPs wanted to be sure that support in their local parties was solid, they did not wish to appear to be in haste so soon after the publication of the terms, and they wanted to demonstrate that they had fully discussed and consulted with their local parties. Heath reluctantly agreed to postpone the decision until October. The party conference was held on 13–16 October, just before the parliamentary vote. Everything demonstrated party support. 69 motions had been received in favour, 25 in favour with reservations, and 4 against. The Conservative Political Centre announced that their two-way contact exercise, whereby the party was able to judge feeling in the constituencies, had shown overwhelming support. The Young Conservatives demonstrated their enthusiastic support—they had always been an important base of European feeling inside the party—and it was a YC motion welcoming entry which was presented to conference. The debate emphasised sovereignty and the political opportunities of membership. The motion was passed by an overwhelming majority, but unprecedentedly Heath demanded a card vote which revealed 2474 votes for and 324 votes against, a vote of about eight to one. The vote was received with wild enthusiasm and a parade of YC 'Eurodollies' reminiscent of an American convention. Thus the pressure was for a maximum Conservative vote in parliament.

Heath insisted on a three-line whip, stating that as entry was a major plank in the government's policy it had the right to insist on the votes of its supporters. However, this policy was widely criticised inside the party, and not only by anti-marketeers. The issue was perceived by many as an issue of such importance that it was an issue of 'conscience', which demanded a free vote. Only after considerable debate with the 1922 Committee, evidence that a free vote would increase the Conservative anti-Europeans by a maximum of only twelve votes, reports that the question of a three-line whip was causing considerable resentment and the persuasive arguments of Francis Pym, did Heath agree to a free vote.

The first parliamentary vote on Britain's membership was held on 28 October 1971, when 282 Conservative MPs voted in favour, with only 39 against and two abstentions. The leading anti-marketeers continued their opposition throughout the complicated process of legislation, but most of the Tory opposition accepted the defeat and did nothing to prevent the passing of the bill. Thus Britain became a member of the European Community on 1 January 1973.

Explanations of the victory of the Europeans within the Conservative party from 1970–2 have been based on the three following factors: the power of the Conservative party leader, the appeal to party loyalty and the strong formal and informal whipping of MPs. These factors were of course important but there were also other neglected factors.

First, the party activists were not 'converted' to Europe between 1970 and 1971. The evidence was that the party members were pro-European, but felt ill-informed about certain specific problems. The internal campaign was conducted not to convert, but to provide information, to create the feeling of consultation, and to deal with the arguments about which the party members felt unsure. The aim of the campaign, and its success, was to change this soft support into hard, firm and sometimes enthusiastic commitment.

Secondly, public opinion shifted in favour of Britain's entry, particularly among Conservatives. The British government, for the first time, attempted to explain the implications of membership to the mass electorate. The rise in public support weakened fears in the party that Europe would be an electoral liability.

Thirdly, the Labour party came out increasingly against membership on 'Tory terms', which aroused partisan feelings among party activists and MPs. One of the most popular party publications on Europe was a Research Department pamphlet called *Words to Remember*, which quoted Conservative and Labour politicians on the EEC. Quotations from it were widely used by Conservative speakers to attack Labour leaders, and it acquired a degree of notoriety with Harold Wilson.

Fourthly, the anti-marketeers proved in fact much weaker than everyone expected. Powell did not emerge as their leader, partly because he was too much of a lone wolf successfully to lead, and partly because the old anti-market leaders did not want to appear as if they were launching an attack on Heath's leadership by following Powell. The anti-market cause had become associated with the Labour party, and especially its left wing. Above all, the anti-marketeers were surprised at how little support they received in the local parties. They had interpreted the expression of doubts and fears as evidence of opposition, which proved not to be the case. As far as the party in the country was concerned, the campaign was conducted with few long-term divisive consequences.

Finally, and perhaps most surprisingly, many MPs were reluctant to vote in favour of entry if it was in total opposition to the position of their local party. After re-election, Conservative MPs are generally considered to act very independently of their local party, even if not of the parliamentary party. Considerable emphasis was placed on full consultation between the MP and his local party, and this was the major factor in the decision to delay the parliamentary vote until October. There seems to be little evidence that these MPs felt their re-selection to be threatened (except perhaps in the case of a few anti-marketeers). No adequate explanation can be put forward here, but an explanation may be sought in the personal relationships and friendships that MPs establish with the leading members of their association. MPs did not want to see these threatened by a divisive political issue. Therefore MPs spent a considerable amount of time and effort explaining their own position, and encouraging the local party to go along with it. This factor is perhaps one that has been neglected in past analysis of the relationship between the MP and his Conservative association.

Thus the internal debate on Europe within the Conservative party in 1970–1 should be seen not as a demonstration of the power of the party leader to lead the party wherever he wishes to go, but as a period of consolidation of support for Europe, and as evidence of sensitivity to local party feeling by MPs and ultimately the party leadership.

The Referendum

The period between entry and the referendum in June 1975 was marked by a number of important events unrelated to Europe. The Conservative government lost office in February 1974, was further defeated in October 1974, and Edward Heath lost the leadership of the party to Margaret Thatcher in February 1975. One significant event was the call of Enoch Powell to vote Labour in February 1974 over the Common Market issue, and he claimed some influence over the defeat of the Conservatives. Within the Labour party opposition to entry grew stronger, even after the election of a Labour government. Eventually Harold Wilson decided to resolve the internal conflict inside the party by renegotiating the terms of entry and holding a referendum.

The Conservatives were placed in a difficult position. The final attitude of the Labour government was not yet clear, and there was the danger that the government would succeed in creating the impression that the Conservatives had entered the Community on poor terms. However, official Labour government support was important to win the referendum, so criticism of the government had to be delicately handled. The second problem was the need to help protect the Labour pro-marketeers. Informal contact with them had been established through the European Movement, and the Conservatives were fully aware of their difficulties. Partisan attacks on the government would make their own position weaker. Thirdly, there was the problem of the growing unpopularity of the EEC among the electorate. Too close an identification with the Conservatives could be electorally damaging.

The decision was taken that the full Conservative campaign should be submerged into the all-party Britain-in-Europe campaign. Britain-in-Europe was highly dependent on the Conservatives for personnel, expertise, and the existence of a national organisation. As the pro-marketeers recognised, 'the Conservative party had the only effective machinery for putting on a nationwide campaign'.[9] Conservatives provided the backbone for very many, if not most local Britain-in-Europe groups, and worked hard for all-party cooperation. The huge pro-European campaign effort would have been impossible without the full support of the Conservative party.

Conservative efforts were directed mainly through Britain-in-Europe, therefore there was little of a distinctly party role to be played. William Whitelaw, Deputy Leader, became the Conservative representative in BIE. Lord Fraser returned to Central Office to supervise the party's contribution to the campaign. A series of leaflets were produced, and twelve regional seminars were held, mainly to revive enthusiasm. Central Office provided much of the professional work, printing and distribution of referendum materials. Generally the party did not seek to play a prominent role in the campaign.

This cannot be said to be primarily due to the strength of anti-market feeling in the party. In only 30 Conservative associations was even one of the three key figures (chairman, agent and candidate) anti-market; only two Conservative associations came out officially against; Neil Marten was the leading Conservative anti-marketeer, and Conservatives Against the Treaty of Rome (CATOR) was created, but played very little role either in the party or in the general anti-market campaign. The fears that the referendum would reopen old wounds were not substantiated.

One issue that did arise during the campaign was the role of Mrs Thatcher. As party leader she did not play an active role in the campaign, in direct contrast to the vigorous campaigning of Edward Heath. Doubts about her own commitment were raised. These doubts were based on little evidence. Mrs Thatcher was a firm supporter of British membership, primarily for political rather than economic reasons. She gave her full support, although usually quietly, to the Conservative involvement in the campaign. The decision on her role was a tactical one, based on two factors: firstly, she did not want to create competition within the campaign between herself and Heath (she asked Heath to lead the Conservative campaign but he refused), and secondly, her advisers suggested that Europe was not a popular issue to be identified with by the electorate.

The referendum on 5 June 1975 gave an overwhelming 'yes' vote of 67.2 per cent. The verdict was interpreted as an overwhelming defeat for the left wing of the Labour party. The Conservatives, despite their major contribution, appear to have benefited little from the campaign. They were simply glad that the campaign had concluded without major internal problems, that Powell had not re-emerged as a major threat and that the issue of British membership had at last been settled.

II CONSERVATIVE RESPONSE TO MEMBERSHIP

Attitudes to Future Development

Debate within the Conservative party about the European Community is no longer primarily concerned with the question of membership, but revolves around the question of the future direction and development of the Community. Attitudes can roughly be divided into four groups: federalists, confederalists, sympathisers and anti-marketeers.

The federalists believe that the European Community is part of the process of the creation of a united Europe, with a European government with limited functions but real powers, exercised in the interests of Europe as a whole. The federalists demand increased powers for the European parliament, the more frequent use of majority voting in the Council of Ministers, and generally a more 'communitaire' policy. Conservative federalists can generally be found in three groups: a number of old, respected Conservatives who became committed federalists in the immediate post-war period, such as Duncan Sandys; business and professional people who feel at home in Europe, many of whom can be found in the Conservative Group for Europe, a pressure group within the Conservative party; and the youth organisations—the Young Conservatives and the Federation of Conservative Students—who have long been enthusiastic Europeans and are both committed to federalism. The federalists are not a numerically strong group and they do not occupy major influential positions, but their primary commitment to the European cause—they are often described as Eurofanatics—has given them a certain degree of influence.

Most Conservative Europeans are confederalists, viewing the Community as essentially an institution for co-operation between nation-states. Mrs Thatcher told the *Times*, 'I believe that we should continue to have a partnership of nation-states each retaining the right to protect its vital interests but developing more effectively than at present the habit of working together'.[10]

The confederalists favour three major areas of cooperation: firstly, foreign policy, with Mrs Thatcher stating 'It is precisely because we want to see Britain making a lively and energetic contribution to the world, as befits her character, that we are working for the success of our European partnership';[11] secondly, defence, primarily to create a greater consciousness of the need for a greater Western European role in its own defence against the Soviet threat; and thirdly economic policy, recognising the British economic dependence on international trade, and the Community's major role in international trade. The confederalists believe that British interests, especially internationally, can best be promoted through the Community, and therefore support further development of the Community. Party policy can currently be described as confederalist.

The bulk of the Conservative party, both members of parliament and party activists, can be described as sympathetic but unenthusiastic towards Europe. Europe has been on the issue-agenda of British politics for so long that most Conservatives seek a rest from it and a return to more traditional Conservative themes. The massive effort in previous years by the party leadership has left a basically positive attitude towards Europe—what has been described as 'common-sense Europeanism'—among party members, combined with a degree of boredom and irritation with the results of certain Community policies, such as the CAP mountains and excessive harmonisation.

Most anti-marketeers have accepted the results of the referendum. They concern themselves with other issues, hope that the Community does not grow stronger, and even welcome elections to the European parliament as a means of demonstrating the limited commitment of the British people. A few anti-marketeers still strongly oppose any new developments in the Community and believe that British withdrawal or Community collapse is only a matter of time. Neil Marten told the House of Commons in April 1976 that Britain has no reason 'to get further enmeshed in a common market which was beginning to break up' and feared 'an immense and decisive shift of power and control from the British parliament to the European parliament'.[12] The anti-marketeers are no longer an influential force, although they are sometimes used as a balance against the federalists.

The position within the Conservative party can be summed up as generally positive, with the anti-marketeers virtually irrelevant, a small but vocal group of federalists, and with party policy in the hands of confederalists. The party leadership is faced with the problem of ensuring that the debate on European developments between federalists and confederalists, inevitable with direct elections, does not cause serious divisions within the party.

Community Policy

European policy has not been a major priority for the Conservative party since the referendum. There are five reasons for this. First, as mentioned previously, the party faithful are somewhat tired of Europe and favour a rest. Secondly, the party is unclear about what its policy should be. Much of their argument for membership has been based on 'spontaneous' benefits, such as increased trade, rather than as a means of new policy initiatives. Thirdly, Mrs Thatcher is certainly a European, but she lacks both the emotional commitment and the intellectual interest towards Europe of the former leader, Edward Heath. Fourthly, party spokesmen on foreign affairs have been disappointing. Reginald Maudling, always known as a reluctant European, was very widely criticised for his inactivity, especially in European affairs. This was noticeable in the reception to his reply to the European debate at the party conference in 1975. His successor, John Davies, while a convinced European, proved to be a well-informed but uninspiring shadow foreign secretary. The appointment of Douglas Hurd as European spokesman in January 1976, however, was widely welcomed in European circles. Fifthly, many Conservatives, including some advisers to Mrs Thatcher, consider that Europe is an electoral liability, with a strongly held public image of the Community as a bureaucratic threat to British interests and values. Thus Europe has not been a major Conservative theme since the 1975 referendum.

Conservative European strategy has been based on four themes: criticism of the Labour government for its anti-Community position, the restatement that the Conservative party is *the* European party in Britain, suspicion of institutional innovations and a set of policies based on reformism rather than new initiatives.

The Labour government is strongly attacked for its lack of European spirit, and Conservative spokesmen have emphasised the continued influence of anti-marketeers like John Silkin, the departure of social democrat marketeers like Roy Jenkins, and the negative attitude towards direct elections of the Labour party conference and National Executive Committee. Douglas Hurd attacked the Labour government in March 1976 'which in its dealings with the Community slithers unhappily between bluster and back-sliding'.[13]

'We are the European Party in the British Parliament and among the British people and we want to cooperate wholeheartedly with our partners in this joint venture' (Mrs Thatcher).[14] Conservative spokesmen, led by Mrs Thatcher, have emphasised that the Conservatives are the only major European party in Britain, and that without the Conservatives Britain would not now be a member of the Community. The targets for these pronouncements appear to be first those Europeans within the Conservative party who may have doubts about the commitment of the present leadership, and secondly to impress on potential European allies that the Conservatives are their only viable partner in Britain.

Party pronouncements seem to favour the present method of decision-making in the Community. Mrs Thatcher told the Conservative Group for Europe, 'It is a Community of nation-states with the Council of Ministers as the chief decision-making body. I believe that this will be true for many years and that national government and national parliaments will continue to have a determining role.'[15] The party has no proposals for institutional reforms, states that 'the European Parliament could not take fresh powers by its own decision' (Hurd),[16] favours closer scrutiny of Community legislation in the House of Commons, and appears to be opposed to decision making by majority vote in the Council of Ministers. Their approach is therefore embedded in a confederalist conception of the Community.

The Conservative delegation to the European parliament, known as the European Conservative Group (ECG), was faced with responding to issues in the parliament where the group was expected to take a position and yet lacked any clear direction from London. Attempts by the group to develop their own policies led to concern that conflict would develop between the policies of the European Conservative Group and the Westminster parliamentary party. The group therefore pursued a low-profile, low-initiative role, which frustrated its ability for coalition-building inside the parliament. The closest the group came to policy-making was the publication, *Our Common Cause*, which identified areas of Conservative interest without giving any clear policy direction.[17] The real impetus for policy formation came from the possibility that as early as May 1978 the party could be faced with European elections. An informal Group on Europe was set up which invited high-ranking Conservatives interested in Europe to present their views on a European policy. In January 1977 a European Policy Committee, chaired by John Davies, was formed to draw up a manifesto for the elections. After the postponement of the elections, the role of the committee was widened to consider European policy and coordinate policy between Westminster and Strasbourg, in effect acting as a sub-committee of the shadow cabinet. By May 1977 a draft campaign guide and a draft manifesto was ready for the elections, and was updated by the end of 1978.

The main themes of the Party's European policies can already be identified: A stronger *foreign policy role* for the Community will be proposed towards the rest of the world, especially the developing countries. One idea being floated is for a foreign policy secretariat to co-ordinate national foreign policies and perhaps even reach a common foreign policy, even though foreign policy is beyond the terms of the Treaty of Rome. This was the major theme of an important speech by Mrs Thatcher in Brussels.

The Conservatives will attack *bureaucratisation* in the Community emphasising attempts at excessive harmonisation, which provoked a highly critical motion at the party conference in 1976 and, exceptionally, an amendment was accepted to the pro-European motion at the conference in 1978 which said that the party should not be afraid to criticise the Community. Mrs Thatcher said in Brussels, 'the cause of European unity is surely not advanced by hundreds of petty internal regulations, such as on the content of ice cream, or the activities of door-step salesmen'.[18]

A major theme will be reform of the *Common Agricultural Policy*, which continues to dominate British discussion of the Community, but not the wholesale replacement of the CAP with a new policy. A number of reforms will be proposed, but the basic structure will be retained.[19]

The view that British *economic* problems can only be solved in concert with our European partners will be given, with emphasis on a Community energy policy.

The Conservative party has developed the institutional mechanism for European policy-making and shows the ability to adapt to the new environment. It is thus far ahead of the Labour party. Future areas of interest will be whether conflict develops between party policies for European and Westminster elections, to what extent the ECG will be inflexibly tied to party policy in their activities in the parliament, and how the party can balance between its general support for the Community and criticism of certain policies.

Direct elections to the European Parliament

The Treaty of Rome provided for the eventual direct election of the European parliament and after considerable pressure from the parliament, the European Council of Heads of State agreed in December 1975 to the principle of direct elections.[20] Conservative spokesmen in the referendum stated party support for direct elections; this was reaffirmed at the party conference in 1975 when Reginald Maudling said, 'We are committed by the Treaty of Rome to the principle of direct elections. There is no going back',[21] and the conference overwhelmingly passed a European motion which included, 'This conference also encourages the Conservative party to work continually for direct elections to the European parliament'.[22]

The Conservatives were thus firmly committed to the principle of direct elections, in marked contrast to the Labour party whose conference in October 1976 rejected the principle of direct elections; not until 26 April 1978 did the National Executive Committee agree to begin the process of preparation.

The European parliament, endorsed by the European Council, had proposed May or June 1978 for the first set of European elections. The Conservatives set up a committee under Sir Anthony Royle, MP, to consider policy towards the detailed aspects of direct elections legislation. The Labour government was very slow to present legislation because of internal differences within the cabinet and the fear that the proposals would reopen the old wounds between Labour pro- and anti-marketeers. The government finally presented the European Assemblies Bill on 24 June 1976.

The bill, however, presented the Conservatives with an awkward dilemma. The Labour government, as part of its compact with the Liberals, presented in the bill two alternative electoral systems. The first was a form of the regional list system, criticised even by supporters of proportional representation for its anomalies, but at least a proportional system acceptable to the Liberals. Most

Conservatives, and especially Mrs Thatcher, are strongly opposed to proportional representation and, therefore, could be expected to oppose the regional list. However, the other alternative, the traditional British first-past-the-post system, required an elaborate process of presentation and appeals for constituency boundaries, which would be unlikely to be completed in time for elections to be held in May 1978 unless the traditional appeal system were abandoned. The Conservatives feared that by voting against the regional list system, the party would be blamed for delaying the elections, which would damage their European image, especially with other centre-right parties. In response to this, influential Conservatives favoured supporting the regional list, or some compromise formula. Indeed, the *Economist* reported that a majority of the shadow cabinet favoured that course.[23] Douglas Hurd argued that it would be a mistake to have a new electoral system for the first election, when a common Community system will be introduced in 1984 which would require yet another change. This argument, together with strong hostility inside the parliamentary party to proportional representation in principle, led to a Conservative free vote but an unofficial whip against it, and an eventual majority for first-past-the-post.

During the passage of legislation, the Conservatives criticised the delay in introducing legislation and expressed fears that the elections would be delayed throughout the Community by the British government's indifference. The debate provided an opportunity for Tory anti-marketeers to repeat their attacks on the Community, but generally there was strong Conservative front-bench and back-bench support for the bill.

The bill, however, faced the opposition with another dilemma. The government presented their guillotine motion for the bill on 26 January 1978. It is, of course, traditional for the opposition to oppose the guillotine motion. However, with strong Labour opposition to the elections, there was a serious danger that the guillotine motion would be defeated, and that the legislation would fail to reach its passage by the end of the parliamentary session. The Conservatives once again wished to avoid the blame for delaying the elections, and therefore for the first time ever the opposition, led by Mrs Thatcher, supported the government's guillotine which enabled the bill to be passed on 16 February 1978. This, however, was too late for a June 1978 election, so the election was postponed until 7 June 1979.

Election Preparations

The party responded to European elections with a new organisational structure, an information and educational campaign and a new selection procedure for European candidates. If the national election had been held, as they expected, in October 1978, then the party would have given top priority to the European elections. The possibility of a general election at any time up to and including the European elections reduced the emphasis that could be placed on the European elections.

The National Union, the voluntary side of the party, responded to the prospect of European elections by setting up high level National and Area Steering Committees on European Elections, with broad party representation, to co-ordinate activity, to brief candidates and activists, and to submit ideas on policy and organisation. The National Union proposed the formation of European Constituency Councils (ECCs), with the six top officers of the (usually eight) Westminster constituencies within the European constituency. The ECC would have responsibility for the selection of the candidate, the appointment of a 'Euroagent' from amongst the Westminster agents, and the organisation for the election. Formation of the ECCs awaited the results of the Boundary Commission recommendations, but intense consultations within probable Euroconstituencies began earlier. One source of friction was that each Westminster constituency was given equal representation on the bodies of the ECC, while contributions to the ECC, in terms of personnel, work and time were likely to be unequal.

The need to educate, inform and stimulate preparations for the elections among party workers was recognised as an important priority, especially considering the positive but unenthusiastic attitude generally prevalent, the widespread feeling that the local parties were not well-informed on developments, and the fact that the elections would be the first for an institution largely unknown to the public, in a constituency different from normal, requiring the establishment of close relations between different constituencies. On 4 August 1977 the Advisory Committee on Direct Elections, chaired by Douglas Hurd, was set up to co-ordinate activities in the field of information and in January 1978 a full-time European Elections Officer, Roger Boaden, was appointed. The main information activities were the distribution of literature produced by the European Elections Office, the European Conservative Group, the

European parliament, the Commission and the Conservative Group for Europe; the organisation of the visits to the Commission and the parliament for party activists and organisers, including everyone expected to play a leading role in the ECCs; and twelve regional conferences with sessions on the parliament, policy and organisation, involving 300 to 400 people at each meeting. Finance for informational activities was available from the European parliament, via the European Conservative Group. A major problem in the ECCs was the problem of raising finance for European elections, along with the other financial commitments.

A Standing Advisory Committee on European Candidates (Euro-SAC) was formed to draw up the candidates list for the elections. In form, it is similar to the system of selecting Westminster candidates. The applicant for the list met first with the vice-chairman of the party responsible for candidates (then Marcus Fox, MP), and then met an interviewing panel with representatives of the National Union and the European Conservative Group. If accepted on the list, the candidate could apply for selection to the ECCs who were expected to form selection committees of two representatives from each Westminster constituency. The selection committee was to present at least five candidates to the ECC, which in turn would select three candidates for recommendation to a general meeting, consisting of a minimum of 25 members appointed from each UK constituency association, and it was recommended that the process of selection should involve as many members as possible.

The selection of European candidates was far more rigorous than for Westminster candidates. The Euro-SAC 'set itself definite objectives as far as the qualifications of candidates are concerned, in order to ensure a high standard and representation of diverse occupations and experience'.[24] The party received well over 2000 enquiries, and had hoped to establish a short list of approved candidates, but the number of applications forced a somewhat larger list than expected. Many applicants were discouraged even from filling in an application form, many highly qualified candidates were rejected, and even those accepted testified to the tough interview. The Euro-SAC was concerned to present a more highly qualified candidate than for the Westminster list, and may have attempted to exercise a greater degree of influence over local candidate selection. Candidate selection was expected to proceed quickly from the final decision of the constituency boundaries (probably November 1978) to the end of February 1979. The party strongly discouraged, but did not forbid, the holding of the dual mandate at both Westminster and Strasbourg.

The Conservative party thus proceeded very rapidly with their preparations for the European elections. At this stage the exact nature of the impact of the European elections on the party is unclear, but a number of interesting questions are raised. Will the structure for the European elections develop an independent and separate status from the Westminster structure? What will be the reaction of party activists to the elections, especially when there will be no obvious concrete result such as the election of a Conservative government? How will the party cope with the finances of the elections, especially at the local level? Will the size of the constituencies change the nature of local campaigning, perhaps towards a more media-oriented campaign? Will the European parliament create a new political career structure? Will the selection procedure lead to both greater control of the candidates by the centre at the early stage of selection, and a more open primary type selection at the end? The impact of European elections on the Conservative party organisation is uncertain, but it will clearly not emerge unchanged.

Centre-Right Cooperation

The Conservative party has no immediately natural allies inside the European Community. The only other Conservative party is the rather small Danish Conservative People's party with whom they form the ECG. The Conservatives strongly seek alliances with other centre-right parties, both to strengthen them during the election campaign and to be able to exert greater influence in the parliament. The party has extremely close relations with the Christian Democrat Union in the Federal Republic of Germany with frequent visits and exchanges at all levels of the parties, and a great deal of agreement on policy questions. The Conservatives therefore seek an alliance with the European Christian Democrats.

The Christian Democrat Parties, however, in Belgium, Netherlands and Italy are opposed to cooperation with the Conservative party. This is for four reasons. First, these parties take the word Christian in their names very seriously, and references to Christian values can be easily found in party pronouncements.

They are therefore suspicious of a secular Conservative party. Secondly, the word conservative translates into their languages as fascist or reactionary, and this view is reinforced by a generally bad press in these countries. Thirdly, these parties have strong left wings associated with Christian trade unions. Fourthly, they have all formed, at one time or other, government coalitions with the socialists. Thus the Conservative party has had to promote an active policy to improve its relations with these parties.

The only international 'organisation' (before the EDU) in which the Conservative party participated was the Inter-Party meeting, which was an annual meeting of centre-right parties to discuss particular policy areas. However, the meetings were only informal affairs, lacking any permanent structure, or decision-making procedure. Sections of the party have created very extensive inter-party links. The International Office of the party maintains extensive links with centre-right parties in Europe and throughout the world. The Women's National Advisory Committee is affiliated to the European Union of Women, with fourteen affiliates in fourteen countries. The Young Conservatives belong to the Democratic Youth Community of Europe, with fifteen affiliates in fourteen countries; and the Federation of Conservative Students belongs to European Democrat Students, with eighteen affiliates in sixteen countries.

At the 1975 party conference the delegates balloted for the motion on inter-party cooperation, and passed the motion overwhelmingly. The motion read:

> This Conference, recognising that Britain is now securely a member of the European Community, urges the Conservative Party to work more closely with our political allies in Europe towards the formation of a moderate centre-right alliance (a European Democrat Party) able effectively to oppose the Socialist grouping in the European Parliament and able to take positive initiatives in the development of Europe.

Mrs Thatcher has played an active role in the search for centre-right cooperation. At the annual conference of the CDU in Hanover on 25 May 1976, she gave a highly successful speech in which she said, 'I am convinced that the Christian Democratic, Conservative and Centre Parties in Europe should now join together in an effective working alliance. I believe that this is a task of historic importance, and one in which we should invest all our energies.'[25] In December 1976 Mrs Thatcher visited the Netherlands for talks with the Dutch Christian Democrats and in June 1977 she visited Rome to meet Christian Democrat leaders and gave a speech called 'Europe as I See It', directly aimed at the Italian Christian Democrat party. 'I would ask those who shy away from the word (Conservative) to concentrate on the common ground which exists between the British Conservative party, and the Christian Democrats and other centre-right parties in Europe.'[26] Thus the question of centre-right cooperation is a major one for the Conservative party, including the party leader.

With British entry to the Community, the Conservative delegation to the European parliament formed their own party group with the Danish Conservatives and did not join the Christian Democrat Group, much to the disappointment of the CDU. Initial problems of mutual misunderstandings, compounded by personal rivalries and ambitions, led to a bad relationship between the two groups. The *Economist* in August 1976 described the Tory-Christian Democrat alliance as being 'in bad shape'.[27] The election of two new group leaders in Sir Geoffrey Rippon and Egon Klepsch led to a much improved relationship. The Christian Democrats and Conservatives invited each other to observe their 'Study Days', and even to give presentations at each other's group meetings. There is considerable contact between the groups in the search for common positions. Group relations, however, have not permeated far beyond the parliament.

The problem of Christian Democrat–Conservative cooperation arose again with the creation of the European People's Party (EPP) in April 1976 as the European Christian Democrat party for the elections. Opposition from some Christian Democrats led to the creation of the EPP without a British member. There were long and intense debates led by the CDU to create the EPP with the possibility of future Conservative membership. The statutes were ambiguous but appeared to allow membership to all who 'share its fundamental concepts and subscribe to its political programme',[28] but there was no possibility that the Conservatives could join the EPP before the first European elections in June 1979.

The search for a European centre-right alliance began in earnest in 1972 when the student and youth sections of nine parties proclaimed a 'Charter' for the European Democrat party in London. The word 'European Democrat' was proposed as the most acceptable to Christian Democrat, Conservative, right-wing Liberal and centrist parties.

In September 1975 there was a party leaders' meeting in Klesheim, Austria, under the auspices of the Inter-Party meeting, which took the principle decision to create a European Democratic Union. After long and difficult negotiations, during which the CDU tried to get other Christian Democrat parties to join, the EDU was eventually formed on 24 April 1978. EDU members at its formation were:

EEC	Full	Permanent Observer	ad hoc Observer
UK	Conservative		
Germany	CDU		
	CSU		
France	RPR (Gaullists)		Republicans (Giscardiens)
Denmark	Conservative		
Italy		South Tirol People's Party Trentino People's Party	
Non-EEC			
Austria	People's Party		
Finland	National Coalition	Swedish People's Party	
Greece			New Democracy
Malta		Nationalist	
Norway	Conservative		
Portugal	Centre Social Democrats		
Spain			Centre Democrats
Sweden	Moderate		
Switzer- land		Christian Democratic Party	

The EDU set up four working commissions on European policy, Eurocommunism, energy policy and unemployment; it created an executive committee under the chairmanship of Dr Josef Taus, the leader of the Austrian People's party, and planned a formal congress. However, the EDU created problems of its own. The majority of EDU members were not within the European Community. Of those who were Community members, the CDU/CSU were committed to campaign for the EPP, and the Gaullists would campaign on a nationalist platform. Thus the Conservatives did not really find the alliance for the European elections that they sought. Some Conservatives never saw the EDU as primarily an electoral alliance at all but wanted it to develop as a centre-right International like the Socialist International, which could play a role in supporting centre-right parties in emerging democracies like Portugal and Spain. However, without the electoral value for European elections, the EDU may lack the impetus for development into a centre-right international role.

Although the EDU will not campaign in the European elections, the other Christian Democrat parties see it as a threat to the EPP. They were seriously upset at the EDU, and strongly urged the CDU to play down the EDU. Some Conservatives believed that the creation of the EDU should have been postponed until the majority of Christian Democrat parties within the Community could be persuaded to join. Others, however, were concerned that continual postponement would have killed the idea completely.

The Conservatives at last belong to an international grouping, the European Democratic Union. However, the problem of broad centre-right cooperation for the European elections, the method by which the Conservatives can conciliate the reluctant Christian Democrats, and the role of the EDU in the future, all remain unsolved.

CONCLUSION

The traditional view of the Conservative party has been a hierarchical one where the initiative lies with the leader and other members of the party follow his lead. With regard to the initiative to join the European Community, the decision has been presented as a personal one taken by the leader against traditional party principles and values. The success in getting the party to support Community membership has been attributed to the tremendous powers of the leader and their use by both Harold Macmillan and Edward Heath. Whilst not rejecting the importance of the role of the leader, it may be more useful to view the party as a collection of interest and attitude groups, which the leader seeks to unite into a coalition behind his policies. The support of all the various groups within the party cannot be assumed but must be sought and wooed, although there may exist a reserve of loyalty which the leader can draw upon.

A leader can successfully lead the party in new directions when he is certain that there is widespread support for his initiative. Macmillan was able to lead his party into support for EEC membership because many of the interests and groups in the party and associated with it were already pro-European. Such groups included the early 'Europeans', the Tory press, much of industry and agriculture, the defence lobby, intellectuals, professionals and young Conservatives. Those groups which opposed entry, such as the Commonwealth group, the 'imperialists' and part of the agriculturalist interest were by no means united in their opposition. Under Heath some Conservatives in parliament and outside objected to unnecessary haste in making decisions committing Britain to EEC membership and only supported membership when their doubts had been conciliated. By the time of the referendum many Conservatives at local and national level had become convinced Europeans and participated in the referendum campaign without the necessity of a strong lead from above. Thus the traditional hierarchical view of the Conservative party may need to be revised towards a more complex, group-based analysis.

Since Britain's entry into the Community, further factors have undermined the hierarchical view, with the development of semi-autonomous decision-making by the European Conservative Group, the creation of a new institutional structure for the European elections and the need to take account of potential centre-right allies in the European parliament. The growth of these new interests will inevitably make coalition-building in the Conservative party more difficult in the future.

NOTES

1. W. S. Churchill, *Europe Unites* (London: Hollis and Carter, 1949).
2. R. Neustadt, 'Whitehouse and Whitehall', in A. King: *British Prime Ministers* (London: Macmillan, 1969) p. 141.
3. H. Macmillan, *Britain, the Commonwealth and Europe* (Conservative Central Office, October 1962).
4. P. Self & H. Storing: *The State and the Farmers* (London: Allen & Unwin, 1962).

5. R. Lieber: *British Politics and European Unity* (Berkeley: University of California Press, 1970).
6. *Conservative Conference Verbatim Report, 1961* (Conservative Central Office, 1961).
7. D. Butler & A. King: *The General Election of 1964* (London: Macmillan, 1965) p. 79.
8. K. Young: *Sir Alec Douglas-Home* (London: Dent, 1970) p. 254.
9. D. Butler & U. Kitzinger: *The 1975 Referendum* (London: Macmillan, 1976) p. 78.
10. *The Times* (January 1977).
11. Mrs Thatcher, Foundation Meeting of the European Democratic Union, Klesheim, Austria, 24 April 1978.
12. Parliamentary Debates (Hansard) vol. 908 (1975–6) col. 969.
13. Douglas Hurd, MP, Norwich (20 March 1976).
14. Mrs Thatcher: *Europe As I See It* (European Conservative Group, August 1977) p. 6.
15. Mrs Thatcher, speech to the Conservative Group for Europe, 24 November 1976.
16. Douglas Hurd, Norwich, (20 March 1976.)
17. European Conservative Group, *Our Common Cause* (September 1974).
18. Mrs Thatcher, *The Sinews of Foreign Policy* (European Conservative Group, June 1978).
19. See publications of the European Conservative Group e.g. *Our Common Cause*, op. cit., 32–4. *Europe As I See It*, op. cit., 6–7. Jim Scott-Hopkins & John Corrie: *Towards a Community Rural Policy* (European Conservative Group, February 1978). Jim Scott-Hopkins: *Food for Thought* (European Conservative Group, April 1978).
20. See Nigel Ashford, *Direct Elections to the European Parliament*, (working paper no. 9 Department of Politics, University of Warwick, May 1976) for the background to the decision directly to elect the European Parliament.
21. *Conservative Party Conference Verbatim Report 1976* (Conservative Central Office, 1976).
22. Ibid.
23. The *Economist* (19 March 1977).
24. Letter by Sir Charles Johnstone, Chairman of the National Union, to the National Union (6 September 1976).
25. Mrs Thatcher, speech to the CDU Congress, Hanover (25 May 1976).
26. Mrs Thatcher: *Europe As I See It*, op. cit., p. 10.
27. The *Economist* (18 October 1976) p. 74.
28. Statutes, European People's Party.

6 Constitutional Reform: Some Dilemmas for a Conservative Philosophy

Nevil Johnson

I INTRODUCTION: THE NATURE OF THE DILEMMA

The Conservative party today finds itself in the somewhat unusual role of protagonist of constitutional reform. This is not to suggest that it speaks with one voice on the matter, nor even that it has entered into serious commitments to reform the constitution as soon as it has the power to do so. But what is beyond doubt is that many Conservatives are worried about the state of the constitution and that in public discussion of what kind of constitutional reforms might be needed, it is Conservatives who have made the running rather than their political opponents. As I shall seek to explain, this puts the party in an unusual stance and indeed presents a serious dilemma for Conservative philosophy.

It is worth beginning with an outline of the nature of this dilemma. Within the tradition of conservative political thinking it has been held that political institutions grow out of and are sustained by social habits and manners: to quote Burke, 'Politics ought to be adjusted not to human reasoning but to human nature'.[1] Political values themselves are rooted in social life and can be learnt only from growing up in a particular tradition of civility. It is a mistake to conceive of political behaviour narrowly as conduct appropriate only to transactions within the confines of political institutions and activity. On the contrary, such virtue as there may be in public life is but the manifestation of principles derived from experience in the family, the school, the club or private association, the practice of a profession, the place of work or business and so on.

Similarly, there is no sharp separation between the institutions of the political realm, the methods by which society is governed, and the infinitely complex network of social institutions and practices[2] through which people are held together in society and enabled to cooperate with each other for the satisfaction of their needs. The political institutions grow out of social arrangements and are sustained by them. It is accepted that political institutions have an important and indeed essential regulative purpose, but their form and *modus operandi* represent a distillation of the wisdom gained in social experience: their shape and character reflect the genius of a people rather than the inspiration of the philosopher or law-giver.

This last remark is important. It has been a persistent theme in British Conservative thought that political institutions should not be constructed on abstract principles. Indeed, more than that, it has frequently been asserted that they cannot be so constructed and that any attempt to do so is foredoomed to failure. The attack on abstract principles is a *leitmotiv* in Burke's writings and is echoed in a similar vein in Disraeli. We find it once more in Salisbury and again in the twentieth century in figures as different one from the other as Baldwin and Oakeshott. No doubt there is a certain plausibility in the view that it is foolish to attempt to shape the political institutions of a stable society by the application of general principles which take no account of time, place and circumstance, nor of the particularity of that society's historical experience. Moreover, the criticism of the appeal to abstract principles is consistent with the emphasis given in conservative thought to the dominant influence of social behaviour and relationships in the complex processes through which political institutions and practices evolve. Nevertheless, the rejection of abstract principles in the structuring of political life reveals an important deficiency in conservative thinking and underlines in an ironic way the dilemmas facing the contemporary Conservative who seeks constitutional reform.

What conservatism in its traditional guise lacks is an adequate explanation of deliberate change. It would be unreasonable to argue either that all change is bad or that all change, good or bad, merely occurs by chance. We have substantial historical experience of deliberate and contrived change, sometimes even contrived with the aid of force and violence, and we know that such change has on occasion been judged beneficial and necessary. We know, too, that people are capable of thinking intelligently about their affairs and in far less dramatic ways than through civil war or revolution have shown themselves capable of establishing new procedures for the regulation of various aspects of their social and political relations. For the Burkean conservative this is all something of a mystery: his postulates require him to decry abstract principles, yet the indulgence in abstract thought and the pursuit of its intimations into practical affairs is a persistent human experience. The difficulty arises, of course, because the conservative view of human nature and behaviour is lop-sided. Too much emphasis is placed on the unreflecting aspects of social life, on 'prejudice' in the sense given to that word by Burke,[3] and not enough on the rational faculties of human beings and their capacity to take thought and to exercise foresight. As a result, deliberate political action and the thinking which may precede and motivate it are seen as peculiarly disturbing irritants, threatening to disrupt the harmonious emergence from the interplay of social interests and habits of such political procedures and policy decisions as are compatible with the underlying preferences of society.

It will be obvious that this traditional suspicion of abstract principles in politics sharpens the dilemma facing the Conservative constitutional reformer. It is difficult to see how he can set about constitutional reform without first undertaking an examination of principles. And, as will be argued later, the condition of the British constitution is such that its reform invites far more than a cautious nibble at abstract principles here and there: on the contrary, it invites the wholesale application of principles for the very reason that it appears to have lost all definition as a body of easily identifiable practices justified by appeal to principles which they can be said to embody. Of course, the traditional Conservative who shares the dislike of theorising in politics might take refuge in Burke's famous remark about the necessary connection between conservation and reform, and recommend that we approach constitutional reform pragmatically, searching in the past for those clues which will unlock the gates to moderate and limited improvement. The difficulty here is that it has become harder to find guidance in the past. Many feel with de Tocqueville that 'as the past has ceased to throw its light upon the future, the mind of man wanders in obscurity'.[4] The rate of social and technical change has depreciated the value of the wisdom of our ancestors, perhaps rendered much of it irrelevant. And as will be argued more fully below, it is the sad fate of an unwritten constitution, resting largely on convention, to be more seriously eroded by a rapid rate of change in social values and habits than one which has greater formality and visibility. Thus, the appeal to the past for guidance in the matter of constitutional change often turns out to be mere romanticism, an appeal to conditions and experiences which have vanished for good. This kind of Conservative constitutional reformer finds himself struggling to put Humpty Dumpty together again and there is no evidence that this can be done.

Before bringing these introductory remarks to a close it is worth commenting on the motives impelling many Conservatives to contemplate various schemes of constitutional reform. It seems not unfair to conclude that what they seek in the first place is protection against radical social change facilitated by political practices and constitutional conventions which no longer impose much restraint on governments. It is not so much that traditional constitutional rules are sharply criticised or rejected, but rather that their inability to achieve the effects they are thought to have had in the past is deplored. Thus the intention expressed in Conservative constitutional argument is generally not radically to change or re-design the constitution, but to seek its restoration or re-invigoration. In this way Conservative constitutionalists tend to be clearly distinguishable, for example, from Utilitarian theorists of the early nineteenth century or a few of the socialist thinkers in the Fabian mould of recent times, all of whom were moved by a desire to re-construct the polity in different ways and to make it substantially better. In contrast the Conservative reformer sees himself as repairing the defences or plugging the dykes; he eschews any optimistic commitment to a better world and hopes to ward off present evils.

Two problems arise out of this defensive and protective approach to constitutional reform. One is that the reformer is liable to be attacked by his opponents as a fraud or special pleader. He will be told that his case for reform is but a smoke-screen for the preservation of vested interests. Fundamentally this is an incoherent and foolish line of attack, but that does not deprive it of weight in day-to-day political controversy. The second problem is more serious and consists in the fact that as the Conservative constitutional theorist seeks to identify what can be restored and how, he is driven to solutions (partial or more far-reaching) which in fact change the ground on which he stands. The would-be protector becomes the innovator, the Conservative risks finding himself playing the part of the radical reformer guided by abstract principles. The individual conservative thinker and even the individual politician preoccupied with day-to-day affairs might be prepared to accept this mutation in his position brought about by the logic of pursuing improvement in a constitution which has atrophied. But there still remains the task of persuading those in the party and those who support it to follow the path of reform. For there is reason to believe that their suspicion of contrived change and their attachment to Burkean 'prejudice' are sufficiently strong to repel most proposals for reform and, what is more, such attachment to prescription and habit extends far beyond the limits of Conservative support in the country. Thus, in a curious way the Conservative constitutional reformer finds himself confronted with the paradox inherent in the Burkean account of the relationship between social life and political institutions: it is social habits and manners which must and ought to determine the course of constitutional evolution. But how then do we explain change and, above all, how can we justify proposals for change to those who believe that it must emerge naturally and mysteriously from the intricate life of the whole society?

In this introduction I have tried to do two things. First, an effort has been made to identify some aspects of conservative political thought which bear most closely on the problem of constitutional rules and their adaptation to new demands or threatening dangers. Second, I have underlined what appears to me to be the difficulty or dilemma in which most contemporary Conservatives find themselves when they think seriously about constitutional problems and how to deal with them. They face the prospect of having to reappraise substantial elements in their own political philosophy should they have the tenacity to work through to a coherent justification of the reform proposals they contemplate. For if constitutional reform is to be serious, and not to remain at the level of pious declamation or unobtrusive tinkering, it must represent an attempt to structure institutions deliberately in the hope of thereby maintaining or establishing political values and practices seen to be desirable. It means recognising that Montesquieu or Hamilton, Madison and Jay—to quote but two famous sources of rational conservatism—are better guides to constitutional re-appraisal than the Burke of the Reflections on the Revolution in France.

II PHILOSOPHICAL FOUNDATIONS AND CONSTITUTIONAL CONSEQUENCES

I want to turn now to a number of the more specific characteristics of conservative political philosophy which can then be linked closely with the contemporary argument about the constitution as well as with some of the ideas which have been put forward for constitutional reform.

It is necessary to present these elements of the conservative political tradition only in summary form since they are familiar and have been discussed by many writers. They can be expressed as follows:

(i) The rights and privileges which individuals and associations enjoy are grounded in property.

(ii) Freedom requires equality before the law. This concept of equality refers as much to the equal protection of unequal claims as to the safeguarding of those rights which can be said to be equally distributed or allocated.[5]

(iii) The successful government of a society depends upon the presence of an elite conscious of its obligations towards the society. Such an elite, no matter how composed, is more likely to enjoy trust (a vital factor in constitutional government) if it has a secure social status.

(iv) Trust in government is created and sustained by appropriate behaviour on the part of officeholders. This is what generates the habits and prescriptions on which constitutional norms. defining responsibility in government rest.

(v) Given the importance of the social foundations of politics and the limited role that can be allowed to government, political or constitutional change should be gradual and evolutionary.

(vi) Just as the health of society requires a diffusion of varied interests and sentiments, so it is desirable to maintain a balance amongst the political institutions in order to ensure that no one interest can impose itself on all others.

It seems to me that these elements—or something like them—together constitute the basis of a doctrine of constitutional and limited government which seeks to maintain freedom under the law. They contain no clear guidance as to the proper limits of government action and perhaps for this reason have rendered

Conservatives too passive and perplexed in the face of the extension of the role of the state during the twentieth century. Nevertheless, they do imply that the role of government should at least be as limited as is compatible with allowing the maximum scope possible for individuals to regulate their lives and relations with each other autonomously. The underlying view of freedom is grounded in a recognition of necessary social differences and of variations in the importance which people will attach to particular rights in virtue of their own situations. The attitude to law expressed in these postulates is for the most part negative, and well within that Common Law tradition out of which much conservative thinking has sprung. Law is seen pre-eminently as codified social practice whether it is the law built up by judges in their decisions or the law laid down in statute by parliament.[6] There is little room, too, for an idea of law as an attempt to achieve a condition of justice or for the argument that positive law might itself be in need of justification by appeal to principles of right or justice. Precisely because so much emphasis is placed on the importance of trust as the cement which binds the polity together, there is a prejudice in favour of allowing to public authorities a wide discretion in the discharge of their functions. This has been held to be reasonable both on practical grounds—we cannot prescribe in detail for the unforeseeable circumstances of the future—and on account of the belief that trust between the rulers and the ruled can develop and survive only when there are present in society, and in the conduct transmitted from social life into politics, implicit restraints determining what it is proper to do. In other words, the conservative theory of limited government does not advocate the institutionalisation of suspicions and mistrust,[7] but instead proposes that those in power are restrained by their own sense of the limits to their authority, as well as by the pressures, moral and material, in society which they have to respect.

It hardly needs to be said that the world has changed since the epoch in which this view of how to maintain an acceptable political order took shape. It has become more and more difficult to ground rights in the ownership and use of property, partly because a more abstract view of rights has begun to exercise a powerful influence over our legislation, partly because the more obvious rights attaching to property have steadily been eroded. The use and enjoyment of property is restricted in innumerable ways; its acquisition and disposal are often rendered difficult; an increasingly large amount of property has passed into public ownership, a trend which has serious implications for the very understanding of the term 'property'. Perhaps the only form of property ownership which might be said to be wholly respectable is the private dwelling—provided it is not too large and is not a second holiday home. There is no space here to explore in detail the ramifications of the changes which have taken place over the past 75 years or so in the status and role of property in British social organisation. But it hardly appears to be an exaggeration to suggest that one of the load-bearing timbers on which the Conservative view of how rights are acquired and secured in society has been infected with dry-rot. And what has replaced it is the claim of the political authority to determine the content of rights abstractly and to alter these in accordance with its view of how best to maximise welfare. By this process the claims of the political authority are exalted and profound changes have taken place in the pattern of constraints on government which exists in society.[8]

In respect of the second point, equality before the law as a condition of freedom, the adequacy of the very principle has been challenged and the discussion of equality, its meanings and application, has become a central preoccupation in political and social analysis. This argument will not be pursued here, but two aspects of the changes affecting the idea of equality before the law which have taken place should be underlined. One is the manner in which the system of adjudication—the courts in more familiar terms—has been fragmented. It will be recollected that one of the terms on which Dicey defined the rule of law was the supremacy of the ordinary courts of the land. It can well be argued that Dicey exaggerated substantially the significance of this condition. Nevertheless, lying behind the argument was an important assumption, namely that the rule of law requires a certain unity and coherence in the law and that this has to be achieved through a system of adjudication which is itself coherent and ultimately subject to a single source of interpretation on appeal. This condition is nowadays fulfilled only in a formal and limited sense. This is because large areas of adjudication have been withdrawn from the ordinary courts of law or never even entrusted to them.[9] This happens, of course, predominantly in the wide field of social provision, in which tribunals of one kind and another abound. However their decisions may be evaluated, one thing is certain: they do not provide an easily accessible and public body of case law. Nor can it be said with confidence that they operate under consistent and equitable general guidelines; instead they apply conventions, statutory requirements and administrative preferences peculiar to their own particular jurisdictions. In such conditions the practical realisation of equality before the law is bound to be heavily qualified: we move steadily towards rule by exception.

The other aspect of this matter to be stressed is the impact of a different view of equality on the older notion of civil equality before the law. I refer to a theory of substantive equality according to which equality is defined in terms of the realisation of a continuing claim by all to an equal share of material benefits in society. Only on this basis, so it is argued, can the inequalities inherent in the idea of formal equality before the law and in the concept of equality of opportunity be mitigated or overcome. It is recognised that if the concept of substantive equality is expressed in radical terms like this, the number of those who take it seriously is far less than of those who merely find it convenient to pay lip-service to the notion. There are many, too, who firmly reject such a view. Nevertheless, it is apparent from the history of the past 30 years that substantive equality in various diluted forms has had a deep influence on many sectors of public policy and to some extent has constituted one of the watch-words in political debate in the country. The outcome has been a shift towards an egalitarian bias in many sectors of social provision, economic intervention by government, taxation policy, education etc., which Conservatives locally and nationally have not been able to check or reverse. Thus we have had the spectacle of Conservative governments pursuing policies they cannot really believe in, hesitating to contemplate changes which might fracture what is held to be a consensus, and encouraging developments which can hardly fail further to undermine confidence in the more narrowly defined idea of equality which has been dominant in the conservative tradition. It is clear that such a situation has implications, too, for the extent to which the party can retain the confidence of its supporters, many of whom see it as too prone to apply the policies of its political rivals, and for the very rationale of a competitive two-party system. Competition there may be, but its object may be simply office rather than the opportunity to pursue the policies that are publicly proclaimed.

There is no need to say much about the third factor. A clearly identifiable social elite has virtually disappeared and though status remains an ubiquitous (and inescapable) social phenomenon its expression in hierarchical relationships is greatly attenuated. The social basis of political careers and of political action has become amorphous and ill-defined, a situation which in different ways affects other political parties as much as the Conservatives. Similarly, it is much harder to talk of a political elite except perhaps in a narrow functional sense. Political scientists may choose to identify 635 or 1000 or perhaps even 2000 persons as constituting the political elite of this country. But to do so is merely to identify officeholders and a group of 'influentials' said to be close to them. This is a narrow concept of an elite, specifying next to nothing of the qualities in virtue of which its members establish a claim to respect and authority *qua elite*. Indeed, the problem which faces the conservative political theorist as well as the conservative politician is that there is no longer a ruling class, something which has nearly always been at one and the same time a social and political phenomenon. There are no longer 'natural rulers' and this does far more than disrupt the foundations of deference. It calls into question the terms on which trust develops in society and can be evoked by those who achieve political office. Yet another of the timbers in the Burkean structure seems unable to carry the weight imposed upon it by this feature of the conservative conception of how political authority can be sustained.

These remarks carry over in their application to the fourth element in a conservative theory of politics. That aspect of the problem of trust in government and responsibility on the part of officeholders that deserves to be stressed is the extent to which political institutions and officeholders are the victims of changes in attitudes and values in society. Even though it is held that trust in those holding office in government is sustained by their conduct, it has to be remembered that we are talking about two-way relationships. Whilst the ability of contemporary politicians to maintain an independent judgement of what is right and prudent to recommend may have been eroded by the gradual breakdown of a well-defined social elite sensitive to its political functions, equally they are exposed to pressures from a society in which the ties of habit have been loosened and agreement on what is appropriate conduct dissolved. The censure of public opinion remains, but it has become more capricious and is formed all too often by disappointment over the non-fulfilment of material expectations which it may not be within the power of the politician to satisfy. Correspondingly public opinion focuses less often on the manner in which politicians and officials have behaved and on the degree to which they have adhered to certain procedures and standards of conduct. The outcome of these trends is that at least part of the basis in society for the understanding of constitutional norms has been taken away; if the constitution is in danger it is as much because many people do not care about it as because politicians have misused it.

Then there is the preference for evolutionary change. No doubt many politicians (and not only in the Conservative party) would still express support for a policy of gradualism. However, it would be naïve to overlook a momentous transformation in the context in which decisions of policy are now taken. Whereas 50 or more years ago there was a widespread presumption that proposals for change had to be justified by those who put them forward, the burden of proof has now shifted to those who oppose change. There is a presumption that change is beneficent or inevitable or both, and if specific changes are under consideration, it is the critics who must make out a case against them. There could hardly be a better example of this than the history of local government reform 1966–74. A conviction took root amongst many of those concerned with local government that some kind of structural overhaul was imperative. Report followed report and finally· a Conservative government carried out a drastic territorial simplification in 1972. If there was an argument of substance in favour of the change, it was that it would promote efficiency and facilitate integrated policy-making in fields where administrative boundaries stood in the way of a unified approach. Whether this argument was well-founded is still hotly contested and, at best, judgment on its validity must be reserved. What is certain is that there was no great popular demand for local government reform and many local authorities opposed their own disappearance or reincarnation. Nevertheless, once the belief in the inevitability of change took root, nobody seemed able to look critically at the case for change or to prevent it happening. And there were Conservative ministers who congratulated themselves on their ability to apply progressive managerialism more effectively than their opponents.[10]

This example illustrates how hard it has become for even a Conservative government to resist what look like well-founded calls for change. Once more the Conservative finds himself in an uncomfortable position *vis-à-vis* the tradition he inherits. He may discern that it counsels scepticism in relation to the benefits presumed to flow from reforming legislation and questions the wisdom of applying to complex social relationships the equalising and centralising remedies of statute law, unless it is clear beyond doubt that only in this way can legitimate grievances be removed or widely supported purposes be fulfilled. But the prejudices of the age are against him and he finds it hard to work against some of those prejudices without resort to more systematic counter-arguments that his tradition has provided.

We come now to the sixth element, the one most directly related to the institutions of government and therefore to the issues of constitutional reform. It is perhaps a fair summary of the whole conservative way of thinking about government from the early eighteenth century down to the present to suggest that the persistent theme has been that of mixed and therefore limited government. At different periods the theme has been expressed in terms appropriate to the existing social and political structures. If we turn to the early writings of Disraeli we find that the idea of popular representation is attacked through an appeal to the historical continuity of estates, each of which was represented in the political institutions of the country.[11] Later the emphasis switches to the balance in parliament between Lords and Commons, and in modern times the balance is sought in the competition of organised parties for popular support within the conventions laid down by the parliamentary system. But, of course, there are other balancing factors: the restraining influence of the monarchy, the independence of the courts, the legal autonomy of local municipal corporations, the freedoms of the professions, the diffusion of interests organised in society and so on. For Conservatives, as indeed for many of different political persuasions, the British appeared to have made a remarkable success of parliamentary government. They had made a peaceful transition to universal suffrage without disruption of the social basis of political life, they had virtually invented the modern political party as a means of mobilising support and enabling the electorate to choose a government or, what is more important, to reject one, they had sustained a sovereign parliament whose powers are in principle unlimited and illimitable, and they had preserved intact a capacity to regulate political life through the conventions of an unwritten and very flexible constitution. They had, in addition, permitted the sovereignty of parliament to be claimed effectively by the government of the day, which increasingly felt entitled to legislate for the extension of public powers in virtue of its popular mandate, and they had devised a bureaucracy for the exercise of these public powers which has been uniquely detached from party political commitment.

Such in outline has been the modern development of the constitution, and Conservatives did, until recently at any rate, approve of it. The achievement appeared to be a tribute to the political sagacity of the nation and to a capacity to work out that accommodation between social needs and attitudes on the one hand and appropriate modes of political action on the other which conservative philosophy recommended as the only prudent course of political development. That Conservative governments presided over much of this evolution no doubt accounts for part of the approval which it has enjoyed. But there was, too, a more substantial reason for satisfaction. The course of social reform as well as the pace of constitutional change was gradual; within and between institutions pressures were at work which maintained a balance, and in society at large there were many sources of obstruction to measures which would have disturbed existing interests too violently, and to procedures which would have short-circuited those laid down by custom and convention as well as by earlier statutory enactment. Within this framework two-party competition was held to be fruitful and itself a mechanism by which moderation was enforced and government subjected to the ultimate control of the electorate. Moreover, when there was clear evidence of deep-seated popular support for changes put through by a radical government, Conservatives were generally prepared to respect such changes and to treat them as part of a new *status quo*. Such, of course, was their attitude to most of the legislation of the Labour government 1945–50.

This satisfaction with the constitutional system and the manner in which it has worked has been replaced by a mood of doubt and anxiety. It is easy to dismiss this as nothing but an expression of the fears and frustrations of a party in opposition, unable to prevent the carrying-out of policies which it dislikes and which in several cases are gravely disadvantageous to interests which it supports (and which in turn tend to support the party). But this is too cynical a verdict on the reasons for Conservative anxiety about the constitution and the present interest in constitutional reform within the party. Some of the actions of the Labour party between 1967 and 1970 when in government, the behaviour of the Labour party in opposition after 1970, the events of 1973–4, the legislative record of the Wilson government 1974–6, and the disturbing developments in several Labour constituency parties during recent years have all conspired to make Conservatives doubt whether there is any longer the will to work the constitution in the accustomed way and to cast a question-mark over the validity of a number of its accepted conventions. Perhaps, too, there are more thoughtful Conservatives who wonder whether the government of Edward Heath with its obsessive pursuit of major legislative changes on the basis of a slender parliamentary majority and a minority of votes in the country did not also contribute to the undermining of confidence in the terms on which the country is governed.

Criticism of constitutional trends has focused on four issues, although there are several less crucial matters which have claimed attention. First, there is the realisation that parliamentary sovereignty can be seriously misused in the sense that it can be harnessed to the fulfilment of a programme for which there is neither a majority in the country nor even an overall majority of the ruling party in parliament. Moreover, there is nothing to stop the authority of parliament being used to push through measures demanded by vociferous interests outside parliament which are subject to little or no popular control at all. The discovery that parliamentary sovereignty is a double-edged sword tends to prompt either or both of two reactions. One is to ask whether there should be formal limits to its exercise, in other words should not some conditions be withdrawn from change at the whim of a transient simple majority in parliament? The other is to consider again the structure of parliament and to look to means of checking the *de facto* claim of the Commons to exercise parliamentary sovereignty alone. This leads, of course, to the question of reform of the House of Lords.

The second issue is linked with the first and concerns the majority principle. If a majority is to be entitled to get its way on virtually anything, should we not look seriously at what constitutes a majority and the terms on which one is produced? Should not the application of the majority principle be subject to certain conditions of reinsurance? Although the experience in terms of electoral statistics is by no means new, it has been demonstrated since 1974 in a remarkably vivid way that a relative majority in the House of Commons may rest on a minority position in the country. Government on these terms is tolerable if the party in power recognises that there are limits to what it is entitled to do. But if it claims that it has a mandate for its programme when in commonsense terms it is clear that it has not, then one of the restraining

conditions on which British parliamentary government has operated collapses. It becomes acceptable for minorities to impose their
will and the majority must put up with it. Faced with the
unpalatable consequences of the lack of congruence between the
parliamentary majority and the majority in the country, it is
impossible to avoid the conclusion that the electoral system has
something to do with it. Hence we find Conservatives considering
whether an electoral system sanctified by centuries of practice
should not be modified in order to provide some assurance that a
majority in parliament will be a genuine majority. Taken together
these two issues—the misuse of parliamentary sovereignty and the
risk of perversion of the majority principle—have been taken to add
up to the danger of elective dictatorship, a matter on which Lord
Hailsham has expended much eloquence.[12] Underlying them is
uneasiness at the manner in which the British competitive two-party
system has developed, increasingly undermining areas of consensus
and discouraging that degree of continuity in policy which is
necessary to good government.

The third issue which has seriously worried many Conservatives
is the way in which particular conventions governing institutional
roles and relationships have been eroded. Collective responsibility
of the Cabinet has occasionally been set aside, a Government has
inclined to condone the actions of those in public office who have
openly flouted the law, the House of Lords has been threatened and
pushed around, political patronage has been extended in the civil
service (and elsewhere for that matter too), adverse votes even on
major issues in the House of Commons appear to entail no
consequences for a government so long as a formal vote of no-
confidence is not passed, the device of the referendum has been
taken up despite its implications for the authority of parliament. No
doubt all these shifts in practice can be presented as justifiable
responses to difficult situations and in no way directed in a spirit of
hostility against existing constitutional conventions. On the whole,
however, this seems to be a rosy view of the matter. The conventions
governing institutional roles have weakened and lost something of
their compelling force: so far nothing much has been put in their
place.

Finally, there is the issue of the role of law in society and in
political life. Here I refer not to the popular law and order theme,
nor to the argument that the Labour party has been less than
wholehearted in its respect for measures passed by a Conservative

government and still on the statute book. It is rather whether the body of law has not become too complex, too uncertain in its effects, too malleable, and not infrequently oppressive. This is, of course, by no means exclusively a British problem and to a large extent it stems from the contemporary view of the role of the public authority in guaranteeing what is regarded as a desirable level of economic and social welfare. But it is not unreasonable to conclude that the more heavily law weighs on society, the greater is the risk that respect for it will decline. To this situation there are two responses, not necessarily mutually exclusive. One is to try to reduce the burden of legal regulation, the other is to try to develop within the legal system regulative principles which the citizen can invoke for his protection. Both these lines of thought find expression in Conservative thinking about constitutional reform.

In summary, Conservative anxieties about British constitutional development stem from the belief that limited and mixed government is in danger. It has been undermined by the vast expansion of state power which has taken place, by the wear and tear imposed by the competition of two disciplined political parties which has magnified the distance between them in respect of political and social values, by the arrogant application of the doctrine of parliamentary sovereignty, and by the erosion of those values and pressures in society which previously imposed constraints on what government felt entitled to undertake. Should present trends continue, many Conservatives would foresee the emergence of a form of populist party oligarchy: the country would be ruled by the dominant minority within a party with a nominal majority, and this minority would justify its position by claiming in some obscure manner to represent the real will of the people. The major political institutions would sink further into the status of dignified parts of the constitution, whilst some might even be candidates for the lumber-room. The effective institution would be the ruling party's central or executive committee and that in turn might be some curious fusion of cabinet and extra-parliamentary party executive. Such a form of government is by no means unknown and it is often claimed to be democratic into the bargain. That such a constitutional outcome would be accompanied by more measures of social and economic regulation to which Conservatives are bitterly opposed would merely compound its disagreeable quality.

III PROPOSALS FOR CONSTITUTIONAL REFORM: THEMES RATHER THAN COMMITMENTS?

The next stage is to examine the reaction of the party in the light of this appreciation of the present position and to assess the significance of the constitutional reform proposals which have been aired within the party.

The initial reaction has been defensive and protective, that is to say, to concentrate on possible ways of warding off the constitutional dangers which are perceived to exist. Proposals have come from various sources and there has been an unusual degree of intra-party discussion and recommendation, some of it officially sponsored by the leadership, some of it coming spontaneously from groups within the party. It must be accepted that so far, despite the intensity of argument and the proliferation of suggestions for reform, very little has been taken over into the party's official policy. This probably reflects more than just caution on the part of the leader and differences of opinion among leading Conservatives.[13] It expresses, too, the hesitations which many experienced Conservative politicians feel once they see where some of the reform proposals may be leading. The dilemma to which I referred at the outset becomes explicit and the result so far is a refusal to enter into policy commitments on constitutional reform. That there are problems is admitted, that they can and should be dealt with by deliberate measures of constitutional innovation and restoration is a conclusion from which many still recoil, sensing, too, that the average party activist would share a similar reluctance to appeal to what look suspiciously like abstract principles.

I propose to discuss briefly only five topics on the agenda of constitutional reform, and one of them, devolution, will be dealt with very briefly as it is a problem receiving separate consideration in this collection of essays.

Reform of the House of Lords is in some respects the easiest to begin with since the nature of the problem is clearly understood and familiar. The primary justification for House of Lords reform is to provide a more effective check on the legislative activities of the government and Commons through the opportunities for legislative revision which fall to the upper house. The present chamber may perform this role tolerably well given the limitations imposed by its composition and working methods. Yet, as we know, it exists on sufferance on account of its composition and is constantly exposed to threats of further attenuation of its powers, or abolition, from the Labour party. Thus it treads softly and recognises how narrow is its room for manoeuvre. Without question the Conservative party prefers to maintain a two-chamber parliament and would support more strongly now than in the fifties the argument that if there are to be institutional checks on the Commons, one at least must be a second chamber. Such a view renders a reform of the composition of the Lords inevitable and it is proposals to that end which an official party committee under Lord Home has recently presented.[14] Essentially these represent a compromise between traditionalists and root and branch reformers. The latter would have a wholly-elected second chamber, the former are very reluctant to see the continuity of the Lords destroyed and some of them would perhaps prefer to risk abolition rather than surrender the concept of a House based on rank and status in society. Thus it is a part-elected, part-nominated chamber which is recommended, though with the elected element preponderant after a transitional period. Only a modest strengthening of the powers through a return to the two-year delaying power is suggested.

In essentials these seem to be prudent and modest proposals, justified in terms of offering the prospect of a return to a more stable balance within a bicameral parliament. That the Labour party should oppose such proposals is not surprising. What, however, of their chances within the Conservative party? It is highly question-able whether they will be implemented, even should the party gain a substantial majority. There are several reasons for this. The Commons collectively (and this includes Conservatives) is very sensitive to any aggrandisement of the upper house. It has lived for three generations and longer in an atmosphere of rivalry and mistrust in its relations with the Lords and as a result will brook no competitor who might claim equal legitimacy in the passage of laws. Thus getting a reform measure through would almost certainly be difficult and perhaps impossible. Then there are the traditionalist sentiments in the party at large, feelings which are bound up with the history of the party and the role which the hereditary peerage has played in it. Those who cherish such sentiments cannot easily envisage their party transforming what is for them a venerable and somewhat romanticised institution. There are influential members of the party, too, who believe that now a Conservative majority has been returned, all will be well. The threat of single chamber government will recede and a balance will be restored naturally.

Finally, there are those who are both practical and sophisticated, discerning that to tackle the House of Lords problem seriously is to embark on a process of change which will have unforeseen consequences and may well entail a far more extensive overhaul of constitutional arrangements than they care to envisage. For they recognise that within the institutions of a country the different pieces are connected one with another; to redesign one is to run the risk that another and yet another will have to be re-fashioned. Inevitably at the end of the day you face the need for a completely revised constitution and on what can that be based if not on abstract principles?

Devolution, about the details of which I will say nothing, presents a marked contrast in intent at least to the approach to the House of Lords issue. The party was early in the field with modest proposals published in 1970[15] for an elected assembly to be associated in the passage of Scottish legislation at Westminster. But in office after 1970 nothing was done and the party's subsequent reaction to proposals advanced by the Labour government has been sometimes ambiguous and generally hostile. In a somewhat desultory way the party has had various internal consultative groups on devolution since 1975, but once the original Scotland and Wales Bill was introduced, the initiative in opposing it shifted to hostile English backbenchers and to those Scottish members who were against the scheme and feared that support for it would merely strengthen the Scottish National party. That some of the Scottish opponents might be described as Tory populists is not without significance. Fundamentally, a majority in the party is hostile to devolution, treating it as a peripheral aberration, a likely source of conflict and an additional burden on taxpayers throughout the United Kingdom.

It is a striking fact that the party of the Union continues to display little sympathy for the claims of the non-English parts of the UK to self-government, and relatively little interest in the question whether the demand for devolution stems from a deep-seated reaction against Whitehall dominance and, if so, whether it could be met in a manner compatible with the survival of the British state. There is another peculiarity of this disinterest in devolution and in the reasons why it has become a major issue which is that a stress on the importance of local self-governing communities as a counter-weight to an over-powerful central government was an important element in Conservative constitutional thinking in the first half of the last century. Not only has the Conservative party in recent years shown little appreciation of local government as an element in our constitutional balance, but it has also failed to see that devolution—assuming that there is a sustained demand for it—could also contribute to restraining the claims of the central authority to know best what policies should everywhere be pursued and how resources should be distributed. If the expansion of central governmental powers is to be checked, here may be an opportunity to make a start.

Yet the party's recent record on devolution is largely negative: the instinctive reactions rooted in the past predominate and no doubt the experience in handling the problems of Northern Ireland reinforced a certain dislike of devolution. However, underlying the critical reaction to the Scotland and Wales Bills is a continuing attachment to the unitary state and the place of parliament within it. More than that, there is the suspicion that to have a genuine scheme of devolution requires a more explicit step towards something like a federal arrangement than the Labour government has been prepared to recognise. However, federalism is associated with legalism, with formal constitutional provisions and with an increased authority for judges in the interpretation of powers. Dicey's polemic against Home Rule continues to echo down the years, even though there are doubtless few active in contemporary politics who have ever read it.[16] The outcome is that it is chiefly a handful of Scottish Conservatives of a liberal disposition and a few of their kinsmen sitting for English seats who actively advocate a devolutionary settlement for Scotland and would be prepared to contemplate a scheme less fussy, ambiguous and inequitable than that which laboured through parliament in 1977–8. For the rest the party remains obstinately attached to the unitary state, even though the price of that may be a minority position at Westminster.[17]

It has already been suggested that the experiences of 1974 strengthened the doubts which some Conservatives had about the simple majority principle and its application in a sovereign parliament. The upsurge in the Liberal vote brought home to the party the danger of being condemned to a permanent minority position should the Liberals decide to give their support to a Labour government. And perhaps the most decisive of all was the belief born of the activities of the Labour government in 1974 and 1975 that there was under the existing system of voting little or no protection against policies judged by many to be doctrinaire and sectarian. These circumstances helped to stimulate a re-appraisal of the electoral system. This, however, has been very much a free-enterprise activity within the party, carried on chiefly by the Conservative Action for Electoral Reform.

This body, which appears to have had generous backers, has not only produced an impressive range of pamphlets and articles, but has also brought over into the electoral reform camp a substantial number of senior figures in the party who have associated themselves publicly with the campaign. It is probable that roughly 80 members of the parliamentary party could in 1978 be counted as supporters or sympathisers.

The details of the reform schemes proposed need not be discussed here except in relation to one aspect of them. That is the strong preference expressed by CAER for the additional member system, i.e. an adaptation of the West German method of combining single-member constituencies with lists to ensure proportionality. The significance of this lies in the retention of single-member constituencies which it facilitates. There seems no doubt that there is a strong attachment in the party to the constituency as the basis of representation and were it ever to support electoral reform, it would certainly be on condition that constituencies of reasonably small size were maintained. Here we can detect a very strong streak of instinctive conservatism, the belief that members do and should represent pieces of territory as they have claimed to do since time immemorial. The fact that they are now mainly detached from their 'territory', people who have no ties of family, education and career with the constituency, is ignored. So, too, is the fact that it is parties which are supported rather than persons. Thus we find the party determined to maintain at least one element in a mode of representation which owes its characteristics to a totally different political context.

The official attitude of the party towards electoral reform remains, however, persistently hostile. The leadership dislikes the idea of coalition (an attitude equally widespread in the Labour party) and questions whether the Liberals would be reliable partners. Indeed it fears that electoral reform might even put the seal of permanence on the minority position to which the party was relegated in 1974. At a more opportunistic level the party's leaders clearly believe that it would be foolish to forego the chance of an overall majority which the British electoral system always has on offer. Thus it is questionable whether the party can be forced into a policy commitment to electoral reform without traumatic experiences. Such might be the case if it found itself again frustrated in office by trade union opposition or if there were a repetition of the 1974 voting pattern, with the party excluded then from office and powerless to prevent Labour policies supported by only a minority of voters from being put into effect. But the root objection to electoral reform remains dislike of a new and unfamiliar style of politics which it would be likely to impose. The politics of genuine as opposed to emergency coalition is not something that the Conservative party cares to contemplate. And it is worth noting that a move to proportionality would seriously affect the behaviour and structure of the House of Commons, perhaps making it impossible to maintain there that fusion of the functions of government with the leadership of the House which has been one of the most decisive characteristics of the British form of parliamentary government.

Finally it needs to be remembered that on this issue the party has officially been unbending in its opposition to proportional voting both for European assembly and for the Scottish and Welsh assemblies.[18] 'No experiments' has been the motto of the leadership and regularly the 'thin end of the wedge' objection has been wheeled out. Clearly there is a long way to go before the party is prepared to accept that if genuine majorities are desired and if competitive two-party warfare is to be moderated or replaced by something more like consensus politics, then electoral reform may well be the only measure capable of bringing about such changes.

Linked to some extent with the electoral reform question is the matter of the referendum. The initial reaction of Mrs Margaret Thatcher to the EEC referendum proposal was one of hostility and she criticised it on familiar constitutional grounds besides condemning it as a device for holding together the Labour party on the EEC issue.[19] More recently she expressed somewhat different views and let it be known that there may be circumstances in which a referendum would be positively desirable. It is probable that Mrs Thatcher is in a minority with her view and that most Conservative politicians still look with suspicion on direct appeals to the people, regarding such methods as subversive of the political responsibility of the government and of the authority of parliament. Nevertheless, it would appear that the party leader is moved by a serious consideration, even though the referendum may not be the appropriate way of dealing with the problem. What worries some Conservative leaders is the prospect of militant opposition outisde parliament to the decisions of a Conservative government, perhaps entailing results similar to those of February 1974. In such a situation the politician is tempted to think in terms of an appeal to the people on a specific issue, something which can rarely if ever be achieved through a general election. Should the appeal be successful, it can then be asserted that there is a definite majority in the country against the militant opponents of a particular policy.

Other elements enter into the referendum discussion. There is in the Conservative party a streak of populism which may be more likely to find expression now that the party in parliament emerges from a socially heterogeneous group. This populist strain sees the people (and quite rightly too) as a bastion against certain types of change and appreciates what kind of fears or resentment can be mobilised both against change and against unpopular or recalcitrant minorities. In addition there is widespread feeling (also probably justified) that government and parliament simply impose on the people nowadays measures, regulations and policies which they dislike and would certainly not agree to support if consulted directly. Thus there is a radical democratic element in the argument for the referendum, too, and it ties in closely with the hostility felt in the Conservative party for the apparently inexorable growth of public bureaucracy.

The difficulties and dangers in the referendum proposal are, however, very obvious. There is the risk of the mobilisation of prejudice; there is the prospect of encouraging irresponsibility in parliament; there is the almost insuperable difficulty of determining what kind of questions really could be put to a popular vote in the hope of mobilising support against the actions of recalcitrant minorities, e.g. a trade union striking for higher pay in defiance of government pay policy. And there are the dangers inherent in all plebiscitary devices when the results go against those who use them. But one obstacle above all stands in the way of the referendum in Britain in a form which would make sense constitutionally and limit the destabilising effects of the procedure. This consists in the impossibility as matters now stand of devising a rule or rules prescribing the conditions under which a referendum might be held. Under our present constitution a referendum can be no more than an expression of will—the will of a majority in parliament. Whether a referendum is decreed and on what issues is a matter of pure discretion and hence of political opportunism. There is no escape from this position without wholesale constitutional change.

Had Britain a written constitution, the amendment of that document itself could be made subject to popular vote. That would be one kind of rule and a perfectly respectable one. Within a formalised constitution provision could be made for a consultative referendum, perhaps related to impending legislation. Similarly within such a framework it would be possible to envisage a form of popular initiative leading to a referendum if certain conditions were met. But what remains a riddle is how to formulate principles to govern the use of referendums within the terms of our present conventional constitution, the only bedrock of which is the sovereignty of parliament. Once again the Conservative reformer finds himself (or herself) in an impasse.

A fifth area of constitutional discussion has been individual rights. In the light of the fairly influential part played by Common Law lawyers in the Conservative party, it is not surprising that there should have been much criticism of the manner in which individual rights have been hemmed in and restricted by the growth of public powers, and more recently by the actions of trade unions demanding compulsory membership, the closed shop. The case for affording a sharper definition of basic individual rights and more protection for them has been mixed up, too, with the fear in some parts of the Conservative party that obstructive groups in society have become more inclined to refuse obedience to the law and to press their claims in defiance of court decisions. So the argument on behalf of individual rights as against collective power, public and private, becomes also an argument about the extent to which the state should use its power to uphold such individual rights, even though to do so may provoke social conflict.

In the era of Mr Heath's leadership there were clear signs that the Conservative party was sympathetic to a more effective and creative use of law for the regulation of competing claims and the adjudication of rights than had been common in the 1950s and 1960s. The 1971 Industrial Relations Act stands as a frustrated monument to that line of thought and it is worth recalling that despite its repeal, much of the approach embodied in it has been followed in subsequent enactments. Nevertheless the experience of that Act has cast doubts over the advisability of using the law in sectors of social relationships where there is strong objection to the intrusion of formalised principles and enforceable adjudication by a court. Rather sadly, the prospects for a more creative use of law in many areas of social life where the public authority intervenes or confers

special privileges on a private body corporate or association do not
look good.

However, there has been another line of exploration which has
attracted support and that is the notion of a Bill of Rights
enforceable through the courts. It is probable that most lawyers
bred in the Common Law tradition still remain hostile to the
proposal, or at any rate find it hard to understand how it might
operate in practice.[20] Similarly, most politicians are instinctively
suspicious, believing themselves to possess a unique insight into how
to resolve conflicts over claims and rights which is mysteriously
denied to judges. Moreover, they sense, too, that the logic of a Bill of
Rights is to enhance the judicial role (though the experience of
Canada since 1960 suggests that such enhancement may be modest
in scale) and they believe for reasons which remain obscure that this
must be harmful to politicians. Thus there are only a few
enthusiastic supporters of a Bill of Rights, amongst whom Lord
Hailsham must now be numbered. What has, however, been
achieved is some awareness in the party that the protection of
individual rights in Britain is often made difficult by the narrowness
of the terms of reference within which cases involving infringement
of rights have to be decided by the courts. Cases often resemble
lotteries, their outcome depending on the attitudes of the judges
who are called upon to reach a decision and on the contingent
statutory conditions out of which a case arises. What a Bill of Rights
offers is at the least the prospect of more general principles being
applied both to the settlement of cases and to the drafting of
legislation. Such principles would be broadly comprehensible to
laymen, and it would be possible to look forward to the development of a case-law in which legal *and* political considerations would
play a part. It is, of course, precisely at the stage when he perceives
such prospects that the Conservative advocate of the protection of
rights draws back. For on the horizon he sees the possibility that
parliament itself will be limited by the terms in which rights are laid
down and interpreted.

IV THE RADICALISM OF CONSTITUTIONAL REFORM AS THE SOURCE OF THE DILEMMA

I have considered only five aspects of constitutional change which
have in different ways been discussed within the Conservative party

and on which in two cases so far proposals have been made by official party committees.[21] Without doubt the discussion of these matters in the party has been beneficial: those involved have felt that serious and worthwhile issues are at stake and on the whole the quality of the arguments used in support of the different proposals made has been high. Yet the practical outcome is meagre: the party appears to believe that the constitution is in some danger and that something should be done. There remains, however, a marked reluctance to enter into firm commitments, and it is hard not to conclude that now the party has returned to power it will concentrate on day-to-day problems and on implementing some of its economic and social policies, leaving the constitutional issues for another day. For a while it will believe that the constitution is not in such a bad state after all and may return to its mood of doubt only if relegated again to opposition.

Why is this so? It seems to me that a purely opportunist explanation is not adequate. The irresolution with regard to the constitutional problems which undoubtedly face this country stems from some awareness of the dilemma with which I began. The social, moral and legal basis of the informal constitution in the shape it gradually acquired after 1832 has been seriously weakened. Political habits and manners have changed; expectations of government have changed; the purposes of government and of law have changed; the balance between state and society has tilted in favour of the former, though the latter increasingly asserts *its* sovereignty. Under the impact of such changes it is not surprising that political institutions cannot operate and relate to each other on the terms still regarded as 'normal' according to the description and justification of the constitution on which we have been nurtured. Most decisive of all, disciplined political parties have come to monopolise the constitution, to treat it as an elusive bit of property to an extent that qualifies substantially the claim so often made in the Conservative tradition that the constitution offers a guarantee of limited government.

I shall not pursue this argument further, if only because I have done so at length elsewhere.[22] The conclusion to which it points is that the constitutional system we have known, the unwritten tradition, is nearing the end of its useful life and that it would be prudent to set in train a radical overhaul. Many Conservatives are reluctant to accept such a conclusion, partly because they retain a streak of optimism, partly because it runs counter to the philosophy they have inherited and to which reference was made at the outset. The course of constitutional argument within the party during the last three or four years does, however, suggest that the very attempt to think pragmatically about this or that feature of our constitutional arrangements forces those engaged in it to recognise that piecemeal reform has become at best very difficult, at worst impossible. For despite the contempt generally shown in Conservative theorising on politics for 'abstract principles', a mature constitutional system reveals a certain coherence and has an internal logic of its own for those who care to reflect on its operation and on the justifications given for it. It is when we begin to contemplate particular reforms in the British constitution that we are struck by the extraordinary coherence which it has or, to be more accurate, which finds expression in the classic expositions of it. Indeed it might even be argued that the informal constitutional tradition has lasted so long and been so successful precisely because it embodied a higher degree of coherence in the understanding of compatible political practices than is usually attainable within a formalised tradition which, almost by definition, must legislate constitutionally for the arbitration of conflict and in this way takes out an insurance policy against the loss of coherence.

But it is possible that the contemporary Conservative reformer contemplates an idealised constitution. This helps to persuade him that the coherence which has been lost in reality can somehow be recovered without radical change, requiring perhaps only a return to patterns of behaviour which once sustained the pattern of limited government which he prefers. There is more than a touch of romanticism in such a conclusion. Yet it is understandable that the Conservative who perceives that the reform of one part of the constitution relentlessly leads on to a scrutiny of another part, should then draw back in doubt. For what then becomes clear to him is that he is engaged in an attempt to establish a new coherence in the structure of institutions and in the principles on which they rest. This is a radical undertaking for which his tradition gives him no taste. Moreover, it would be worse than useless to embark on it if society at large is not yet ready for such a work of reconstruction. This is why it is reasonable to ask what might be the political cost of such an attempt and whether there is indeed strong popular support for such an endeavour. It is perhaps at this point that the traditional Conservative view of political and constitutional evolution reasserts itself: a constitution consists of rules and conventions sanctified by understandings, values and practices in society; it is not an artificial or contrived product but the natural expression of the political skills of a people; and it is dangerous to uproot what you already have, not just because to do so is to risk instability, but because extensive reconstruction can proceed only through the clarification of principles and the definition of how they are to be applied. Here the circle closes itself: the Burkean Conservative is trapped by the postulates of his own argument.

Such seems to be the dilemma which inhibits an active commitment to constitutional reform by the Conservative party. Conservatism is a very English phenomenon, at any rate under that name. Yet there are other traditions of political thought which in their outcome are conservative and which in different ways have overcome the fear of abstract principles which has been such a prominent feature of English Conservatism. We owe to Montesquieu the principal elements of a powerful theory of limited government which is perhaps still the soundest basis for an alternative to the thoroughly Hobbesian theory of parliamentary sovereignty. And from the most penetrating of all conservative political thinkers, Hegel,[23] we can learn that it is possible (and indeed necessary) to distinguish between abstract principles and rational principles. But to pursue that distinction would require another paper.[24] Let it suffice to suggest that the British constitution in its present condition reveals a deficit of rational principles and that even a Conservative in the British tradition need not fear the reproach of inconsistency if he embarks on the pursuit of a more rational pattern of constitutional arrangements. For that means that he would through reform be seeking practical conclusions more consistent with his political values and better adapted to their maintenance and survival than is British constitutional practice today.

NOTES

1. E. Burke: *Observations on a Late State of the Nation* (London: J. Dodsley, 1769).
2. Social institutions include, of course, legal relationships established in England through the development of Common Law.
3. Burke quite rightly emphasised the crucial role of prejudice—acquired and unreflecting habits in social behaviour—in holding society together. He was probably right, too, to argue that we can find wisdom in prejudice. But to grant this much still does not justify neglect of man's reflective and critical capacities.

4. De Tocqueville, *Democracy in America* (London: Oxford University Press, 1961) p. 593.

5. It seems to me to be important to point out that inequalities of condition, position and prospects in life can be justified on Utilitarian grounds, e.g. in terms of the beneficial consequences of such a situation, but that such is *not* the primary justification in the conservative tradition. That tradition takes its stand on a view of the diversity of human nature and on the necessary quality of inequalities in social life: to deny inequality is equivalent to denying to human beings natural opportunities for self-development and for satisfying their desires. A precise and restricted view of equality is entailed by this.

6. It might be held that this understanding of law is now obsolescent and fails to take account of the extent to which much modern public law is a form of deliberate social engineering, resting on formalised norms and bureaucratic procedures for implementation.

7. It should be noted that the theory of the separation of powers in its various forms is directed to the institutionalisation of mistrust in the interest of liberty.

8. One of the more profound political consequences of policies of redistributive equalisation in society is precisely that many of the political obstacles to the increase in centralised governmental power are dissolved in the process. Tocqueville shows this more clearly than any other writer.

9. See, for example, on this point L. Scarman, *English Law: the New Dimension* (London: Stevens, 1974).

10. Local government reform is only one example of 'non-evolutionary' change and of the tendency to believe without conclusive evidence that some kind of changes must be made, e.g. also the reorganisation of the National Health Service and of the Water industry in 1973-4.

11. For example, in B. Disraeli, *Vindication of the English Constitution* (London: Leadenhall Press, 1835), Chapters XII to XVI.

12. Most recently, Lord Hailsham, *The Dilemma of Democracy* (London: Collins, 1978).

13. Whether caution stems from doubts about the value of constitutional reform proposals in terms of electoral advantage of disadvantage is a matter not discussed here. It seems doubtful whether any conclusive judgment is possible.

14. *The House of Lords*, Report of the Conservative Review Committee chaired by Lord Home, published by the Conservative Central Office, March 1978.

15. *Scotland's Government*, Report of the Scottish Constitutional Committee under the chairmanship of Sir Alec Douglas-Home, March 1970.

16. A. V. Dicey, *England's Case against Home Rule* (London: John Murray 1886). The most notable contemporary expositor of Dicey's denial of the possibility of reconciling Home Rule (= Devolution) with a unitary system of parliamentary government is Mr Enoch Powell. There is no doubt some irony in the fact that he now sits for a Northern Ireland constituency and that this is attributable in some degree to the destruction of the Unionist party political fabric which resulted from the abolition of Stormont in 1972 by a Conservative government.

17. There is almost certainly more support amongst Conservative MPs for some form of Scottish devolution than for Welsh devolution. But this reflects the widespread belief, confirmed by the referendum result, that the demand for

devolution is weaker in Wales and in addition the Conservative party is unlikely to lose support there through opposition to the scheme.

18. The disapproval of the leadership did not prevent some Conservative MPs from supporting a list system for elections to the European assembly and amendments to provide for proportional voting for the Scottish assembly. In the House of Lords amendments were in fact passed to ensure proportional representation in Scotland, but the Conservative party allowed a free vote in the Commons which effectively meant helping the government to override such amendments.

19. Parliamentary Debates (Hansard) vol. 888, 1974–5, cols. 304–17.

20. It is worth noting that the most persistent exponent of the codification of basic rights on the judicial bench (Lord Scarman) has to be described as a liberal and perhaps even as a libertarian too. The most recent discussion of the Bill of Rights proposal is to be found in the report of the House of Lords Select Committee on a Bill of Rights, H.L. 176, 1977–8.

21. A committee to examine the referendum was set up in April 1978 by the party leader. Its report, *The Referendum and the Constitution* was published in September 1978 as a Conservative Research Department Paper (no. 16). The other committee was, of course, the Home Committee on the House of Lords referred to previously.

22. Nevil Johnson, *In Search of the Constitution* (Oxford: Pergamon Press, 1977).

23. It is in some respects inaccurate to describe Hegel as conservative. Yet his great achievement was to encompass the fact of change and the experience of rational thought within a political theory which vindicated the claim that all serious reflection on the practice of politics must in its outcome be 'conservative' in respect of the political order it justifies. On this basis a thoroughgoing programme of constitutional reform can, in some circumstances, be justified as 'conservative'.

24. This is the appropriate point at which to note that I have in this paper deliberately avoided drawing comparisons between the dilemmas presented by the pursuit of constitutional reform, and those presented by the attempt to formulate a coherent view of the limits of state action in relation to the economy and the provision of social benefits by government. The effort to develop something like a social market economy philosophy to guide a Conservative government in the formulation of its economic and social policies has run into objections which, *mutatis mutandis*, are similar to those brought against the constitutional reformers on the Conservative side. It is somewhat surprising that Sir Keith Joseph and others who share his commitment to the redefinition of the economic and social aspects of Conservative philosophy appear to show little interest in the constitutional implications of their arguments: the impression is often conveyed that political institutions are rather secondary bits of organisation which a management consultant can re-jig according to need. In contrast the political and constitutional dimension was always central to the arguments of the German neo-liberal advocates of the *soziale Marktwirtschaft*. Once more, there is here a topic for another and far more extensive paper.

PART TWO

PARTY POLITICS

7 Approaches to Leadership in Opposition: Edward Heath and Margaret Thatcher[1]

Martin Burch

I INTRODUCTION

The opposition context is relatively neglected in studies of major British political parties.[2] It is often assumed that the party as opposition and the party as government, while differing marginally, are broadly equivalent types of organisations. Though there are substantial and important elements of continuity, it is worth emphasising that when a major party enters or leaves office certain aspects of the structure and purpose of the party are radically altered. Indeed, it can be reasonably argued that in some areas of party activity, for example policy-making, the transformation is of such a degree that it makes more sense to speak of the system of party politics in the UK over the post-war period as being characteristically a four- rather than two-party one.[3]

As far as Conservative politics is concerned, this neglect of the opposition dimension is further compounded by a strongly held view amongst some observers that the Conservative party is the natural and proper party of government. It is the *natural* party of government because historically it has been in office for longer than any other party. About two-thirds of the period since the 1884 Reform Act has been dominated by Conservative or Conservative-led governments. It is the *proper* party of government because, it is alleged, Conservatives traditionally regard their party as being the best qualified and most suited to govern, so that any period out of office is seen as a temporary break in the usual ruling pattern and an opportunity to rest and regroup before the normal situation is resumed once more.[4]

The assumption that the Conservative party is pre-eminently a party of government is based on observations made in the 1950s and early 1960s. From the perspective of the late-1970s, however, this assumption no longer appears quite as tenable. In particular the Conservatives' experience of opposition can no longer be regarded as negligible and, therefore, abnormal. In the post-war period, for instance, during the almost unbroken thirty-three year span of the two-party parliamentary system, the Conservatives have actually been in opposition for nearly half that time. Moreover, since the 1964 election defeat, mindful perhaps of possible changes in the electoral base of the two-party system, many Conservatives seem to have lost much of their alleged confidence about their party's future and its central place in British politics. It seems, therefore, that if labels are to be given, then there is as much justification for describing the Conservative party as a party of opposition as there is for calling it a party of government.

The following involves a small attempt to remedy the neglect of the opposition perspective by considering the nature of Conservative leadership during two periods in opposition: from 1964 to 1970, and from 1975 to the present.[5] A central concern is with the approaches to opposition leadership adopted by Edward Heath and Margaret Thatcher. Initially, attention is given to the broad context in which leadership operates and to the tasks Conservative leaders may be expected to perform when their party is in opposition. Thereafter the examination moves to consider the approaches of both leaders to the problems of opposition leadership and to provide some contrast between them. Analysis is concentrated upon certain particular aspects of leadership activity including party organisation, policy production, and public relations. The conclusion examines some explanations of the difference in approach exhibited by these two leaders of the Conservative opposition. Readers might note that there will be no attempt to provide a searching analysis of the psychological and personality factors involved;[6] rather the discussion will stick to the staple diet of political science with an emphasis upon institutions, processes, and policies.

II THE CONTEXT OF LEADERSHIP

A good prime minister does not always make a good leader of the opposition and vice-versa. Not surprisingly, the leadership skills required are different. In part this is because each context of party action (government or opposition) provides a different framework of constraints and potentialities within which leadership must operate and this framework serves to shape and guide the approach developed by each particular leader. To understand the context of leadership in the Conservative party as opposition it is necessary to consider at least two sets of factors. First, those which generally apply to opposition leadership in the UK two-party parliamentary system, and secondly, those which apply particularly to the Conservative party as opposition.

Party Leadership in Opposition

An obvious but central distinction from which much else follows is that in opposition party leaders are ultimately concerned with *winning* power whereas in government, as prime ministers, they are generally concerned with *maintaining* it. These differences in purpose are important because they require the development of distinctive strategies of party action and organisation in line with the different resources available to the leader in government and opposition. The party as government, for instance, in attempting to maintain power, is primarily to be judged on the basis of its performance in office, so that the tried calibre of its personnel and its general competence in managing the country's affairs are liable to be of central importance and, therefore, of vital concern to the leader. In opposition, however, the leader is not concerned to oversee the development of a detailed legislative programme, and he or she[7] lacks the patronage available in government, and the initiative in establishing the issue and terms of debate. So in opposition the leader must find other means of achieving his party's return to office.

Broadly speaking, two models are available, and each involves a different perception of the proper strategy and organisation of the opposition party.[8] First, there is what might be termed a *critical* approach to opposition, whereby the leader chooses to concentrate resources upon criticising the governing party in order to exploit its weaknesses with the aim of undermining its support amongst the electorate and of maintaining the unity of the opposition party. This concept of opposition strategy has some connection with the extreme nineteenth century view that it is the duty of an opposition 'to oppose everything and propose nothing'.[9] In its modern form, however, the critical approach is not quite so negative, for the opposition may be expected to have some alternative proposals to put forward, if only in broad outline. The critical strategy is based on the assumption that it is principally governments which lose elections and not oppositions which win them, and closely related to this is a concept of party organisation in opposition which places great emphasis on the need to exploit the benefits to be had from being no longer responsible for the day to day administration of the country. In particular, the leader should avoid appointing a rigidly defined shadow administration and should allow his colleagues a degree of freedom in debate and argument[10] so that, as in the nineteenth century notion of 'men in opposition', a measure of flexibility is preserved and broad ideas can be considered and developed.

The second model might be labelled the *alternative government* approach. According to this view, the leader should concentrate resources upon presenting the opposition as a real, responsible and viable alternative to the existing administration with the aim of strengthening party support and morale and, in time, gaining victory at the polls. The alternative government strategy has developed in parallel with the party system and is, therefore, largely a twentieth-century phenomenon.[11] Its increased acceptance in recent years reflects in part the programmatic approach to party politics initiated by the Labour party and the demands of modern mass communications for instant, but informed alternative re-actions to government pronouncements.[12] It is based upon the concept that the opposition can win elections or, at the very least, cannot credibly criticise the government without having a well thought-out alternative to put over. As far as party organisation is concerned, it is the leader's task to develop an alternative team and alternative measures. Hence policy should be produced in some detail and leading members of the opposition should be given specific shadow ministerial duties to perform. Moreover, the opposition must act responsibly and avoid purely negative tactics if it is to appear credible as an alternative government.

In choosing whether to place primary emphasis upon the critical or the alternative government approach, a party leader needs to consider carefully the problems inherent in each. Too great an emphasis upon the critical viewpoint, for instance, may result in the party returning to office without being fully prepared, while over-negative, 'ding-dong parliamentary battles'[13] may undermine the party's credibility amongst the electorate and, at the same time, devalue the reputation of the parliamentary system. Additionally there is the problem of party management: too much flexibility and too deep a discussion of the fundamentals of party belief may lead to division and a lack of control from the centre.

The alternative government approach is no less problematic. A responsible approach to opposition may fail to satisfy party supporters, while the desire to project a real and distinct alternative to the existing administration may lead to the adoption of extreme positions impossible to maintain or to implement when returned to office. There are also problems involved in the production of an alternative programme: for instance, the difficulties of producing realistic policies without the information and assistance available in government, or the difficulties of producing proposals in the present to be implemented in a future situation, the exact circumstances of which cannot be foreseen.[14] Overall there is the danger of limiting the freedom of manoeuvre of a future administration by encumbering it with too many detailed policies, publicised and committed to in advance. A too closely organised shadow administration may also have its drawbacks. Some members may feel constrained by the lack of flexibility allowed them, and the opportunity to re-examine intelligently the fundamentals of party belief which opposition affords may be smothered in the detail of particular policy responsibilities.

Conservative Party Leadership in Opposition

Although both the critical and alternative government models are applicable to the exercise of opposition leadership in either of the two major British political parties, there are at least two other considerations which are peculiar to the Conservative party and are especially relevant to an understanding of the context within which Edward Heath and Margaret Thatcher have developed their own distinctive approaches. First, there is the tradition of past practice bequeathed by previous leaders of the Conservative opposition in the post-war period. Secondly, there are certain important structural features of the Conservative party as opposition which, relative to the situation in government, serve to alter the resources available to the leader and the channels of communication and contact between him and his followers. These also may be expected to affect the nature and operation of leadership.

As far as past practice is concerned, the 1945–51 experience provides two influential precedents. More importantly, there is Churchill's example which conforms broadly with the critical concept of opposition leadership. Churchill was greatly concerned to avoid giving hostages to fortune by making commitments which could not be fulfilled in the future, and his main objective was to preserve flexibility. He therefore declined from establishing a system of sharply defined shadow ministries, preferring instead to command a front-bench with loosely determined responsibilities, and whenever possible he preferred to avoid making precise policy statements.[15] A slightly contrary approach was developed by R. A. Butler, to whom much of the responsibility for policy production was delegated. Butler veered towards the alternative government perception with a strong belief in the need to formulate a distinct alternative programme, although not in great detail.[16] The aim should be to give a general impression of intent rather than to set out a series of precise proposals.

As opposition leader, Douglas-Home showed a marked preference for Butler's viewpoint. He considered that an opposition could only make an impact if it suggested itself as a 'competent alternative' by acting constructively and responsibly and by presenting a substantial alternative programme. Furthermore, for Douglas-Home the opposition could only be 'effective' if it remained united, for nothing would harm potential support more than disunity.[17] Hence he placed great emphasis upon matters of party management, and introduced measures designed to increase the degree of coordination between the leader and the various sub-sections of the party. His concern to create a competent and effective alternative was reflected in his initiation of a wide-scale reassessment of party policy under Heath and the establishment of a shadow administration of 60 (including a 'shadow cabinet' of nineteen members) with clearly defined responsibilities.[18]

As well as being influenced by past performances, Conservative opposition leaders must learn to operate within the changed structure of the Conservative party as opposition. Most obviously, instead of presiding over a cabinet and ministerial team, the leader is in command of some kind of shadow administration organised around the leader's Consultative Committee or shadow cabinet. Although the size, organisation and membership of the opposition team are matters for the leader to decide,[19] relative to the situation in government, his status and prestige and his powers of appointment and patronage are greatly reduced and consequently his hold over his senior colleagues is somewhat weakened.

In opposition there are also important differences in the organisation of the parliamentary party which serve to extend the contacts between the leader and his front-bench colleagues on the one hand and their back-bench followers on the other. In particular, the party's back-bench subject committees are chaired by the relevant front-bench spokesman, whereas in government the chairman is elected by the back-benchers. In addition, since the 1945–51 period it has been customary to establish a Business Committee to liaise between the leadership and the back-benches. According to Punnett, the membership of this committee in the October 1964 to July 1965 period included all front-bench spokesmen not in the Consultative Committee together with the elected officers (vice-chairmen, secretaries and sometimes treasurers) of the back-bench committees. It met weekly at 6.15 on Wednesday after Consultative Committee meetings, when a senior member of the latter would report to the Business Committee on the decisions of the Consultative Committee regarding the following week's business in the House.[20]

Contacts between the leader, the front-bench and the party bureaucracy are also transformed, especially those involving Research Department personnel. For, in lieu of the advice and assistance of the permanent civil service, the leader and his colleagues fall back upon the services of the Research Department: the leader has first call on the resources of the Department, while each front-bench spokesman is able to call upon the assistance of the desk officer relevant to his subject area. The same desk officer also serves as minutes secretary to the relevant back-bench subject committee so that through the Department the network of relationships between front and back-benchers is further extended. In addition, Research Department officers are involved in servicing the various committees in which the leader and his colleagues are involved, such as the Steering Committee and the Consultative Committee. Of course, in government, party officers are usually excluded from cabinet and ministerial meetings and the contacts between the leadership and Research Department officers (with the possible exception of the director) are not as close nor as frequent as they are in opposition.[21]

In general, in opposition the structure of the Conservative party changes so that the network of contacts and the channels of communication and potential influence centring upon the leader are more closely located within the party than is the case in government. In particular, the contacts between the leader and his front-bench colleagues, and the back-benches and the Research Department are significantly extended and the leader is thus brought closer to party opinion than is the case in government. At the same time the formal relations with extra-party organisations (especially the civil service and major pressure groups), which the leader is subject to in office, are either severed or altered in terms of their nature and intensity.

It is within this broad context of the Conservative party as opposition that both Edward Heath and Margaret Thatcher have developed their own distinctive approaches to the party leadership. How did they set about the tasks in hand? What contrasting approaches to leadership have they exhibited?

III EDWARD HEATH AS OPPOSITION LEADER 1965–70

Heath was elected to the leadership by the parliamentary party in July 1965. He had already been deeply involved in the development of the opposition under Douglas-Home when, following the party's October 1964 general election defeat, Heath was appointed chairman of the Advisory Committee on Policy (ACP) and was given charge of the party's policy review. He also, as opposition spokesman on economic affairs, led the Conservatives' effective examination and critique of the Labour government's 1965 Finance Bill. Heath thus promised to be a well-rounded leader of the opposition capable of providing effective criticism of the Labour government on the one hand and a thorough presentation of the Conservative alternative on the other. His distinctive approach to opposition leadership can be best exhibited in relation to certain key areas of activity, most especially, policy-making and the organisation and operation of his front-bench.

In the policy field, Heath was deeply concerned with both the machinery and content of policy-making. As chairman of the ACP prior to his election as leader Heath launched a systematic and organised re-examination of party policy and remained the driving force behind this policy exercise throughout the opposition period. He kept a close interest and involvement in the machinery of policy-making and its operation, even though formal responsibility was delegated to the subsequent chairmen of the ACP: Edward Boyle until late 1968 and Reginald Maudling thereafter. Heath's concern that the review should be extensive and intelligently organised is reflected in the machinery that he established which in terms of its nature and scale was an innovation in British opposition politics. The building blocks of the exercise were the various policy groups (23 before the 1966 election and 29 thereafter) which brought together Conservative parliamentarians and outside experts to develop detailed proposals in specific areas such as agriculture, housing and industrial relations.[22] In theory these groups reported to the ACP, though in practice their reports often went directly to the leader. Heath also actively encouraged the establishment and operation of two policy research projects: the Conservative Systems Research Centre and the Conservative Public Sector Research Unit.[23] These were directly responsible to the leader and they were concerned with, amongst other things, the compatability of different policies and the problems of implementing them once returned to power.

Heath's interest in the organisation of policy-making was further reflected in his concern with the forward planning and management of policy development. He was concerned that the exercise should be timetabled well in advance and, that as far as possible, schedules should be kept to. In the period prior to the 1966 general election, as an election was expected at any time, the exercise was planned around the production of a policy statement which could serve as an election manifesto if the need arose, but otherwise would be published in the autumn of 1965 as an indication of the party's altered policy direction. After the March 1966 election, with the prospect of a long spell in opposition, plans could be made with greater certainty and it was decided that from the autumn of 1966 to the early part of 1968 the policy group exercise would continue, but its work would not be publicised or emphasised. In the summer of 1968 the various policy group reports were to be drawn together in the form of a generalised mid-term manifesto to be published in the autumn. Thereafter, until the next general election, particular policies were to be refined in preparation for office. This plan was more or less adhered to throughout the post-1966 period of opposition.

The concern with the organisation and planning of the machinery of policy-making had consequences for policy content. In initiating the policy review in 1964 Heath was concerned to establish the broad outline of future Conservative policy at an early date so that the policy groups could take over the job of filling in the details. The first draft of this outline in part reflected Heath's analysis of the reasons for the party's 1964 election defeat, and it was later re-drafted by the director of the CPC, David Howell, into an 8000-word skeleton manifesto which was approved by Douglas-Home in January 1965. The approach developed in that document formed the basis of the autumn 1965 policy statement, 'Putting Britain Right Ahead', which contained most of the major policy themes (with the particular exception of machinery of government questions) that were further refined throughout the opposition period. In particular, two central objectives were emphasised: the encouragement of individual initiative and enterprise and the creation of 'a new dynamic within industry' by measures of increased competition. These objectives were related to certain elements of policy such as tax reductions and incentives, selectivity in the social services, trade union reform and entry to Europe.[24]

By establishing the broad framework of policy production at an early stage, Heath was able to keep a close hold on the policy exercise. In addition, he was able to limit discussion upon the fundamentals of party belief: the broad purposes had been determined, and thereafter it was a matter of refining and developing them. Partly for reasons of party management, Heath was anxious to avoid wide ranging debates about the nature of Conservatism. They seemed to him likely to create deep division within the party which in turn might serve to undermine the credibility of the opposition in the eyes of the electorate. He thus tended to limit or proscribe debates on certain key issues, especially in the economic sphere, such as incomes policy and economic planning. His attempts to avoid the discussion of contentious issues sometimes led to the adoption of ambiguous policy positions, for rather than risk splitting his front-bench, he tended to try to avoid decision and keep the options open.

The emphasis upon thorough policy work in opposition reflected a view that policy should be prepared in some detail in readiness for office. Considerable and fairly detailed proposals were prepared in some key areas, such as taxation, industrial relations and the reorganisation of the social services, but this did not mean that the details had to be made public beforehand. In fact, a good deal of detailed work, especially on taxation, was kept secret. Heath's emphasis upon the machinery of policy-making and the thoroughness of the policy exercise suggests a view that policy problems are capable of right solutions and that once the fundamental moral framework has been decided the 'best policy' can be formulated if the right information and expertise are united.

Like all party leaders, Heath was more interested in certain areas of policy than others. Entry into the EEC was a major interest and this helps to explain a good many of the policy proposals produced during the opposition period, such as those on taxation and agriculture.[25] Machinery of government questions were also matters of importance to Heath and he seemed as much concerned with the technology and efficient organisation of government as he was with questions of its purpose and control. Economic policy was a further, major concern and was regarded by him as the central key part of the party programme.

Heath's interest in organisation and party management is further evidenced in his approach to the nature and operation of his front-bench team. He rejected Macmillan's advice to 'do what Winston did' and preserve flexibility and, like his predecessor, he maintained a large shadow administration,[26] initially appointing 72 spokesmen each with clearly defined responsibilities, the only exceptions being Maudling as deputy leader (an innovation) and Hogg, who was without departmental responsibilities. Heath divided his front-bench into a number of specialist teams on each of the major subjects under a leading spokesman. This also was an innovation in opposition politics but it was abandoned after the 1966 election and the front-bench was cut down to 37, though each remained responsible for specific policy areas. Later the front-bench team was extended once more so that by 1970 it numbered 50.

To some degree, Heath attempted to operate his shadow administration in accordance with the proceedings of cabinet government. Consultative Committee meetings tended to be fairly brisk and were tied to a specific agenda; the idea was not to have broad debates as in Churchill's period, but to deal competently with the business in hand. He continued Douglas-Home's arrangement whereby meetings were held twice a week on Wednesdays, mainly to discuss parliamentary business, and on Mondays to discuss broader issues, usually questions of policy. Decision-making tended to be collective except in some areas, such as the decision to keep incomes policy off the agenda and the commitment to a Scottish assembly, where the leader exercised his right to make policy decisions in isolation. The doctrines of collective and ministerial responsibility were applied and front-benchers were expected to keep within the confines of their policy areas and to support the collective policy of the party in public. Some clearly felt constrained by the lack of freedom to debate and argue that this arrangement allowed, and both Maude and Powell, though the circumstances of each case were different, lost their position on the front-bench partly because of their failure to stick to the rules and keep within their allocated responsibilities.[27]

Under Heath, the contacts between the leader and certain sections of his party were extended and developed. He involved the back-benchers in the work of the party to a greater degree than had been the case in any previous period of opposition. Many were engaged in the detailed policy work being undertaken by the policy groups. For instance, in the 1965–6 period, 181 MPs and Peers were brought into the policy groups exercise and 191 in the years thereafter.[28] Heath also developed the practice, especially after the 1966 election, of bringing forward back-bench committee officers to speak on a temporary basis from the front-bench. In this way new talent could be spotted and back-benchers had an added opportunity to make their mark in the party. Heath continued the operation of the Business Committee and began the practice whereby the leader generally attended in person to report on the decisions of the Consultative Committee. However, the Business Committee was mainly used as a means by which the leader could inform his followers and not as a forum for policy debates or as a two-way channel of communication between front and back-benches.

As Heath was relatively unknown to Conservatives in the country when he became leader, one of his major tasks was to develop close contacts between himself and the mass party. According to his biographer, Heath travelled more extensively visiting local branches and attending party functions than any previous Conservative leader.[29] He was also the first leader to attend the annual party conference in full (this he did in 1965 and every year thereafter), he was a frequent visitor to Central Council meetings and he made a habit of speaking at some of the annual conferences of the various sub-sections of the NUCUA, such as the Young Conservatives and the Women's section.

In his concern with policy production, the operation of the front-bench and in developing contacts with the party in the country, Heath was greatly assisted by a relatively substantial personal machinery of leadership. His private office, in terms of its scale, was an innovation in British opposition politics and was modelled on the Prime Minister's office at No. 10. The office was headed by John MacGregor until early 1968 when Douglas Hurd took over and at its full complement in 1969 it had a staff of thirteen, including seven secretaries and Heath's two PPSs, Prior and Kershaw. As well as dealing with press and campaign arrangements, members of the private office carried out a number of executive functions on behalf of the leader. They deputised for Heath on various committees and organisations, they briefed him on current issues and policy proposals and they were often involved in the preparation of speeches, though this task was usually in the hands of Michael Wolff. In addition to his personal staff, Heath depended on a relatively small group of individuals for advice and assistance, though most were drawn from within the Conservative party, often from the front-bench and the Research Department. The machinery of leadership established by him enabled Heath to delegate a great deal of activity and work to a loyal and efficient team and thus, in the formal organisational sense, he was able to extend his leadership potential more considerably than any previous leader of the Conservative party in opposition.

Heath's emphasis upon policy production should not be taken to mean that he was unaware of the need to attack and criticise the Labour government. Though not averse to the cut and thrust of parliamentary opposition, he tended to adopt more 'critical' tactics mainly in response to demands from his followers for a more vigorous approach. This was particularly the case during the period from March 1966 to 1968, when policy-making was at a low key and the party was divided over defence, Rhodesia, immigration and incomes policy. But Heath never seemed happy with a substantially negative approach and tended to use the parliamentary tactic of a reasoned amendment, rather than outright rejection. While this may have served to preserve the unity and credibility of the opposition it did not always satisfy his parliamentary followers.

A further difficulty was Heath's approach to putting the party's message across to the electorate and his followers in the country. He was not easily persuaded to adapt to the requirements of good public relations, and unless the subject was Europe, he seldom seemed to inspire the party faithful. His major speeches were often rather dry catalogues of policy proposals and, according to his biographer, he was more comfortable and effective when briefing small, informal groups.[30] Heath perhaps lacked facility at one of the major skills required of the opposition leader, that of using words to inspire and persuade. He never seemed happy with many of his set speeches, continually re-drafting at a late stage. Overall he was more interested in concentrating on the business of policy production than on the development and delivery of speeches.

In general, Heath was a classic exponent of the alternative government approach to opposition leadership. This is reflected in his desire to create a real and viable alternative involving a well-tried team of men and a thoroughly considered, though not necessarily publicised, alternative programme. He never publicly advocated the adoption of an opposition for opposition's sake posture, preferring instead vigorous opposition conducted in a responsible and constructive manner. His major interest seems to have been concentrated on preparing for regaining power in the future, hence his concern with the details of policy and with issues relevant to the machinery of government and policy implementation. It could be said in criticism that Heath was too much interested in what was to be done once the party got back into power and did not give enough attention to how the party was to get there. He was poor at communicating the party's programme and potential, seemed frustrated by opposition and showed a lack of concern with the vital persuasive aspects of opposition politics. Heath also placed great emphasis upon the need to preserve the unity of the opposition. This concern with party management and control was reflected in his tight hold over the organisation and operation of his front-bench, his concern to limit discussion on party fundamentals, the development of a substantial personal machine and the establishment of closer lines of communication between the leader and, in particular, his parliamentary followers.

IV MARGARET THATCHER AS OPPOSITION LEADER 1975–9

A major difficulty in analysing Margaret Thatcher's period as opposition leader is that it is not yet over and the events involved are too recent to be either easily accessible to outside observers or capable of supporting a rounded judgment. However, some generalisations can be made, if only tentatively. It is important to stress that there are substantial areas of continuity and significant similarities, especially in terms of policy content, with the 1964–70 period. In fact, Thatcher's leadership of the party as opposition has involved extensions in many of the initiatives introduced by her predecessor, though she has of course introduced her own distinctive approach—particularly in relation to policy presentation and contacts with the parliamentary party.

In comparison to Heath, Thatcher has shown relatively little interest in the organisation and machinery of policy-making. Although the policy review has been as extensive as in the 1964–70 period with over 60 policy groups operating at one time or another, the leader has not been intimately involved and she has delegated organisational and day to day responsibility to Sir Keith Joseph (chairman of the ACP) and Angus Maude (chairman of the Research Department). She tends to take part in the policy process at a relatively late stage, usually after a report has gone through Joseph's policy steering committee and before it proceeds to the policy sub-committee of the Consultative Committee which she chairs. She may on receipt of a report decide that it should not go further and send it back for reconsideration or re-drafting, though this is unusual. Equally, she has not concerned herself with the detailed forward planning of policy development. This has tended to be left to others especially the director and other key officers of the Research Department.

One significant change in the organisation of the policy review under Thatcher's leadership is the greater attention given to matters of party management. For example, back-benchers generally play a more central role in the policy groups and outside experts tend to be used on a consultancy basis. Moreover, the groups' membership tends to be selected, not only on the grounds of expertise and interest, but also to keep a balance of views between the various divisions within the shadow administration. Though questions of party management were also a concern of the Heath period, they were not as strongly emphasised, whereas under Thatcher it is not only a question of what is the best policy but also what is acceptable to the party.

As far as policy content is concerned, Thatcher is less involved in the details of policy than was Heath. She seems to dislike giving too much attention to specifics and is concerned to avoid making precise public commitments which may limit the flexibility of a future Conservative administration. Her approach is to develop the general philosophical outlines of policy, what some have termed a 'broad brush' approach which involves getting the general objectives right in readiness for office while providing some impression of the details.[31] The solutions to the problems of carrying through the party's purpose if returned to office are seen as depending more on developing and refining the right set of values which can then be applied to the particular situation, rather than on preparing detailed plans in the present. There is, however, one exception— economic policy—for it is on the success of this that all other policies are seen to rest. Hence, the leader has been greatly concerned with detailed policy development in this area, especially in relation to taxation and public expenditure control.[32]

Thatcher's apparent unease about the production and publication of detailed policy has not been wholly carried through in practice. Under her leadership about as much detailed policy has been produced as in the 1964–70 period and a substantial, though more selective, amount has been publicised.[33] The difference is in terms of presentation and the more cautious tone adopted. Policy statements tend to be couched in a language which stresses the qualifications involved in implementing the policy: that it may take a full parliament, that present plans can only be tentative, that much depends on getting the general economic framework right, etc. These types of preliminary cautions were trundled out during the 1964–70 period, but they were not so heavily underlined.

In relation to the organisation and operation of her shadow administration, Thatcher was initially faced with a major problem: she inherited the substantial membership of her front-bench from her predecessor and she may well, especially in the Consultative Committee, have found herself in a minority on some issues. Hence a central concern has been to find ways of managing and developing her front-bench team so as to by-pass or counteract the initial bias against her. She has gradually altered the composition of her shadow administration. Initially, six members of Heath's previous team were excluded and new members unconnected with the Heath leadership (such as Maude and Neave) were brought in. There have since been important changes in the nature of the team, and although the re-distribution has taken account of the need to balance the various tendencies within the parliamentary party, it is today more sympathetic to the leader's command and authority. Thatcher has continued Heath's practice of bringing forward back-bench committee officers and, like Heath, she has maintained a large shadow administration numbering 45 initially (including a Consultative Committee of 21) which has now expanded to a total of 50, most with precisely defined responsibilities.

The pattern and proceedings of Consultative Committee meetings remain much the same. Decision-making still generally tends to be collective, though the leader has shown a tendency to make broad policy pronouncements in advance of committee discussions, as in the case of immigration, with the consequence that either the leader must back-track or her colleagues must go along with her. She has also, like Heath, taken the initiative on certain issues such as her proposal on the use of referenda in the case of major industrial troubles and her Glasgow speech rejecting the idea of a planned incomes policy.[34]

An added difficulty for Thatcher on becoming leader was that she was relatively unknown to members of the party generally in parliament, in the bureaucracy and in the country. Previously she had tended to be a specialist front-bencher and had not been greatly involved in party affairs. Additionally, a major point in her leadership election platform was that Heath had lost contact with the various sections of the party.[35] Thus a central feature of her approach to opposition leadership has been the development of contacts between the leader and her followers, and the closer co-ordination of the three major parts of the party.

As far as contacts with the parliamentary party are concerned the leader has made some important innovations. She has made a point of holding twice-yearly meetings with all front-bench spokesmen not in the Consultative Committee and she has held occasional meetings with all Conservative spokesmen in the House of Lords. She has attempted to involve the back-benchers in the policy process to a greater extent than was the case under Heath. Their increased role in the policy groups has already been noted. In addition, however, the back-bench subject committees have to some extent been brought into the formal process of policy-making by the introduction of the practice whereby each year the chairman of a particular policy group will report to the appropriate back-bench committee on current progress within the group and seek the comments of the assembled back-benchers, while the leader has sometimes encouraged front-bench spokesmen to check the attitudes of their back-bench committee before proceeding with an initiative.

Thatcher's concern with gauging back-bench opinion is further reflected in the changed status and operation of the Business Committee. This is treated far more respectfully and is used less as a means of providing back-benchers with information about front-bench thinking and more as a two-way channel of communication with greater opportunity for back-bench comment. Generally the whole of the Consultative Committee will attend the meetings unless there are other pressing engagements, and the leader will report to the committee collectively on behalf of her colleagues on the opposition's proposed approach to the parliamentary business, for the coming week. The leader tends to use the committee quite positively as a sounding board to take the temperature of the party and often asks for comments to be expressed and sometimes asks the relevant front-bench spokesman to reply. In one or two cases the strength of the views expressed by the back-benchers have led to the Consultative Committee reconsidering an issue and occasionally changes have been made in the original proposals. During the early months of Thatcher's leadership, before she had extended her influence over her front-bench, on certain items of business, the expression of back-bench opinion through the Business Committee occasionally served to strengthen the leader's position *vis-à-vis* a dominant and opposing view in the Consultative Committee.[36]

Thatcher has managed to build up a relatively close liaison with the Central Office and Research Department, though she does not depend upon the latter's assistance to the same degree as Heath did and has tended to delegate responsibility for the operation of the party bureaucracy to Thorneycroft, Joseph and Maude. She has, like Heath, attempted to develop contacts with the party in the country. For example, since becoming leader, Thatcher has visited more than 200 constituencies and has dropped the rule that the leader does not take part in parliamentary by-election campaigns: she has attended every one. She has also extended Heath's initiative by attending almost all the conferences of the major sub-sections of the mass party. Her concern with contact and co-ordination between the various elements of the party is reflected in the establishment of a new co-ordinating committee under her chairmanship. It usually meets once a fortnight, and has a membership of about eight, including the chairman of the 1922 Committee, the chairman of the National Union Executive Committee, the deputy leader, the chief whip and the chairman of the party. The committee may occasionally discuss strategy but is mainly used as a sounding board for opinions and as a channel of communication.

Like Heath, Thatcher runs a substantial private office: including her two PPPs (Stanley and Butler), the office has a staff of about fourteen and is under the overall control of Airey Neave, though the management of the office is in the hands of Richard Ryder. It differs from Heath's office in two principal ways.[37] First, the head of the office is a political figure, a close confidant and adviser of the leader, a front-bench spokesman and member of the Consultative Committee. Secondly, the remaining staff tend to fill more of a secretarial than an executive function: they are mainly concerned with briefing the leader, arranging schedules and campaign tours and handling correspondence. For information and advice Thatcher tends to rely on a more varied range of sources than was the case with Heath. As already noted, though relationships are necessarily close, she is less dependent on the party bureaucracy and tends to draw on sources outside her own front-bench and sometimes from outside the formal party structure. For example, speech writing involves the leader in drawing together many drafts which may be submitted by, in addition to party specialists (front-benchers and officials) and some back-benchers, others from outside the formal structure of the Conservative party including sympathetic journalists and academics and certain individuals closely connected with the party such as the director of the Centre for Policy Studies. Considerable press attention has been given to the leader's briefing sessions prior to Prime Minister's questions which usually involve certain back-benchers.[38] Overall, in comparison to Heath as opposition leader, Thatcher has tended to use sources of assistance and advice drawn from outside the traditional mainstream of the party.

Her approach to criticising the Labour government has not been noticeably more vigorous than Heath's, and during the early period of her leadership the lack of effectiveness of the opposition was much criticised. She has developed a distinct critique of her opponents around the label 'Socialism' and under her leadership the Conservatives have occasionally developed aggressive parliamentary tactics as in the case of the refusal of pairing arrangements, though this seems more likely to reflect the problems of minority government than to indicate a tendency to adopt a predominantly critical approach to opposition leadership.

In articulating the Conservative message to followers and the general public, Thatcher seems to have proved herself more capable than Heath in exploiting the persuasive aspect of politics. She is more amenable to the demands of public relations and on such matters she is closely advised by the party's publicity director, Gordon Reece. She has undertaken a number of extensive campaign tours with particular attention being given to Scotland and the 90 or so key seats which the Conservatives, in order to return to power, must hold or win in any future general election. For Thatcher, speech writing and delivery are clearly seen as important tasks for the opposition leader and she spends a great deal of time drawing together the various drafts submitted. She is often capable of inspiring a party audience, though sometimes her speeches seem too partisan to have a broader appeal. While clearly having a strong appreciation of the importance of words to the opposition politician, the major weakness tends to be in terms of presentation and style of delivery.

In general, compared with Heath, Thatcher's approach to opposition leadership places less emphasis upon the alternative government concept. In her attitude to policy-making, her concern to avoid precise commitments and her desire to develop the broad outline of Conservative purpose, Thatcher has more in common with the type of leadership developed in the 1945–51 period. In terms of her attitudes towards the organisation and development of the front-bench, however, there are marked similarities between Thatcher and Heath. Moreover, while she has developed a distinctive critique of the Labour government, she has not shown a marked preference for tactics of opposition for opposition's sake, seeming instead to regard opposition as an opportunity to consider and re-examine the fundamentals of party belief. This is a major contrast with Heath and his concern to avoid deep ideological debates. Thatcher seems more in the tradition of the 'men in opposition' concept, allowing for the discussion and development of ideas, but with the important proviso that the pace and direction of the discussion should be superintended and controlled from the centre.

Like Heath, she has also shown great concern about the problem of party unity, though this is to be achieved not through limiting discussion on fundamentals, but by increased measures of co-ordination and contact between the various sections of the party and particularly the leadership and the back-benchers. The consequence is, however, not simply to achieve agreement, but also to alter the balance of dominant attitudes and values within the party. In general a central feature of her approach to opposition has been a concern with party issues and party questions. A clear danger of such an approach is that it may prove too partisan to ensure either a return to power or, if returned, a successful period in office thereafter.

V ACCOUNTING FOR DIFFERENCES IN APPROACH

The different approaches to opposition leadership exhibited by Heath and Thatcher are necessarily the product of a complex and varied set of factors and it would be foolish to argue that any one factor can be judged to be primary or dominant. However, there are certain issues which are clearly important and these concern both the changing political and party context and the personalities of the individuals involved.

Most obviously both leaders have had to come to terms with different political situations. The more certain parliamentary situation operating from 1966–70 with an overall Labour majority of 96, for instance, allowed for a more planned and systematic approach than has been possible during the post-1975 period, with an initial overall Labour majority of three subsequently reduced to a minority. Moreover, the electoral circumstances of the Conservative party have changed radically. In the 1964 general election, the Conservatives received 43.4 per cent of the votes cast; by October 1974 their share had declined to 36.5 per cent and was more substantially concentrated in suburban and rural areas in the south and west of England and amongst the more aged and middle-class sections of the community.[39] These alterations in the electoral base of the party have presumably had some consequences for policy presentation and public relations.

The intellectual climate within which policy-making takes place has also altered substantially. In the 1960s much political and academic debate was concerned with the efficient operation of economic and political institutions, and about how changes in the scale and organisation of the machinery of government might facilitate a more rational and intelligent use of resources.[40] Heath's concern with the organisation of policy-making, his problem solving approach to policy issues and his interest in machinery of government questions was very much in keeping with the managerial emphasis of current thinking in the 1960s. By contrast, the debate in the 1970s has been concerned not so much with the potentialities of government but more with its problems and limitations. Attention has been given to the difficulties of establishing clear criteria for the operation of public services and the problems of carrying through or implementing policies.[41] At the same time, broader and more traditional questions about the purpose and control of public agencies have once more become central issues of debate and argument. Thatcher's emphasis upon broad philosophical themes and her cautious approach to policy presentation and commitment is in line with a wider debate about the nature and capability of government.

Both leaders have learnt from past experience, but from a different vantage point. For Heath a prime example was the Labour party's period in opposition under Gaitskell and Wilson and the relatively substantial amount of policy work that was carried out under their leaderships. Thus Heath, by indulging in a detailed policy review, was simply further extending what had already become a major trend of British opposition politics. Equally, the Labour party's deep divisions over Clause IV and disarmament provided telling evidence of the dangers to party unity involved in allowing wide-ranging debates about party beliefs. Thatcher, on the other hand, has had the experience of the 1964–74 period to learn from. The development of detailed policy commitments in that earlier period of opposition and the failure to carry some of them through later in office has undoubtedly influenced her development of a broad brush approach, her wariness about policy details and her belief in the need to get the overall strategy right in readiness for office.

In addition to these broader considerations, the circumstances of Heath's and Thatcher's emergence as leaders of the Conservative party can help to explain both some of the similarities and some of the differences between them. Both have had to contend with the problem of exercising power in opposition and they share the unusual distinction of having become Conservative leaders during such a period.[42] The Conservative leader who emerges in opposition can hardly expect to command the same moral authority as one who emerges in government, for he is in a sense a leader on trial who has yet to prove his quality and potential by winning and holding office. This variation in leadership status may in part explain why, relative to earlier Conservative leaders, both Heath and Thatcher have been greatly concerned with developing closer liaison and contact with their followers.

Other aspects of the circumstances surrounding, and the nature of, their rise to power were, however, significantly different. Heath came to power as an insider drawn from the accepted and dominant group within the Conservative hierarchy. As chief whip and later as a senior minister in the Macmillan and Douglas-Home administrations, he had been at the centre of Conservative party affairs. His succession to the leadership meant a continuation of the mainstream in the Conservative power structure. Thatcher, by contrast, came to the leadership as a challenger and an outsider in opposition to the overwhelming majority of the existing leadership group and as a result of what amounted to a back-bench revolt.[43] She inherited a split party and a party machine still dominated by supporters of her predecessor. Hence, relative to Heath, she has shown a greater concern with matters of party management and co-ordination and has tended to call on advice and assistance from outside traditional party channels.

By virtue of being a challenger to the existing power structure within the party, the task of Thatcher as opposition leader has had an added dimension, namely the need to produce a dual alternative: to the Labour government on the one hand and to the policies of the previous Conservative government and leadership on the other. A central part of the policy approach enunciated by Thatcher has been a rejection of the 'conventional wisdom' of the 1960s and 1970s, so that to a large extent she has been reacting against sections in her own party at the same time as developing an alternative to the existing administration.[44]

The different approaches to leadership exhibited by Heath and Thatcher have developed in accord with the changing power structure of the Conservative party. One of the most important changes, strongly emphasised in this paper, has been the gradual extension of back-bench influence both under Heath and Thatcher. In addition to the points noted in earlier sections of this paper, this development is further reflected in the progressive expansion in the number of back-bench committees from less than 27 in 1964 to 36 in 1978, and in the important part played by back-bench groupings in influencing and shaping official policy, especially during the post-1975 period in relation to immigration and devolution.[45] This growth of back-bench influence may in part reflect a more frequent and prolonged experience of opposition for, as already noted, the formal opportunities for back-benchers to influence the policy and practices of their party are substantially greater in opposition than in government. However, the extended role of the back-bencher appears to be a cumulative development and is not simply or wholly to be explained as a product of the party's political circumstances. To some extent it is an inevitable outcome of the 1965 reforms in the leadership selection process, for once the facility to choose and, later, replace the leader was given to the back-benchers, the nature of the power balance within the party was significantly altered with certain important consequences for the practice and operation of leadership. Both Heath's and especially Thatcher's approaches to opposition leadership indicate a recognition of this change.

Finally, approaches to leadership must in part be regarded as a product of the different personalities involved and one or two brief, but relevant, points may be noted. Heath, with his background as an ex-civil servant, chief whip and effective and active minister, seems more concerned with getting things done rather than extensively exploring the principles and philosophy involved. An energetic organiser and administrator with an 'inborn taste for order, system, preparation, planning',[46] he takes a problem-solving approach to political matters and is said to be capable of an amazing grasp of details. By contrast, Thatcher, with her legal background, tends to deploy facts as part of a wider argument and tends to move from the general to the particular. Though very cautious and careful in making decisions, she seems both more romantic and more impulsive than Heath and more at home with ideas and general statements.

To conclude briefly, although this chapter has been concerned with the differences between Heath and Thatcher, some references have been made to the important continuities in approach especially in relation to the organisation of the front-bench, the development of a personal machinery of leadership and the concern to develop wider contacts within the party. Naturally as both have been subject to equivalent demands and limitations as leaders of the Conservative party as opposition their behaviour displays certain similarities. In particular, under their leaderships, the Conservative party as opposition has emerged as an institution in its own right with its own distinctive machinery and purposes. It is an interesting speculation as to whether, as a result of the more frequent and sustained experience of opposition, the values of an opposition party have increasingly begun to dominate the practices and operation of the Conservative party.

NOTES

1. This paper was written in June and marginally revised in September 1978. I should like to thank those Conservatives, both parliamentarians and officials, who kindly answered my questions on the subject matter of this paper.
2. An obvious exception is R. M. Punnett, *Front Bench Opposition* (London: Heinemann, 1973). See also, Saul Rose 'Policy Decision in Opposition', *Political Studies*, vol. IV, no. 2 (1956).
3. As long as it is specified which area of party activity is being considered.
4. See Andrew Gamble, *The Conservative Nation* (London: Routledge Kegan Paul, 1974) p. 9; S. H. Beer, *Modern British Politics*(London: Faber, 1965) p. 299; Nigel Harris, *Competition and the Corporate Society* (London: Methuen, 1972) pp. 254–62.
5. I have left out the February 1974 to February 1975 period of opposition because (a) from February 1974 to October 1974 the party was more a government in exile and the strong coalition flavour of leadership-thinking suggested a change in their perception of the two-party parliamentary system; (b) from October 1974 to February 1975 the party was almost wholly taken up with the leadership question. Thus the 1964–70 and 1974 to present day periods are the most strictly comparable.
6. See, by contrast, J. H. Grainger, *Character and Style in English Politics* (London: Cambridge University Press, 1969) p. 3 ff; A. F. Davies, 'The Concept of Administrative Style', *The Australian Journal of Politics and History*, vol. XII (1966).
7. To be consistent, the third person singular will subsequently be in the male gender.
8. For an early outline see Bernard Crick, 'Two Theories of Opposition', *New Statesman* (18 June 1960).
9. Attributed to George Tierney, quoted in H. J. Hanham, 'Opposition Techniques in British Politics: 1867–1914', *Government and Opposition*, vol. 2 (1 January 1967).
10. Churchill's view, see Lord Butler, *The Art of the Possible* (London: Hamish Hamilton, 1971) p. 133.
11. See G. Ionescu and I. de Madariaga, *Opposition*, (London: Watts, 1968) pp. 102–21.
12. Alan Beattie, *English Party Politics* (London: Weidenfeld & Nicolson, 1970) p. 235ff.
13. Kenneth Young, *Sir Alec Douglas-Home* (London: Dent, 1970) p. 239.
14. See speech by Reginald Maudling *NUCUA 84th Annual Conference Report*, 1966, p. 126.
15. J. D. Hoffman, *The Conservative Party in Opposition 1945–1951* (London: McGibbon & Kee, 1964) pp. 135–6.
16. Butler, op. cit., p. 135.
17. Robert Rhodes James, *Ambitions and Realities* (London: Weidenfeld & Nicolson, 1972) p. 116.
18. Punnett, op. cit., Appendix D.
19. Subject, of course, to the usual considerations of party management etc; for a thorough examination see ibid, p. 234.
20. Ibid, p. 303. The senior member of the Consultative Committee who liaised

with the Business Committee in 1964–5 was Selwyn Lloyd.

21. There are no significant formal changes in the relations between the leader and the NUCUA when the party is in opposition, though of course, in the absence of the demands of government, the leader will have more time and opportunity to develop contacts with his followers in the country.

22. For a full list see D. Butler and M. Pinto-Duschinsky, *The British General Election of 1970* (London: Macmillan, 1971) p. 67, f. n.

23. The former was under Mervyn Pike and Michael Spicer and the latter involved Ernest Marples, David Howell and Mark Schreiber. It is difficult to ascertain precisely what contribution these organisations (as distinct from the individuals involved) made to Conservative policy-making. However, they do indicate Heath's concern with problems of policy production and the machinery of policy-making.

24. *Putting Britain Right Ahead* (CCO, 1965) pp. 7–8, 11, 13 and 20.

25. On Heath's European commitment, see Andrew Roth, *Heath and the Heathmen* (London: Routledge Kegan Paul, 1972) ch. 15.

26. George Hutchinson, *Edward Heath: A Personal and Political Biography* (London: Longmans, 1970) p. 172.

27. Punnett, op. cit., p. 302 suggests two junior spokesmen, Channon and Fisher, may also have fallen foul of the individual and collective responsibility rules.

28. Butler and Pinto-Duschinsky, op. cit.

29. Hutchinson, op. cit., p. 190 ff.

30. Ibid, p. 186.

31. Patrick Cosgrave, *Margaret Thatcher* (London: Hutchinson, 1978) p. 168ff.

32. Ibid.

33. Considerable detail has been published in relation to housing, education, social security, structure of industry, immigration and certain aspects of law and order. Also see the relatively detailed economic proposals contained in *The Right Approach to the Economy* (CCO, 1977).

34. See, 'The Making of Tory Policy: 1978', The *Economist* (15 April 1978).

35. For Thatcher's leadership election platform see George Gardiner, *Margaret Thatcher* (London: Kimber, 1975) Appendix C.

36. For some indication of these changes see, Geoffrey Smith, 'The hey-day of the party rebel', *The Times* (12 May 1978).

37. There is the additional difference that Airey Neave had been Thatcher's leadership campaign manager and that originally her two PPSs were Fergus Montgomery and William Shelton, both of whom, particularly the latter, were closely involved in initiating and organising her successful bid for the party leadership. Thus initially her private office mirrored very closely her election campaign organisation. In Heath's case there was less continuity between his campaign team and his private office.

38. Certain MPs are usually mentioned such as George Gardiner, Geoffrey Pattie and Norman Tebbit. Despite speculation to the contrary, there is nothing new about this practice; most opposition leaders have prepared for prime minister's questions, though they are not generally advised by back-benchers.

39. For detailed figures and analysis see D. E. Butler and Dennis Kavanagh, *The British General Election of October 1974* (London: Macmillan, 1975) p. 330ff.

40. This managerial emphasis was in part reflected in a large number of official reports and papers, including the Fulton Report on the Civil Service, the

Redcliffe-Maud Report on local government and the Seebohn Report on the social services.

41. See, for instance, Jeffrey L. Pressmen and Aaron B. Wildavsky, *Implementation* (University of California Press, 1973); Christopher Hood, *The Limits of Administration* (Wiley, 1976); A. J. Culyer, *Need and the National Health Service* (London: Martin Robertson, 1976); Anthony King, *et al.*, *Why is Britain Becoming Harder to Govern?* (London: BBC, 1976).

42. Heath was the first to become leader of the Conservative party during a period in opposition since Bonar Law in 1911; though this is arguable, there is the problem of Conservative leadership in the Lords and the case of J. Austen Chamberlain in 1921. However, the point is clear: it's a long time since a Conservative leader has emerged in opposition. Heath and Thatcher also share the distinction of being the first to be elected to the leadership by the parliamentary party.

43. For informed accounts of the 1975 leadership battle see Gardiner, op. cit., chs. 13, 14 and 15; Cosgrave, op. cit., ch. 2; 'The selling of Margaret Thatcher', *The Sunday Times* (9 February 1975).

44. Though it is worth noting that the policy change that has taken place under Thatcher's leadership, at least in economic affairs, is not altogether different from that which took place during the 1964 to 1970 period. There is the additional point, that it is a tendency of opposition parties to break away from policies previously pursued by them in office.

45. In the case of devolution and the dropping of the party's commitment to a directly-elected Scottish assembly, an important and influential role was played by the Union Flag Group—an ad hoc and unofficial back-bench group of about 70 members, which as well as influencing opinion within the Conservative parliamentary party also liaised with Labour and Ulster Unionist opponents of devolution in a successful attempt to impede the passage of the 1976 Devolution Bill.

46. Hutchinson, op. cit., p. 172.

8 The Conservative Elite, 1918–78: Does Unrepresentativeness Matter?

David Butler and Michael Pinto-Duschinsky

I INTRODUCTION

Are measures more important than men? Do we judge our parties more by what they do than by who the people are who do them? The answers to such questions are complex and unclear. Yet a party's destiny, as well as its public image, certainly rests partly on its leaders. It is instructive to consider how the Conservative party in and out of parliament has changed or failed to change over recent generations.

When the Conservative strategists set about the task of re-establishing the party after its defeat in 1945, they did so in two ways: firstly by reformulating Conservative policy, and secondly by attempting to widen the social composition of the party. This two-pronged approach reflected a long-standing tenet that the party's electoral success demanded not only a popular programme but also the recruitment of men and women from differing backgrounds into the party leadership. Accordingly, two major documents were produced. *The Industrial Charter*[1] dealt with policy; *The Maxwell-Fyfe Report*[2] proposed far-reaching internal organisational reforms.

Looking back at these landmark reports 30 years later, there is a clear contrast between the importance of *The Industrial Charter* and the lack of impact of the changes proposed by Sir David Maxwell-Fyfe's committee. Firstly in terms of policy, the leftward move inaugurated by *The Industrial Charter* has proved more decisive than its authors could possibly have foreseen. Their acceptance of the Welfare State and a mixed economy has conditioned every subsequent Conservative manifesto. But, secondly, the party has altered slowly in its social composition. The absence of working-class representatives and dominance of the upper-middle-class in the senior Conservative ranks, both in parliament and in the constituencies, is nearly as marked today as it was in the late-1940s when the Maxwell-Fyfe proposals were introduced. Moreover, there have been few broad changes since the period after the First World War.

This chapter first outlines the main Maxwell-Fyfe reforms of 1948-9 and their aims; secondly, it charts the changes—or lack of them—in the composition of the Conservative hierarchy in the House of Commons and in the constituencies; and thirdly, it considers whether the unrepresentative pattern of Conservative leadership is a serious handicap to the party.

II THE MAXWELL-FYFE REFORMS 1948-9

The desire to end the social elitism of the pre-war Conservative party was a major motive for many of the organisational innovations during the late-1940s, when Lord Woolton was party chairman. This aim lay behind several of the Maxwell-Fyfe proposals.

The Special Committee on Party Organisation, which met under the chairmanship of Sir David Maxwell-Fyfe (later Lord Kilmuir), was set up in June 1948. Its Interim and Final Reports were approved by the 1948 annual conference and by a special meeting of the Central Council in July 1949.

The main reform emerging from the Maxwell-Fyfe Committee was the removal of financial burdens from parliamentary candidates. Clauses 1, 5 and 6 of the new rules stipulated that:

1. The entire election expenses of Conservative candidates in every constituency shall be the responsibility of the constituency associations . . . and no subscription shall be made directly or indirectly by the candidate to the fund for statutory election expenses . . .
5. Candidates may, by arrangement with their constituency associations, make nominal subscriptions each year, but the

subscriptions must in no case exceed £25; the annual subscription of members of parliament to their associations shall in no case exceed £50.

6. In no circumstances shall the question of an annual subscription be mentioned by any constituency selection committee to any candidate before he has been selected.[3]

The objective of these regulations was to remove the financial barriers which had, it was thought, prevented working-class and ordinary middle-class Conservatives from standing for parliament before the Second World War. As Lord Woolton wrote in his *Memoirs*, 'it was no use saying that the Conservative party was not a "class" party if a working-man Conservative could not afford to stand as a candidate'.[4]

The pre-war situation—which the new rules aimed to alter—had been highlighted in a memorandum written in 1939 by Ian Harvey.[5] According to Harvey, a young Conservative who was later to become a Conservative MP, the Conservative constituency associations operated 'A plutocratic system'. He claimed that there were three categories of would-be candidates:

Class 'A': those willing to pay all their election expenses (£400–£1200) and to subscribe £500–£1000 a year to the local association;

Class 'B': those willing to pay half their election expenses and to subscribe £250–£450 per annum;

Class 'C': those unable to pay any election expenses or to contribute more than £100 per annum.

According to the memorandum:

' 'A' Class have always an excellent chance of being adopted . . . 'C' Class hardly any chances at all'.[6]

Harvey complained that the system resulted in bad, unrepresentative candidates and led to the defection of Conservative voters. This was an analysis which Lord Woolton and Sir David Maxwell-Fyfe apparently accepted in the late-1940s. According to Lord Woolton's *Memoirs*, the banning of local subscriptions by candidates:

was revolutionary and, in my view, did more than any single factor to save the Conservative party . . . the Conservative party had become at least as broad-based as the Socialist party . . . Here was Tory democracy in action. The way was clear for men and women of ability to seek election to Westminister.[7]

Besides this change in the financial arrangements of candidates, the Maxwell-Fyfe Committee sought to democratise the party in other ways. For example, a 'quota' scheme was introduced to encourage local associations to contribute to the funds of Conservative Central Office. (At the same time it was proposed to publish annual party accounts since, according to the committee, this was 'the only effective basis' from which to persuade the local parties to contribute to the central funds.[8] This latter proposal was, however, not implemented for another twenty years.)

The ban on financial payments by candidates and the quota scheme both imposed heavy extra burdens on the constituency associations and gave them the incentive to find new members. Before the Maxwell-Fyfe Committee was set up, and while it was sitting, vigorous recruitment campaigns were in progress. These were to raise membership levels to an all-time record.

The reforms of the late-1940s have had some lasting effects:

1. The ban on the 'selling of seats' to candidates by local associations appears to have been completely effective.
2. Widespread, small-scale fund-raising at the constituency level has replaced the common pre-war system of funding by a few rich supporters. The new methods have not only provided for the needs of the local parties but have also produced surpluses for 'quotas' to Central Office. Between 1966 and 1977, constituency quotas provided £3½ million. This was about a fifth of total central party income.
3. Although party membership has dropped considerably below the temporary peak of 2.8 million, which was recorded in 1953, it has remained high by pre-war standards and by comparison with other parties. According to the constituency survey carried out for the Houghton Committee, there were about 1½ million Conservative members in 1974—nearly five times the Labour total and eight times that of the Liberals.[9]

Yet, all these democratic developments have had relatively little effect on the social composition of the party, either within or outside the House of Commons. Lord Woolton's claim that the Conservative party has 'become at least as broad-based as the Socialist party' is without foundation.

III THE MIDDLE-CLASS HIERARCHY

In post-war elections approximately half of all Conservative voters have been working-class (the percentage has varied between 52 per cent in 1950 and 44 per cent in October 1974). But the working-class Conservatives have remained almost completely passive adherents. Moreover, Conservatives from the lower middle-class (social group C/1) have made little impact upon the party hierarchy, though (unlike working-class Conservatives) they seem to have been active as party members. The only change of any significance is the gradual decline of aristocrats and of rich businessmen and their replacement by professionals and managers. This seems to have happened both within the parliamentary party and in the constituency associations. But it must be emphasised that this development has left the solidly upper and upper-middle-class nature of the party elite almost unchanged.

Conservative MPs and Front-benchers

'The country has been transformed but the Tory MP stays the same.' This assertion is patently untrue, in all sorts of ways. Yet it is easy to offer evidence for it. Consider Table 8.1:

TABLE 8.1   Conservative MPs 1923 and 1974

	Con. MPs.	Education			All Univ. %	Occupation		
		Etonian %	Public School %	Oxbridge %		Profes- sional %	Manual %	Women %
1923	258	25	79	40	50	52	4	1
1974 (Oct)	277	17	75	56	69	46	1	3

NOTE

1923 was the interwar year with the fewest Conservative MPs. It is cited here because it comes nearer to matching the 277 Conservative MPs of 1974 than 1922 (345) or 1918 (358). But the comparison would be almost the same with other elections in the 1920s or 1930s as the Appendix on p. 207 shows.

The educational and occupational background of Conservative MPs appears to have altered little over 50 years. The most striking feature of the table is the absence of working-class Conservative MPs. In fact, the proportion with origins in manual labour, never substantial, has shrunk almost to nothing. In all the years since the Maxwell-Fyfe reforms, there have only been two working-class Tory MPs. At the other end of the social scale, the proportion of Etonians has gradually fallen—but this one school still provides nearly a fifth of the parliamentary party and the public school element has hardly diminished. The biggest change lies in the increase in MPs with a university education, but the Oxbridge dominance has not been challenged.

Of the 277 Conservatives elected in October 1974, 208 went to Headmasters Conference Schools and 159 of them went to Oxford or Cambridge. A further 23 went to Oxbridge from other schools. Thus, only 46 Conservative MPs (under 17 per cent) had neither of these elite labels 'Public School' or 'Oxbridge'. The proportion of women remains negligible. The picture of 1923 and 1974 alike is of a party that draws its representatives from male members of the upper-middle class.

The same is even more true of the party's leaders as Table 8.2 shows:

TABLE 8.2   Conservative Leadership 1924 and 1978

| | | Class | | | Education | | | | |
	Total	Aristo-crat	Middle-class	Working-class	Eton	All Public School	Ox-bridge	All Univ.	Women
Cabinet 1924	21	9	12	—	7	21	16	16	—
Shadow Cabinet 1978[1]	20	3	17	—	6	18	15	16	2

See Appendix for definitions.

NOTES

In May 1978, of the front bench spokesmen outside the shadow cabinet and party whips—39 in all—33 were from public schools and 26 were from Oxbridge. This means that 84 per cent of front-benchers, inside and outside the shadow cabinet, were from public schools.

Mrs Thatcher now, like Mr Baldwin after the First World War, is surrounded by a public school, Oxbridge elite. They are less aristocratic than 50 years ago, but the shadow cabinet before the May 1979 election includes, besides Mrs Thatcher, only one who did not go to a Headmasters' Conference school.

Of course there have been changes in the body of MPs that Table 8.1 does not reveal. In 1924 there were 35 sons of hereditary peers on the Conservative benches. In 1974 there were only nine. In 1923 a significant proportion, perhaps a fifth of Conservative MPs could only be classed as of 'private means'. Now almost every MP can claim to have had a genuine occupation. There has been a significant move from the aristocracy to the professional classes. Yet one reservation must be made. There was only one heir to a peerage and eight other sons of hereditary peers among the 277 Conservative MPs elected in October 1974, yet of the first 26 selections made to replace Conservative MPs elected in October 1974, six went to sons of hereditary peers, four of them heirs to the title. Is the pendulum swinging back?

Twenty years ago one encountered Conservatives who lamented the Maxwell-Fyfe rules, which ended the purchase of seats, on the ground that free constituency choice meant uniform choice. The identikit candidate was replacing the diversity of aristocratic eccentrics, country squires, self-made men and successful QCs who brought their way into parliament. Working-class people, women, Jews and Catholics now found it hard to be selected.

In recent years the religious barriers have diminished. From one practising Jew in 1959 the number has jumped to twelve—a number comparable to pre-war. But there were only seven women out of 277 Conservative MPs in October 1974 (in 1964 there had been eleven out of 304), and the working class still had to be content with Ray Mawby and Sir Edward Brown as their only Conservative representatives.

One other change has come over Conservative MPs. They are not only more university educated: they are, by general consent, of a higher level of average ability than they used to be. The relatively dumb knight of the shire is said to be a dying breed, replaced by the thrusting city banker or advertising man. The Conservative benches are filled by competent and, usually, enlightened men: the number whom their colleagues have cause to blush for in terms of their intelligence or their prejudices is probably smaller than ever before. The job of an MP has changed even in the last ten years. It is incompatible with most occupations: certainly it is no place for the captains of industry or the wealthy idlers who were a recognisable element in pre-war parliaments. But there has been no compensating move towards a more diversified party.

The uniformity of Conservative MPs is not the fault of the party hierarchy. Constituency democracy is hard to control. Central Office has long since learnt how hard it is to place meritorious candidates. Constituency chairmen and their shortlisting groups, while agreeing that the party needs more women, or more working-class MPs, will always feel that their seat is not the one to make the sacrifice. And selection committees, composed in a fairly similar way across the country, seem to have fairly similar tastes when it comes to choosing a candidate.

This is not the place to argue the merits of alternative electoral systems. But it is relevant to point out that, all over the world, when parties have to put up a slate of several names rather than an individual candidate, they produce a balanced ticket, with some consideration for sex, class and race. It is, for example, not a matter of regional prejudice that there are more women councillors in the north than the south but merely a reflection of the fact that many more councils in the north have multi-member wards, selecting three candidates at a time instead of one.

Constituency Leaders and Activists

Biographical information about party activists in the constituencies is much more difficult to obtain than for members of parliament. In particular, it is not possible to collect full data about the pre-war period and the 1940s and 1950s. An accurate time-series cannot, therefore, be constructed. However, material is available from a number of sources about the social composition in the 1960s of Conservatives at various levels of the party outside parliament.

This shows, as might be expected, that the higher the level of the party, the smaller the extent of working-class and lower-middle-class participation. The pattern, based on information collected between 1964 and 1969, is shown in Figure 8.1:

Since there were about fourteen million Conservative identifiers and about 300,000 Conservative activists during 1964, the statistics in Figure 8.1 indicate that roughly one out of 105 working-class Conservatives carried out some kind of activity on behalf of the party. Middle-class Conservatives were nearly four times as likely to be active in support of the party. The ratio of identifiers to activists

TABLE 8.3   Occupations of Conservative Constituency Chairmen, 1969, and Parliamentary Candidates, 1966

	Constituency Chairmen %	Parliamentary Candidates %
Professional		
Barrister	–	16
Solicitor	7	8
Chartered Secretary/Accountant	7	5
Civil Servant/Local Government	1	5
Armed Services	3	6
Teaching (university, adult and school)	3	4
Other	3	3
	24	47
Business		
Large proprietors and directors	17	13
Medium proprietors and executives	16	11
Commerce, insurance, salesmen	3	7
Small proprietors, shopkeepers	16	2
Managers, clerks	14	2
	66	35
Miscellaneous White-Collar		
Farmer, landowner	9	7
Other (journalist, private means etc.)	–	10
	9	17
Manual workers	1	1
Total	100%	100%

SOURCE
As for Figure 8.1 for constituency chairmen and for candidates, D. Butler and A. King, *The British General Election of 1966* (1966) pp. 208–9.

NOTE
Former officers in the armed services are categorised under their existing occupations unless retired. Wives are categorised under their husbands' occupations. Apparent inconsistencies in the total result from rounding.

was one to 30 for lower-middle-class (C1) and one to 27 for upper-middle-class Conservatives.

Apart from the expected difference between middle-class and working-class participation, the notable aspect of the figures is the perhaps unexpected extent of lower-middle-class involvement in

FIG. 8.1   The social pyramid: working-class, lower-middle-class, and upper-middle-class participation in the extra-parliamentary Conservative party, 1964–9.

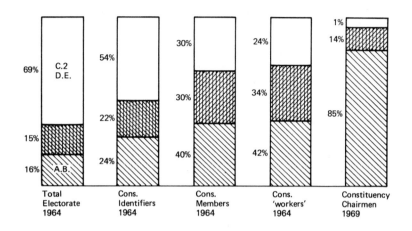

SOURCES

(a) D. Butler and D. Stokes, 1964 survey for *Political Change in Britain* (cols. 1–3);
(b) a private survey carried out for the Conservative Research Department by the British Market Research Bureau, *The Determination of Political Attitudes and Voting Behaviour: Party Workers*, (1966), (col. 4) and
(c) interviews carried out by M. Pinto-Duschinsky with area agents in England and Wales in 1969, which produced information on 380 constituency chairmen (col. 5).

NOTE

The division between social groups A and B on the one hand and C1 on the other hand needs to be treated with caution for col. 5, as information on occupations given by area agents was sometimes not sufficiently precise to determine social group. For example, the social group of a shop-keeper is determined by the number of his shop-assistants—information which was not available. The C1 category of constituency chairmen consists of clerks, and a third of those identified as small business proprietors, shopkeepers, salesmen and managers.

party work. Conservatives in social grade C1 were nearly as likely to participate as those in grades A and B. However, the distinction between the lower and upper-middle-groups emerges very clearly further up the constituency hierarchy. The constituency leaders, especially in Conservative-held seats, are predominantly upper-middle class. The ratio of constituency chairmen to ordinary party workers is about five times greater for upper than for lower-middle-class Conservatives. This is seen in the contrast between columns 4 and 5 of Figure 8.1. However, constituency associations are elaborate organisations and the statistical information given in Figure 8.1 ignores several intermediate levels of the hierarchy—the branch officers, the women's leaders, the association officers and the constituency agent (all of whom can have important roles), and the local organisations of Conservative trade unionists (which are generally small and insignificant despite encouragement from above). A complete account would also require an analysis of Conservative local councillors, of Young Conservatives and members of the area and national committees of the National Union.

Special attention is given below to constituency chairmen because they are the local leaders about whom the most comprehensive information has been collected. The chairman is, during his normal three-year term of office, the most important single officer. But the dependence of most associations on finances raised by ward branches generally ensures an important role (for instance in the selection of parliamentary candidates) for the branch chairmen. Their backgrounds seem, from case studies of particular constituencies, to be halfway between those of party activists and of chairmen. This conforms with the general 'filter' pattern whereby each higher level is more socially exclusive than the last.

A closer look at the constituency chairmen reveals broadly the same solidly middle-class, male pattern as for Conservative MPs, although constituency chairmen as a group are a notch lower on the social scale.

Apart from a few constituencies, most of them Labour-held, local associations generally have middle-class, male chairmen. Of local party chairmen in 1969, 94 per cent were male. Only 1 per cent of chairmen were skilled or unskilled manual workers (the same percentage as for MPs). Like MPs, the vast majority of chairmen were professionals or businessmen. But there was a marked difference in the balance. Whereas MPs and candidates were strongly professional, the majority of chairmen were businessmen, executives or small proprietors. This emerges from Table 8.3 which compares the occupations of all Conservative candidates in 1966 and of 369 chairmen in 1969.

An examination of their educational backgrounds shows that 95 per cent of chairmen in Conservative-held seats had been to public or grammar schools. The proportion of chairmen in all seats who had been to such schools was 84 per cent. However, the proportion with public school backgrounds was distinctly lower among chairmen than among parliamentary candidates or MPs. For example, 50 per cent of chairmen in Conservative-held seats in 1969 were from public schools as compared to 80 per cent of Conservative MPs.

TABLE 8.4   Educational Background of Conservative Constituency Chairmen, 1969

	Public Schooling %	Grammar Schooling %	Elementary Schooling %	%
Safe Conservative	52	44	3	100
Marginal Conservative	44	47	9	100
Marginal Labour	25	56	19	100
Safe Labour	20	49	30	100
All Constituencies	36	49	16	100

NOTE
The definitions of 'grammar' and 'elementary' school used here are cruder than the classifications of MPs' schooling in the Nuffield election studies. This is because the table is based on information about local party chairmen supplied by area agents, often speaking without exact information. The table is therefore not strictly comparable to, or as reliable as, Table 8.1.

Have these social patterns changed over recent decades? Accounts of individual associations suggest that there have been significant developments both in urban and rural constituencies. In the rural areas, the influence and participation of leading local aristocrats and landowners seems to have declined gradually and steadily. In urban areas, the pre-war leadership of substantial businessmen has largely disappeared. In the 1920s and 1930s, and to a lesser extent after the war, large proprietors were frequently the financial mainstay of their local Conservative associations and, to all intents and purposes, employed the agent. The modern constituency leaders are expected to contribute their time rather than their money. They are normally well-established, respectable professionals and businessmen—solicitors, accountants, executives and proprietors of small or medium-sized companies. But they are a different breed from the landowners and business magnates who controlled many associations before the war.[10]

In summary, it appears that the pre-war influence of aristocrats and of very rich capitalists has given way both in the parliamentary party and in the constituencies to the dominance of the 'ordinary' upper-middle-classes. The hierarchy includes fewer sons of peers, millionaires and men of leisure. But this change has not opened the party to participation by members of the working class and the lower-middle class. Although these groups provide three-quarters of the party's voters and over a half of its constituency workers, they have continued to be almost completely excluded from the constituency and parliamentary leadership.

IV DOES UNREPRESENTATIVENESS MATTER?

Ought the uniform social character of the party hierarchy to be a matter of concern to Conservative strategists? Are voters really influenced, either directly or indirectly, by the absence of working class voices on the Tory benches in the House of Commons and among the constituency leaders? Besides the possible electoral consequences, does Conservative unrepresentativeness harm the party in other ways? This concluding section will list some of the opposing arguments about these questions.

Why a party's social composition is unimportant

Elections in Britain are being won and lost to an increasing extent on the basis of policy issues. It is by no means certain that the continued predominance of the upper-middle classes has led the Conservatives to advocate unpopular or unrepresentative stands. Etonians, though untypical in their backgrounds, are not necessarily so unrepresentative in their opinions. Some of the party's leading moderates have been drawn from the upper-classes (one example is Lord Boyle), whereas some of the most vocal right-wingers in the party have recently been those with relatively modest social origins. Defenders of the large group of Etonians in the present hierarchy have even gone so far as to suggest that their exit, if it ever occurred, would lead to a rightward lurch in policy and to a loss of popular support for the party. This claim is exaggerated. There have been right-wing aristocrats among Conservative MPs and ministers (the late Lord Salisbury and the Hon. Nicholas Ridley, for instance) as well as left-wingers with less elite backgrounds (such as Peter Walker). In reality, there is no clear connection between the class and the policy views of MPs. In any case, to the extent that issues determine votes, the socio-economic backgrounds of the senior Conservatives are irrelevant. Moreover, statistical demonstrations like those of Table 8.1 and 8.2 are limited to a comparison of readily measurable facts. Whether an MP hated his father may influence his politics far more than where he went to school. Whether he is a kind man may signify more than whether he had a manual occupation. It is at least possible that in many essential personal characteristics Conservative MPs are closer to being mirrors of the population than these tables suggest.

Insofar as personalities are significant, the party leader is the only person who really matters. The leader makes as great an impact on the voters as all his (or her) cabinet colleagues put together. Individual MPs, candidates and constituency chiefs are of even less account, as the uniformity of constituency swings in general elections demonstrates. This means that the social composition of the party's front-benchers, MPs and local leaders makes virtually no direct impact on votes.

Moreover, the popularity of party leaders seems to be determined by their personal qualities and only to a small extent on the basis of their class. This is seen in the case of Sir Alec Douglas-Home—one of the less popular and more aristocratic Conservative leaders of recent times. Survey evidence indicates that Sir Alec's unpopularity was not connected with his background. When asked to list what they liked and disliked about him, respondents included few mentions of his class (and a majority of them were positive); the unfavourable mentions were mostly about his personal defects:

Some Favourable and Unfavourable References to Sir Alec Douglas-Home, 1964[11]

	Class background	Personal qualities
Favourable	Upper class, well educated.	Strong, decisive, courageous, good PM.
	132	218
Unfavourable	Educational background—snobbish.	Weak, indecisive, bad PM.
	25	546

Modern political campaigns concentrate on national propaganda. The image of the typical Conservative more often reaches the voter on television than via the old-style doorstep canvass. If the image-makers at Central Office wish to present a picture of a broadly based party they can use party political broadcasts to feature interviews with working-class supporters, regardless of whether they represent a large section of the constituency organisations or not.

The high social status of the Conservative hierarchy is a positive attraction to some electors who give their 'deferential' support to the party.

The arguments suggest that the social composition of the hierarchy is largely irrelevant to the party's electoral appeal and, insofar as it is relevant, it may lead to a gain rather than a loss of votes.

It can also be argued, in more general terms, that there is no reason why legislators should resemble their electors. Being an MP is a specialist job, requiring education and finesse. If we wanted parliament to be a microcosm of the nation we should choose its members by lot from the electoral rolls. But the qualities that make a man or woman want to be an MP and the qualities that make them a good MP are not distributed at random throughout the population. There is, on this argument, nothing wrong with MPs being an elite drawn from the more highly-qualified segments of society. Sociological indices that show how unrepresentative MPs are by their high status in education and occupation can indeed be turned into evidence of how well-fitted they are to their jobs.

Why a Party's Social Composition is Important

General attitudes and beliefs about the parties are still more important than specific policy issues in determining voting choice. This holds true despite the fact that party alignments and class images have been diminishing in their hold over votes, despite the growing volatility of electoral behaviour, and despite the growing importance of issues and other short-term factors.

Surveys continue to indicate that, among these general images about the major parties, those relating to class are enormously important. The belief that parties represent class interests or class norms remains especially strong among working-class Labour supporters, over 90 per cent of whom express this view. Moreover, the majority of responses about the link between parties and class interests are favourable to Labour and unfavourable to the Conservatives. There can be no doubt that the Conservatives are damaged by being seen as a class party.

The association of the Conservative party with middle-class interests has been built up over a long period and in many ways. It is uncertain what part the social composition of the party's hierarchy has played in this process. However, it seems obvious that the exclusive image of the Conservatives held by most working-class Labour voters must have been reinforced by the style and accents of Tory spokesmen, which have inevitably reflected their Oxbridge, public school backgrounds.

In the post-war period the two major parties have reached very similar positions on many policy issues. Their electorate appeal has therefore concentrated in the claim that they will perform better than their opponents. Both sides acknowledge the need to reduce unemployment, inflation, and strikes, and to increase economic growth. Each attacks the record of the other and promises to do better. Since there are few differences in policy positions, the credibility of each party's message becomes all-important. This is particularly the case in the vital area of economic policy. There can be no serious doubt that the Conservative party is considerably handicapped in presenting their views on the economy by the failure to recruit any senior or well-known member of the working class into its ranks. It can hardly escape the notice of trade union members that, notwithstanding the efforts of Central Office, there is not a single trade union leader who publicly backs the Conservative party.

Although the appeal of the Conservative leader does not seem to be directly affected by his (or her) social class, it is indirectly affected by the social structure of the party. A British political party is a closed institution. The leader must choose the vast majority of his ministerial team from the ranks of his MPs. It is not possible for the British prime minister or leader of the opposition to follow the practice of US presidents in recruiting outsiders from a variety of backgrounds (and popular with a variety of electoral groups). When choosing the members of the cabinet or shadow cabinet a British leader is stuck with the talent already in parliament. Moreover, the MPs of a party must all pass the gauntlet of a constituency selection committee. There is no alternative pathway to the House of Commons such as that provided to would-be US congressmen by the primary system. It is this exclusive power of candidate selection that gives particular importance to the constituency leaders.

The Conservative party (like the Labour party) thus forms a world of its own. The party leader must spend a great amount of time in the party milieu and is likely to be influenced by these contacts. They are likely to affect his language and manner. Some of the leader's pronouncements must be directed not to the electorate but to the party faithful. But these party speeches are also monitored by the press and television. The leader's speech to the party conference is also seen by the electorate at large. Party demands prevent a leader from straying too far from the views and attitudes of the Conservative faithful. Thus, even if—as with Mr Heath and Mrs Thatcher—the party elects a leader who did not go to a public school, that leader is under pressure to adopt the upper middle-class accents and styles which dominate the party hierarchy.

It will be seen from these complex arguments that the absence of working-class representatives is not an automatic disadvantage to the party electorally. Where the Conservatives adopt popular policies and choose personable leaders, the narrow social composition of the hierarchy becomes irrelevant; and, insofar as the party appeals to deferential voters, it may even be a positive advantage. On the other hand, the lack of a broad social base is potentially a very serious handicap, because of three features of the British system: first, the importance of general class images, second, the importance of valence issues and third, the exclusive control of the constituency associations and the parliamentary party over access to cabinet office and the premiership (and consequently their influence over the style of party leadership).

The uniformity of the Tory hierarchy also damages the party in the ways that are unrelated to considerations of electoral advantage. It arguably limits the party's ability to formulate policy and to govern effectively. The problem is not that some social groups (particularly the working class) are under-represented in the upper ranks of the party. They are hardly represented at all. There is no compelling reason in democratic theory or in political practice for the senior office-holders of a party to reflect in their social composition that of the party supporters at large. The fact that half of all Conservative voters are working-class does not mean that precisely half the party's MPs should be working-class as well. The absurdities of this position were demonstrated at the 1972

Convention of US Democrats which tried to apply conditions of social representativeness to state delegations. However, it seems reasonable that a group that forms such an important section of the party's voters should at least have some voice in the top councils of the party. It is the virtually complete absence of working-class representation that is the core of the Conservative problem. The constituency associations have selected only two working-class MPs since the war and neither has gained cabinet rank.

There can be little doubt that recent Labour government have gained by having in their ranks a few members—like Mr Lever—whose experience of business has given them a rapport with the business community. No senior Tory has had similar experience of the shop floor. There are several other areas about which few senior Conservatives have first-hand knowledge or expertise, such as education and the social services. In these fields Labour is left to make the running. On the other hand there is a wealth of knowledge among MPs and local leaders about finance, defence, business, agriculture and the law. Similarly some of the discussions about industrial relations in the Conservative cabinet of 1970–4 would surely have been very different if among its members there had been a single figure with the background and prejudices of an Ernie Bevin or, even to pitch it far lower, of a Jimmy Thomas, to remind ministers of how other people reacted.

The uniformity of their backgrounds gives members of the Conservative elite in the House of Commons and the constituencies an unduly restricted frame of reference which limits the party's ability to formulate policies or to put them into operation.

The narrower band of choice exercised by constituency associations in recent years has probably hurt the Conservative party more, through an increase in uniformity, than it has helped it through an increase in ability. Likemindedness can be a hazard to a party that seeks to guide a diverse nation.

Although the Labour parliamentary party has had its own problems as it has moved from an overwhelmingly working-class group to one that has almost as many graduates as the Conservatives, it has always had and continues to have a far wider social, educational, and economic diversity than its opponents, and that has been a genuine strength.

Following the concerted efforts of the 1940s to broaden the social base of the Conservative party, the attempts to attract members of the working class into the higher ranks of the organisation and into the House of Commons have flagged. It is in the interests of good government and probably the electoral advantage of the Conservative party that they should be renewed.

NOTES

1. *The Industrial Charter* (Conservative and Unionist Central Office, 1947).
2. *Interim and Final Reports of the Committee on Party Organisation* (The National Union of Conservative and Unionist Association, 1949).
3. Ibid., pp. 13–14.
4. *Woolton, Earl of, Memoirs* (London: Cassell, 1959) p. 345.
5. The Harvey Memorandum is reprinted in J. F. S. Ross, *Parliamentary Representation* (London: Eyre & Spottiswoode, 1943) pp. 236–8.
6. Ibid., p. 237.
7. Woolton, op. cit., p. 346.
8. *Interim and Final Reports of the Committee on Party Organisation*, op. cit., p. 15.
9. *Report of the Committee on Financial aid to Political Parties*, Cmnd. 6601 (HMSO 1976) p. 31.
10. J. Ramsden, *The Organisation of the Conservative and Unionist Party in Britain 1910–1930*, Oxford D.Phil. Thesis, 1974. According to Ramsden there was a move towards democratic financing of Conservative associations during the interwar years. But it was not until after 1945 that the decisive steps were taken.
11. D. Butler & D. Stokes, *Political Change in Britain* (London: Second Edition, Macmillan, 1974) p. 359.

Appendixes

1 Main occupations of Members of Parliament 1918–74 (percentages)

	Conservative				Labour			
	1918–35 Average	*1945*	*1950*	*1951*	*1918–35 Average*	*1945*	*1950*	*1951*
Employers and Managers	32	32½	30½	32½	4	9½	9½	9
Rank and File Workers	4	3	3	4½	72	41	43	45
Professional Workers	52	61	62	57½	24	48½	46½	45½
Unpaid Domestic Workers	–	½	–	–	–	1	1	½
Unoccupied	12	3	4½	5½	–	–	–	–
	100	100	100	100	100	100	100	100

(continued)

(*continued*)

	Conservative								Labour							
	1951	1955	1959	1964	1966	1970	Feb. 1974	Oct. 1974	1951	1955	1959	1964	1966	1970	Feb. 1974	Oct. 1974
Professional	41	46	46	48	46	45	44	46	35	36	38	41	43	48	45	49
Business	37	30	30	26	29	30	32	33	9	12	10	11	9	10	9	8
Misc.	22	24	23	25	23	24	23	20	19	17	17	16	18	16	15	15
Workers	–	–	1	1	1	1	1	1	37	35	35	32	30	26	30	28
	100	100	100	100	100	100	100	100	100	100	100	100	100	100	100	100

SOURCE
Data for 1906 and 1910 are based on J. A. Thomas, *The House of Commons 1906–1911* (1958). From 1918 to 1950 J. F. S. Ross provides the data on university education in *Elections and Electors* (1955) and on public school education for Conservatives. The figures for Labour public schoolboys up to 1935 have been calculated afresh for this table. All figures from 1951 onwards are taken from the Nuffield studies. See also C. Mellors, *The British MP 1945–1975* (1978).

2. Public School and University Education of Members of Parliament 1906–74 (percentages).

| | Conservatives | | Labour | |
	Public School	University Educated	Public School	University Educated
1906	67	57	0	0
1910 Jan.	74	58	0	0
1910 Dec.	76	59	0	0
1918	81	49	3	5
1922	78	48	9	15
1923	79	50	8	14
1924	78	53	7	14
1929	79	54	12	19
1931	77	55	8	17
1935	81	57	10	19
1945	85	58	23	32
1950	79	62	22	41
1951	75	65	23	41
1955	76	64	22	40
1959	72	60	18	39
1964	75	63	18	46
1966	80	67	18	51
1970	74	64	17	53
1974 Feb.	74	68	17	56
1974 Oct.	75	69	18	57

SOURCE
As Appendix 1

3 Social and educational composition of British Cabinets 1895–1974[1]

Date	Party	Prime Minister	Cabinet Size	Aristo-crats	Middle Class	Working Class	Public School		University educated	
							All	Eton	All	Oxbridge
Aug. 1895	Con.	Salisbury	19	8	11	—	16	7	15	14
Jul. 1902	Con.	Balfour	19	9	10	—	16	9	14	13
Dec. 1905	Lib.	Campbell-Bannerman	19	7	11	1	11	3	14	12
Jul. 1914	Lib.	Asquith	19	6	12	1	11	3	15	13
Jan. 1919	Coal.	Lloyd George	21	3	17	1	12	2	13	8
Nov. 1922	Con.	Bonar Law	16	8	8	—	14	8	13	13
Jan. 1924	Lab.	MacDonald	19	3	5	11	8	—	6	6
Nov. 1924	Con.	Baldwin	21	9	12	—	21	7	16	16
Jan. 1929	Lab.	MacDonald	18	2	4	12	5	—	6	3
May 1931	Nat.	MacDonald	20	8	10	2	13	6	11	10
Jun. 1935	Con.	Baldwin	22	9	11	2	14	9	11	10
May 1938	Con.	Chamberlain	21	8	13	—	17	8	16	13
May 1945	Con.	Churchill	16	6	9	1	14	7	11	9
Aug. 1945	Lab.	Attlee	20	—	8	12	5	2	10	5
Oct. 1951	Con.	Churchill	16	5	11	—	14	7	11	9
Apr. 1955	Con.	Eden	18	5	13	—	18	10	16	14
Jan. 1957	Con.	Macmillan	18	4	14	—	17	8	16	15
Oct. 1963	Con.	Home	24	5	19	—	21	11	17	17
Oct. 1964	Lab.	Wilson	23	1	14	8	8	1	13	11
Jun. 1970	Con.	Heath	18	4	14	—	15	4	15	15
Mar. 1974	Lab.	Wilson	21	1	16	4	7	—	16	11
Apr. 1976	Lab.	Callaghan	22	1	13	7	7	—	15	10

(continued)

Date	Party	Prime Minister	Cabinet Size	Aristo-crats	Middle Class	Working Class	Public School		University educated	
							All	Eton	All	Oxbridge
Average 22 Cabinets			19½	5	11½	3	13	5	13	11
12 Con. Cabinets			19	7	12	–	16½	7½	14	13
6 Lab. Cabinets			20½	1½	9½	9	7	¼	11½	7½
2 Lab. Cabinets			19	6	11½	1	11	3	14½	12½

NOTE

This table is largely based on W. J. Guttsman, *The British Political Elite* (1963). Aristocrats are those who had among their grandparents the holder of a hereditary title. Working class are those whose fathers appear to have had a manual occupation when they were growing up. Schools are classified as Public Schools if members of the Headmasters' Conference.

9 Conservatives and Trade Unionists

Andrew Rowe

I INTRODUCTION

In February 1974 the determination of a government not to give in to a trade union was one of the issues contributing to its defeat. Several trade union leaders made it clear that they would do all they could to prevent the Conservatives from winning the general election. A few have gone even further and suggested that it will be impossible for a Conservative government to work with the trade unions or vice versa. This is one of those judgements the public statement of which looks rather like a threat. These facts alone would suggest that the Conservative party should take seriously the trade union movement not only in its policies but also organisationally.[1] If we add to them the facts that the Labour party derives about eleven-twelfths of its national income from trade unions, that union block votes account for seven-eighths of the votes at Labour conferences, and that eighteen of the 29 members of the NEC are elected by union votes, the case for an effective Conservative response becomes overwhelming.[2]

The Conservative Trade Unionists organisation is part of that response and this paper seeks to explain what it is and how it works. Part of my task is to make clear also what it is not, since many people, including some Conservatives and some industrial correspondents, have sometimes implied that the CTU is in some way an embryo alternative to the TUC. It is not, of course, and never can be. It is rather a voluntary organisation composed of paid-up members of trade unions who believe in Conservative principles and who seek a Conservative victory at the next general election, but whose priority is activity within their unions.

The CTU believes in free and responsible trade unions and its members work hard for their unions. They also believe, however, that there is plenty of room for argument about where the best interest of trade unions and their members lie politically. For example, they may point to a long series of polls among trade union members declaring their firm opposition to further nationalisation and ask why so many union leaders support it.[3] They may look at the problems posed for free trade unions when a government is the only large employer and ask if it might not be better for trade unionism if the government's share of the economy were cut back relative to the private sector. They may compare living standards here with those in other advanced industrial countries and ask whether the century-old link between the Labour party and the trade unions[4] has necessarily been in the best interests of their members. Looking at voting patterns in successive general elections, they wonder why it is that, with so many trade union members obviously voting Tory, the Labour party can so confidently claim to have the trade union movement behind it at election time. Polls also show stronger belief in union membership than in current union leadership.[5]

Most of the answer is to be found in the history of the two main parties. Despite the fact that many of the laws which allowed trade unions to form and flourish were passed by Conservative governments,[6] it is the fact that the Labour party is the child of the unions—the political arm of organised labour—which has dictated its history so far. Moreover, among union activists, the commitment to socialism, at least in theory, has kept the link secure. It may be true that the link is sometimes one of rhetoric rather than one of substance, but rhetoric is particularly important in the Labour movement. It is one of the more remarkable failures of the Labour party's opponents that it is still possible for union leaders to pretend that Labour governments achieve more, even in economic terms, for trade unionists than Conservative ones.[7] The myth has been sustained partly because, however slow the rate of growth in the general economy, it has at least grown a little each year so that the fairer shares for all implicit in the commitment to a form of socialism did not mean that significant numbers of union members might have to receive less. Further, trade unions are deeply conservative in their practices and habits of mind so that, even without going as far as the family fiefdom of the General and Municipal Workers Union, many major industrial unions have preserved a fairly long, Labour-oriented, line of succession among their leaderships. It is an important paradox that the newer white-collar unions often produce more radical leaderships who, at the moment, frequently lean a good deal further left.[8]

It would be foolish to suggest that this had changed already but the old system is coming under pressure. A combination of the closed shop, the switch in employment from blue to white collar occupations (with a consequent drive by unions such as the Transport and General Workers Union to spread their base) and a realisation by managers and professionals that they need protection too, is sweeping into the unions millions of people who not only have no background of working-class solidarity against 'exploitative' bosses but who have probably joined unions to protect their privileged earnings and status. This increasing unionisation of non-manual workers presents a challenge to the Conservative party as it does to the trade union movement.

The tensions are showing in some of the larger unions and in the competition between unions for merger partners. Some unions, like the Amalgamated Union of Engineering Workers, may break into some of their constituent groups. If they do, they may then float free until they join up with other fragments to form new unions based on skills or earning levels. How long, for example, can TASS (Technical, Administrative and Supervisory Section) be expected to remain part of the AUEW?[9]

Furthermore, there are a number of pressures, including cash flow difficulties, often caused by technological changes reducing membership, which are likely to force mergers. It is already true that sizeable numbers of union staff are recruited directly from graduates and others who seek union employment either for ideological reasons or as a step in their own professional career rather than as a climax to a long period of voluntary service to the union. It seems possible that, if unions grow larger and their management more technical, the gap between a union leadership tempted to look outwards to the wider political scene and the members concerned overwhelmingly with their own problems will grow wider.[10] It is vital that the CTU succeed in mobilising trade union members who are prepared to work hard to secure the sort of official they really want and to mobilise support for non-socialist solutions. Otherwise, the radical left will increasingly dominate the unions.

As unions grow and their influence at least appears to extend into more and more sectors, the general public will become increasingly aware of the need to find acceptable and effective restraints. Already, strikes and go-slows in the Health Service or local government, widely covered by the media, have increased public awareness of the problem. Members, too, will find the bureaucratic restrictions on their activities imposed by their unions increasingly irksome.

Thus the unions are faced with difficulties created by what their early champions would have called success. Furthermore, huge employers, whether government or multi-national corporations, may make union organisation easier but they also wield sanctions capable of making even the largest unions cautious. The organisation of half the country's workforce already, with the promise of many more, certainly boosts the unions' claim to representativeness, but carries with it new problems. For example, they not only have to balance the claims of one section of members against another but, as we saw at the 1978 Labour party conference, there is also the appalling difficulty of balancing what is perceived to be the government's interest against that of the union members.

For the Conservative party, too, the changing union structure presents problems. Should Margaret Thatcher and Jim Prior really encourage activism among people who accept most, if not all, the principles and practices of trade unionism? Can Tories really argue, not only for the closed shop, as a good number of members did at the CTU conference in 1977, but also for the use of sanctions by one group of people in restraint of the trade of another, especially if both vote Conservative? How much of the present practice of trade unions can Conservative trade unionists accept either in the short or the long term? There are Conservatives who will argue passionately that the attempt to build an effective CTU on the basis of loyalty to trade unionism is to build a Trojan horse filled with corporatists who will spill out one dark night finally to subdue the Conservative liberal tradition of individual freedom.

There is no room here to discuss this crucial question properly but many CTU members would, I think, approach an answer as follows. The principle and practice of individuals coming together to secure jointly benefits which would not accrue to them separately have been accepted by Conservatives for over a century. It was indeed the Conservative party which made trade unions legally possible and encouraged them legislatively, even if, for a variety of reasons (some of which are looked at later), they remained unconvincing champions to many wage-earners. Moreover, the same principle has been regularly used by skilled or professional people and by capitalists to further their own interests. Indeed, the absence of effective anti-trust legislation in this country and the blurring of outline between professional associations and trade unions make many of the arguments between supporters and opponents of the closed shop resemble those between pots and kettles.

The closed shop chiefly exists because large numbers of people wish to enter and maintain one at their place of work and because many employers find it convenient to deal with one. The CTU, like Jim Prior, is clear that there are aspects of the closed shop, as at present operated, which are unacceptable and, if unions will not moderate its ill effects upon individuals, legislative action may be required to protect individuals. CTU members would certainly prefer that abuses were modified by action from members within unions rather than by intervention by government, but they readily accept that the government has an overriding responsibility for its citizens.

What is urgently needed in Britain is a new solution. A closed shop is regarded by many trade unionists as such as good thing in itself that they pursue one at their place of work with a single-mindedness which excludes any consideration of personal choice, personal responsibility at work, or the changing conditions in which they work. Skill has long ceased to be the basis for membership but at the same time technology has increasingly put the power to stop an industry or the country into the hands of groups so small as to make a mockery of claims to be representative of the workers, the nation, or even of the majority of the particular union's members. In these circumstances, it is essential that some forward-looking compromise be reached. CTU members believe that no solution will work which is imposed from above but they are anxious to resolve a dilemma which is increasingly burdensome to Conservatives and the country. Jim Prior may have more room to manoeuvre than has sometimes seemed likely, in that public opinion in general seems hostile to some of the effects of the closed shop, including trade union members themselves. Thus, in the Opinion Research Centre poll 74 per cent of the total sample thought it wrong for an employer to sack someone who does not belong to a union, if a closed shop agreement is brought in, and 60 per cent even of active trade unionists thought the same.

CTU members tend to believe that strikes are an undesirable

method of reaching settlements but they also believe that there are occasions on which employers will only negotiate properly under threat of strike. The CTU looks to secure responsible trade union leadership which will use the strike as a weapon of last resort in matters of proper industrial concern and not in pursuit of political aims. The pendulum of opinion about strikes swings relentlessly. Once unofficial strikes were everybody's bugbear, yet any successful attempt to regulate or postpone official strikes will inevitably increase unofficial strikes.

Again, however difficult it may be to draw a dividing line between behaviour acceptable and unacceptable to good trade unionists who are also Conservatives, there is no doubt that with over four million Conservative voters already involved in their unions, there can be no question of withdrawing from them and that therefore many practices which may be difficult to accept in principle have to be accepted in the short term. In many unions, for example, it would probably be fruitless at this stage even to debate the propriety of the block vote at the Labour party conference since it is the foundation of the present establishment, and it is much more important to secure limited objectives which lie within one's grasp than reach, like Tantalus, for the fruit beyond one's scope.

In a party system which has developed the three-line whip and the guillotine to their present effectiveness, MPs' strictures on the corporatist tendencies of trade unions seem somewhat selective. Their problem, too, is to enforce voting discipline. What is needed is to build the CTU to a point where it can press realistically for changes. Who knows, it might end up seeking change in more than just the constitution of trade unions.

II THE DEVELOPMENT OF CONSERVATIVE TRADE UNION ORGANISATION

The Conservative party's history shows at least two previous attempts to organise to meet the challenge of a largely hostile union movement: the Unionist Labour Movement of the inter-war years and the Conservative Trade Unionists' organisation formed shortly after the Second World War; yet Disraeli himself grappled with a problem which still bedevils the CTU: 'I have never been myself at all favourable to a system which would induce Conservatives who are working men to form societies confined to their class'. He wanted, above all, to have constituency associations 'of whom a very considerable majority (would consist) of working men'.[11]

After a number of experiments based mainly in Lancashire, there was formed on 22 July 1919 the Central Labour Committee as a sub-committee of the National Union and a National Labour Organiser was appointed to head a Labour Department at Central Office.

At the very beginning it was clearly hoped that Conservative trade unionists might succeed, if properly organised, in counteracting the use of the political funds for the benefit of the Labour party but as early as 1922 the emphasis had swung towards a contracting-out campaign. Its other great aim was to strengthen the representation of working men at every level in the party including parliament. *Plus ça change* . . .

Throughout its existence, the Central Labour Committee fought a losing battle against the middle-class dominated constituency organisations and by 1939 there were only 113 constituency Labour Committees throughout England and Wales. A further problem which remains with us was the fact that so few effective wage-earners could afford the time and money needed to sustain full participation in the party on terms equal to volunteers working for other sections.

After the war the last remnants of the Unionist Labour Movement were allowed to die and a new organisation was attempted. One of its principal objectives was 'to promote non-political trade unionism'. This time Central Office tried to ensure that the 'Councils of Conservative trade unionists should not be an integral part of the constituency association and formally linked to it by rules'. The attempt was, however, a failure and it became obvious that the trade union organisation had no chance unless it were linked to and cooperative with the constituency associations and agents.

In 1953 the National Union Executive Committee published a report by Sir Edgar Keatinge recommending a reversal of policy and urging that where a constituency had a Divisional Council of Trade Unionists (DCTU) its chairman should be ex officio a vice-chairman of the constituency association. While in theory this was very valuable, in practice it raised fierce opposition in the constituencies. Moreover, as with every innovation in the party, the existence of a DCTU threw extra work upon the agents. As a result more effort was put into the formation of industrial groups and by the mid-1960s it was claimed that there were over 15,000 of them. At the same time the DCTUs were renamed Trades Union Advisory Committees (TUAC). Yet by 1964 the party itself was already running the organisation down and by 1975 the two remaining paid staff took their old age pensions and left. Why?

Partly it was snobbery: snobbery allied to ideology. In many constituencies, the TUAC was regarded as a nuisance, a boring if necessary device for bringing into the fold the kind of person who would not ordinarily fit in with the association. If a trade unionist did fit in well with the association, he or she probably devoted increasing amounts of time to ordinary association work rather than the TUAC because that was where the rewards lay. And most Conservative activists were not only ignorant about trade unions, but also they came from the very groups most obviously threatened by their spread. People of independent means, small businessmen and professionals were ideologically unsympathetic to trade unions. There are examples of constituencies which refused to set up a TUAC because the model rules enjoined upon them the duty of giving it a seat on the executive, and this seems to have been for reasons of snobbery as much as any.

Yet three years after its demise, the organisation was back in business with 270 branches, seven full-time executives, all with union backgrounds, and a new hope and vigour. How was the Conservative trade union organisation re-established, and can it succeed this time where it failed before?

The decision to try to revive the party's trade union organisation owed something to the persistence of the voluntary members of TUNAC (Trades Union National Advisory Committee), including Ron Benson of the NUR, convenor of the shop stewards' committee at York; Tom Ham, ex-president of the Stevedores and Dockers Union; and Fred Hardman, the present national committee chairman. It also owed something to Jim Prior's determination that his activities in relation to trade unions should be backed up by a field force of trade unionists with knowledge and experience in a position to offer him accurate information. It owed most, however, to the chairman of the party, Lord Thorneycroft, who took the decision to re-establish the Central Office machinery. From then on both he and Mrs Thatcher gave the CTU considerable support and Mrs Thatcher appointed John Page, MP for Harrow West, as her liaison officer between the parliamentary party and the CTU. A key step was taken when John Bowis, at that time national secretary of the Federation of Conservative Students, was appointed director of the CTU, responsible to the director of Community Affairs.

To try to answer the question whether this initiative will be successful I look at what we are trying to do and how we do it, and I start with three questions which we are often asked. First, who does the CTU represent and how representative is it? Second, if the Conservative party believes in lessening the involvement in party politics of trade unions, are there dangers in setting up an organisation within them open only to people who are prepared to be attached to the Conservative party? Third, how can the party justify such interference in the internal affairs of an independent trade union?

The CTU represents itself. However often and however realistically it may claim to be the voice of a large minority within trade unions, the truth must be that its elected officers from local to national level represent strictly only the CTU, except in cases where the views of others have been explicitly sought and conveyed on their behalf by the CTU. Yet this is not necessarily a derisory position to be in. When we talk of the CTU, we are not talking of an alternative nor a rival structure to that of the trade unions. We are talking about a voluntary gathering of members of the existing structure who happen to share a number of beliefs. Chief among these, of course, is that the country, including the trade unionists, would benefit from a Conservative government. This is not widely shared by the union leaders themselves, at least in public, and since they have a strong grip upon the union structures and resources, members who wish to challenge the establishment's anti-Tory orthodoxy need to organise themselves to make their potential strength effective. Hence the CTU which, if it can attract its due proportion of able union activists, will become as capable of effecting change as the Protestant reformers became within the late mediaeval church, although, we must hope, not to the point of schism!

In many respects, the CTU is a voluntary organisation more representative of its membership than the unions themselves. It is after all more voluntary than many trade unions. Nobody joins the CTU because he or she must. None can lose a job or face a disciplinary hearing for not belonging. It is at least as democratic. Every voluntary officer in the CTU is elected every year, so that when the national chairman speaks, he is speaking as the representative of all the members and there is no question of his holding his office for life. It must obviously be our aim to ensure that more and more Conservatives become active in their unions until it ceases to be even mildly surprising to find Tories everywhere within their union structures. There are already scores of branch officers and shop stewards in the CTU as our annual conferences show. Equally, we must try to make certain the CTU at every level is represented by effective and successful trade union activists. (The CTU represents its members within the Conservative party and, in that respect, is fully representative.)

It is no use pretending, however, that all is cosy for the CTU within the party itself. It is a great advance that so many candidates and an increasing number of MPs are pleased to claim union membership as part of their credentials, but there is still some way to go before trade union activism is regarded by selection committees as a powerful reason for selecting a parliamentary candidate. Sir Edward Brown and Ray Mawby have carried the torch of Conservative trade unionism into the House of Commons but the years since they were first adopted, in 1963 and 1955, have not seen any considerable trade union figure selected by a constituency and this lack needs to be made good soon if the CTU is to carry real weight within a Tory government. The independence of con- stituency selection committees seems often incredible to outsiders but is well attested by many unsuccessful candidates.

It is, of course, a chicken and egg problem. In the present Labour-orientated trade union hierarchies, it will be rare for an official to reach the highest levels with declared Conservative sympathies and anything short of that will make selection for a constituency hard to secure. A very great deal will depend on how the next Conservative government handles its relations with the trade unions.

In the meantime, most constituencies need to take much more trouble than hitherto to support (and use) their CTU branch. The Penistone by-election, in which the area CTU put in 200 hours of work, showed how the use of trade unionists to canvass and work in areas which have been traditionally unsympathetic to the Con- servative party could achieve impressive results.[12] There is a great deal of work to be done to help the CTU and constituencies work out the best ways of mutual support, but that brings us to the much wider question of how the party organisation should respond to the modern world.

The answer to the second is easier to give on pragmatic grounds than in pure principle. The UK is the only advanced industrial nation in which trade unions are linked exclusively with only one of the great political parties. Norman Atkinson, treasurer of the Labour party, put it explicitly:

> The Labour party is the trade unions and the trade unions are the Labour party. We are an integral part of each other and there has never been an attempt by either part to dominate the other.[13]

There are signs that the Labour party is not always as happy with a relationship which seems to be more one of involvement by the unions in the affairs of the party than vice versa. It was, for example, suggested at the time that Harold Wilson set up the Houghton Committee partly to seek a means of lessening the financial dependence of the Labour party on the unions. Yet, as the government increasingly dominates the employer's side of wage negotiations, it is hard to see the relationship continuing without the unions losing some important freedoms to the government as employer, especially in periods of Labour rule. This provides a respectable ground on which even Labour supporters can stand to criticise the relationship. For Conservatives, the argument is a great deal stronger. While the trade union leaders persist in maintaining automatic links with one political party, even to the point of financing it, members of other parties are entitled to organise to challenge them. It would be as unrealistic to imagine that, if Conservative supporters decide to organise themselves, they would not seek help from their own organisation as it would be to expect Labour members of unions to refuse help from Transport House. The key here is whether any action is undertaken with the best interests of the union at heart or for some other purpose and CTU members believe that there is plenty of room for constructive argument about where the best interests of their fellow union members and of themselves lie. In theory, two outcomes at least are possible. Either the unions will end up as determinedly non-party political as chambers of commerce and many other voluntary organisations, or the existence of political factions within them will be openly recognised and accepted, as they are in other countries. A third possibility would be for union members to be organised in unions according to their political allegiance, but that seems too alien to the British tradition to be likely. I discuss the question of reciprocal influence on the Conservative party later, in the context of finance.

The third question referred to Conservative 'interference' in the internal affairs of trade unions. It is often asked, and is usually taken to mean trying to alter the union's practice to fit an outside body's purposes. The best way to answer this is to look at how such 'interference' might work in practice. If the Conservative parliamentary party or a shadow minister wished, for example, to persuade a union to strike or to postpone a strike in order to affect the result of a general election they could, in theory, ask the national committee of the CTU to advise all its members in that union to work to achieve the agreed end. Unlike the Labour party, on whose National Executive the trade unions are represented and which is, in theory, bound to take heed of its National Executive, the Conservative party has no constitutional relationship with the CTU national committee which could evoke the desired response. If the advice appeared sound, the CTU national committee might agree to recommend it to its member groups, but each of them would have to make an individual decision on whether to accept or not. And what they decide begs the question of how effective any decision could be in relation to the union's policies, even if the CTU were a good deal stronger than it is now. The point is that the members of the CTU are volunteers in only an advisory relationship with the party. They have no power beyond any influence they earn with the quality of their advice. If the party's policy-makers succeed in persuading them to act in a particular way, they still have the task of persuading their fellow trade unionists to agree with them and, in those circumstances, the term 'outside interference' becomes meaningless.

The only other type of issue on which it might be possible for the Conservative policy-makers to persuade the CTU to exert an influence is in the election of union officers. And on this matter the present union leaders are understandably, if erroneously, touchy.

Although many unions have national journals, information about the candidates at their regional or national level elections is often sparse and quite hard for the ordinary member to acquire from sources which he regards as trustworthy. Moreover, since many unions, probably in a tradition dating from their non-party political origins, forbid canvassing, candidates have no opportunity publicly to proclaim their experience or loyalties. There is, therefore, a need for information which is met at present by a haphazard series of devices, such as magazines of the far left[14] urging a slate of candidates or, occasionally, national newspapers doing the same for the centre right. In these circumstances, it is hardly surprising if CTU members ask for help from their fellows in their own union through the central secretariat and, where it is available, *factual* information about the records of all candidates for union office is circulated to CTU members who ask for it. It would be much more satisfactory if the unions themselves organised their elections in ways which ensured that every member had easy access to enough information to make an informed judgment although, even so, many members would want to know, for example, about the voting record of a National Executive member.

III THE ORGANISATION OF THE CTU

Within the Conservative party, the CTU has an assured place. The rules of the National Union lay down that the national CTU committee is to be regarded as one of its major advisory committees and this is reflected at area and at constituency association level. Every constituency association is, of course, autonomous, but in the 220 which have CTU groups, the guidance of the model rules is followed and the CTU has an automatic place on the constituency executive committee.

There may still be a handful of constituencies which think of trade unionists as I described earlier, but the effect of Margaret Thatcher's constantly repeated appeals to Conservatives to become active in their unions, combined with the spread of union membership, makes these a dying breed. Over 40 parliamentary candidates in England and Wales and some seventeen in Scotland claim union membership now as part of their credentials and the number of card-carrying union members at the April 1978 Central Council meeting was surprisingly high.[15]

Constituency based groups of Conservative trade unionists meeting together regularly serve some useful purposes. For example, they allow, rather as a Trades Council allows, members to discuss issues of common local concern. These may be industrial, such as the effect of incomes policy on wage levels generally, or more general, such as the response of CTU members to an invitation to join a newly-formed branch of the Anti-Nazi League. They are also valuable for organising recruitment drives, social events, rallies, etc. and for the part they play in the local association. Yet despite these activities, local groups of the CTU are not enough. If Conservative supporters are to make their influence felt, groups based on their union or on their industry must also exist. That is why we have so far created at national level the following groups:

Teachers	Local Government	Communications
Railways	ASTMS	Firemen
Post Office	Civil Service	

Several more have been formed locally or are in the process of formation. This will have increasingly important effects within and without the party. First, within, it will be a rare urban constituency which will be able to sustain a CTU group based on a single union or even group of unions. It is much more likely that a COHSE or NUM CTU group will draw members from quite a wide area, covering several constituencies. If the groups thrive and perform their function properly, they will, for example, have several MPs and candidates to brief on the affairs of their union and their employment. It seems probable that, because such groups correspond with union organisation, they will gradually take up the time and resources of CTU members, except for special efforts, such as local elections or a general election campaign, and the general CTU group will become a kind of holding company for a number of specialist groups. It will remain an essential part of the structure because progress within the Conservative party will still depend, to a large extent, on the contribution made to the local association's affairs.

IV THE FUNCTIONS OF A SPECIALIST GROUP

What will a CTU specialist group do? So far, we have only limited experience on which to draw, but it seems likely that its functions will include briefing themselves and the Conservative party, at whichever level is appropriate, about the affairs of their union or their place of work. In the past, the party has got into unnecessary trouble because it has had no source of reliable information about the strength of feeling within a union or a shop floor on a particular dispute nor whether the leadership's view is representative of the members, nor whether the public pictures of the issues presented by the press or the union leaders fits the real position. Again, the party has often lacked information about the hopes and fears of union members about such matters as dumping or technological change or the thousand and one issues on which unions pronounce opinions, often more in accord with the political leaning of their research staff than of their members. Good CTU groups can begin to change that.

One particularly vital job for CTU groups in the future will be to elucidate for the Conservative party the tangled skein of inter-union disputes. These are likely to become more bitter and complex as financial pressures force mergers and competition upon unions.

All this is vital because trade unions are now a formidable power within the state, with leaders determined to work against a Tory victory, and because of the Conservative party's need to brief itself about every aspect of their work if it is to live with them successfully. But there is an even more important job to do. As union membership grows, so do the anxieties of many members about the way in which the unions go about some of their business. See for example, responses of union members to a poll in 1977.[16]

	Agree %	Disagree %
Unions have too much power in Britain today.	68	27
Unions are mostly controlled by a few extremists.	58	33
The closed shop is a threat to individual liberty.	66	26
The Labour party should not be so closely linked to the unions.	57	34

Hugo Young, political editor of *The Sunday Times*, wrote on 25 June 1978:

> One cannot underestimate the high cost of the interim victory over inflation: a steady, often pernicious, usually unchallenged advance of collective over individual rights . . . Since 1974, unions have not only got more power. They have succeeded in suppressing honest outrage about how they sometimes use it.

If a union has this power over the life of its members, is it satisfactory that the disciplinary procedures of most unions allow the union itself to act as judge and jury in its own cause? A recent case in ASTMS illustrates the dangers. The executive had ordered an enquiry into the behaviour of a member accused of conduct 'likely to bring the union into disrepute' and of 'interfering in the affairs of another union'. When the enquiry began, not only did the union executive provide the chairman of the enquiry, but the tribunal under his chairmanship ruled virtually all disputed points of order in favour of the executive, even the central fact that the other union had not only lodged no complaint, but sent witnesses from their own national executive committee to say so. More important still, the proceedings, which had been started as a complaint by the executive against the member, were turned quite arbitrarily by the tribunal into a hearing at which the member was expected to justify his behaviour without the executive feeling bound to establish that there was a proper case to answer. It is right that there should be public anxiety about allegations of corruption in union elections or maladministration but there are rotten apples in most barrels. It is much more worrying when the legitimate operation of normal procedures appears to fly in the face of natural justice.

If trade union members successfully campaigned for reforms to bring their practices up to date and to make their leaders more in tune with members' opinions, trade unions would be strengthened by becoming less disliked by the public as well as more relevant to the members. It might also put them and the TUC in a stronger position to play a full part in the development of a competitive British economy in contrast to their largely negative strategies of the present moment, but it will only come if enough union members seek it from within.

Constructive resolutions demanding change are needed to come up through the union structure for debate at annual conferences and elsewhere and, in this process, the CTU should be able to play a useful part. Speedy action will be needed because of financial pressure on many unions which will create opportunities to look at the rules and structures which should not be missed.

V FINANCE

Like most voluntary bodies with no capital, the CTU is perennially short of money. To act effectively, CTU groups must be able to act at national level as well as local level and travel is desperately expensive. Union members do not get paid leave nor expenses if they are engaged on CTU business and several CTU loyalists spend substantial sums of their own money on their work for the party.

In these circumstances, the possibility that the political levy could provide support for the CTU as it has in so many unions for the Labour party, is bound to be attractive. There are, however, problems. These do not lie in the legal status of the political fund. The law is careful not to stipulate any party and, indeed, is not even couched in terms which imply that political activity equals party activity, except in the use of the fund to sponsor an MP or candidate. The rules of some unions may raise problems, but the fact that the NUT, for example, until recently sponsored Tory MPs as well as Labour, shows that there is no difficulty for many.

Paradoxically, the problem lies at the other end. The Conservative party has always kept itself carefully aloof from any suggestion that money could buy influence in the party. The largest contributor cannot, by his contribution, achieve a seat at the party conference nor an office at any level within the party. Moreover, the party is not structured to give any group within it power in return for its support. All policy stems from the leader and bodies like the CTU or the party conference are simply invited to offer advice and help. They have no direct control over any party decision. Indeed, the divorce is even wider than this. As the debate over the Conservative party's stance in relation to the Joint Committee Against Racialism emphasised, the party has no corporate identity. It cannot belong to another organisation and it, as a whole, cannot declare an opinion nor receive affiliations from outside. Full affiliation, therefore, of a union to the Conservative party, is not possible. Nevertheless, there is no good reason why a union branch should not decide to contribute from its political fund to a Conservative meeting or other activity and perhaps this will be one way of meeting some CTU expenses, although it could never solve the problem. A union could also act as collecting agent for subscriptions to the CTU.

Whatever happens, the financial future of the CTU is bound up with that of political parties in general and is likely to remain on the agenda of constitutional discussion.

VI CONCLUSION

This discussion has deliberately avoided the difficult philosophical questions of whether either or both the Conservative party's dominant traditions can come to terms satisfactorily with the corporatist tendencies of the most powerful pressure groups in the country but I hope that this brief account of what the CTU is gives some pointers to what could be done.

The goal is an ambitious one: to break eventually the automatic link between the Labour party and the trade unions. It is important to remember that the link is not quite such a simple one as at first sight appears.[17] From the earliest days, the TUC has eschewed a structural attachment to the Labour party although the last few years have seen the creation of the Liaison committee on which TUC representatives sit with members of the National Executive committee and the parliamentary Labour party. The creation of the Liaison committee was followed by the Social Contract and, at the 1978 TUC conference, by the Trade Unionists for a Labour Victory committee. Indeed, the whole conference resembled nothing so much as a pre-election rally for the Labour party.

The important point to notice, however, is that it is still possible for the TUC to take a step back again and seek to preserve its independence from the Labour party. And it is in connection with the stance of individual unions that the CTU must work. At the moment, it is taken for granted at most union meetings that if politics arise at all, they will be Labour politics. How many union branches, for example, have ever heard a report on CTU activity, let alone on Conservative party activity? Yet many branches expect to hear a report on Labour party operations. Moreover, one-third of the parliamentary Labour party is sponsored by trade unions.

For all practical purposes, it is wishful thinking for Conservatives to imagine that a serious rift will open up (at least for electoral purposes) between the Labour party and any of the large unions for some time to come, but the goal of persuading enough trade union members that Conservative governments may do better for them than the Labour party, and thus of changing the nature of union alignments in this country, remains a proper and, I believe, an attainable one. We believe that a majority of the country and nearly half of trade union members would like to see this done. We also believe that it would be good in the long run for the trade unions to break the link. On the way to the goal, there is much that can be, and is already being, usefully done. Conservative spokesmen, MPs, candidates, students, Young Conservatives, and others are receiving better briefs on industrial matters, including disputes. Conservatives at every level are actually meeting trade union officials and activists in much greater numbers than ever before. The specialist groups are beginning to appear at union conferences, often to a warm welcome from members who had little idea that the CTU existed. More important still, CTU members are beginning to challenge the present leadership in their branch meetings and even, occasionally, at annual conferences. ASTMS's decisions against nationalisation owe something to CTU members (acting as loyal trade unionists first and Conservatives second). If we can spread that kind of attitude and build the self-confidence of Conservatives in their trade unions, the prospects both for successful Conservative government and for fully representative unions enormously increase.

If the CTU can bring both pressure and first-hand understanding of union life to bear on the Conservative party, which often appears quite long on legal and constitutional knowledge but disastrously short on personal experience of union matters, it will have done much of value to strengthen the whole constitution. It was a proud moment for CTU when, on the Post Office Bill recently, it persuaded the party to change its whipping intentions because of advice from UPW members of the CTU. More of that and the union-bashing epithets trotted out so readily by trade union leaders, uneasily aware of the gap between themselves and their members, will become impossible to use.

NOTES

1. In 1975 there were 488 registered trade unions with an average size of 24,000 members. At the end of 1974 there were 11,950,000 members claimed by trade unions of whom 10,364,000 belonged to unions affiliated to the TUC. However, only 111 unions were affiliated to the TUC—see Department of Employment Gazette (November 1976) and the Bullock Report on Industrial Democracy (1977) quoted in R. Taylor, *The Fifth Estate* (London: Routledge Kegan Paul, 1978).

2. In 1976, 59 of the TUC unions were affiliated to the Labour party, accounting for 5,800,069 of the party's total membership of 6,459,127—R. Taylor, ibid.

3. The British Election Study directed by Ivor Crewe and quoted by P. Kellner in the *New Statesman*, 23 June 1978, p. 839, shows that support for more nationalisation among those with 'very' or 'fairly' strong Labour party

identification had fallen from 64 per cent to 50 per cent between 1964 and 1974.

4. MORI poll—*Sunday Times*, August 1977: 57 per cent of union members believed that 'the Labour party should not be so closely linked to the unions'. (354 trade union members out of interlocking quota sample of 2248 electors.)

5. MORI poll (15-19 October 1975)—a probability sample of 3761 adults in 240 constituencies throughout Britain, of whom 29 per cent (1103 people) were trade union members. Of all the trade unionists, 47 per cent believed that 'everyone who works should have to belong to a trade union', but 56 per cent of them believed that 'most trade unions today are controlled by a few extremists and militants' and 66 per cent of them believed that 'trade unions have too much power in Britain today' (72 per cent of non-activists).

6. Repeal of the Anti-Combination Laws—1824.
   Truck Acts—1831.
   Legalisation of Peaceful Picketing—1859.
   The Conspiracy Act (right to strike)—1875.
   The Mines Regulations Act ('Miners' Charter')—1875.
   The Unemployment Insurance Act (benefit a right)—1887.
   The Contracts of Employment Act—1963.
   The Industrial Relations Act (right to join a union and compensation for wrongful dismissal)—1971.

7. Some of the facts, at least, suggest otherwise. In real terms the improvement in average take-home pay in sixteen years of Labour rule is 6 per cent, in sixteen years of Tory rule, 60 per cent.

8. See for example L. Minkin, *New Left Unionism and the Tensions of British Labour Politics*, paper delivered to a conference on Eurocommunism and Eurosocialism at the City University, New York, November 1976.

9. See, for example, the conflict between docker and driver members of the Transport and General Workers Union, where drivers talked of having their own union, quoted in R. Taylor, op. cit. At the same time, Taylor stresses the considerable cohesive strength of the TGWU and it may be that, despite its size and diversity, the TGWU will manage to hold together.

10. But there is, for example, considerable confusion among union members. In the ORC poll of October 1977 (quota sample of 1051 electors, 10–19 September 1977), 67 per cent agreed that 'trade unions should concern themselves only with the pay and working conditions of their members and not with political problems', but 42 per cent agreed with the proposition that 'trade unions should be just as much concerned with politics as with looking after their members' interests'.

11. J. Greenwood, *The Conservative Party and the Working Classes: The Organisational Response*, Working Paper no. 2, Department of Politics, University of Warwick, (June 1974).

12. Penistone by-election, 13 July 1978: Labour 19,424, Conservative 14,053, Liberal 9241. The increased Tory vote on a reduced poll in this highly trade unionised constituency (steel, coal etc,) was in part due to the very active campaign by CTU members in the by-election.

13. World at One, BBC Radio 4 15 June 1978.

14. e.g. In the CPSA elections in 1976 there was a double page spread in the left-wing newsletter canvassing for a whole slate of left-wing candidates. It was

called *Redder Tape* in a direct satire of the official CPSA magazine *Red Tape*.
15. Conservative MPs in 1978 included members of APEX, ASTMS, TGWU, EETPU, NUJ, IPCS, AUT and BALPA.
16. *Sunday Times* MORI poll, August 1977.
17. L. Minkin, op. cit. L. Minkin and P. Seyd, 'The British Labour Party', in W. Paterson and A. Thomas (eds.), *Social Democratic Parties in Western Europe* (London: Croom Helm, 1977).

10 Factionalism in the 1970s[1]

Patrick Seyd

I INTRODUCTION

It is rather unusual to observe Conservatives involved in intense intra-party dispute, but in 1978 press stories of party bureaucrats' responsibilities being amended, of party officers being excluded from 'all-party committees', and of policy documents being 'leaked' were not mere instances of sensational political journalism, but rather were a reflection of serious internal party division usually more common in the Labour party.

Conservatives have continually placed great stress upon party unity. Perhaps the degree of unity has been overstated but nevertheless, whilst differences of opinion have existed, the Conservative party in contemporary times has not suffered from breakaways or expulsions. The party has had its differences of opinion on particular issues but it has maintained its overall unity. Consequently some observers argue that whilst factionalism is apparent in the Labour party, it has no counterpart within the Conservative party. For example, Richard Rose argues that the Conservative party is a party of tendencies rather than factions: that it contains constant sets of political attitudes but lacks groups of organised members united in attitude towards a range of issues over a period of time.[2] The purpose of this chapter is first, to challenge this argument and second, to assert that the incidence of factionalism within the Conservative party has increased since 1964.

II CONSTRAINTS ON FACTIONALISM

One important reason why party unity has been maintained has been the low priority party members have placed upon ideological discussions. Conservatives tend to deny the existence of any single cohesive body of ideas which might provide the basis for party programmes; instead they rely upon such general guidelines as tradition, intimation, or common sense. Whilst the existence of a Conservative ideology is open to considerable academic debate, the important point when considering intra-party conflict is that the practitioners have placed little emphasis upon its importance. Appeals to an underlying 'Conservatism', except at the most general and superficial level, are rare, thus making it easier for the Conservative party to adapt to changing political circumstances without intense intra-party disputes. Thus in the past it has not experienced the soul-searching over objectives which, for example, affected the Labour party in the 1950s.

Nevertheless the party is not monolithic; tendencies do exist. It is possible to distinguish authoritarian and populist, imperial and nationalist, tendencies. It is common to distinguish the Tory from the Liberal in domestic politics by the stress placed upon collective or individual action in the economic and social fields. The Tory view is of an organic society—a corporate entity with interrelated functional parts and each part operating to preserve the unity of the whole. The state plays a positive role in co-ordinating these various sections, thus achieving the necessary stability, harmony, and order. From this springs the Tory belief in the state's responsibilities in economic policy, such as planning or a prices and incomes policy, and social welfare involving the general Disraelian commitment to the 'welfare of the people'. In contrast, the Liberal view is individualistic, in which the state plays a limited role. Liberal values are those of competition, incentive, and conflict, and the function of the state is limited to 'holding the ring'. Thus the Liberal is concerned to stimulate economic competition, to curb the amount of government expenditure, and to encourage personal initiative by reducing taxation and restricting the universal provision of social welfare.

Whereas revisionist and fundamentalist tendencies in the Labour party have become organised into factions, such bodies are not so common in the Conservative party. Various studies of the voting behaviour of members of the *parliamentary* party between 1945 and

1970 reveal the absence of factions.[3] However, such conclusions about the parliamentary party should not lead on to the generalisation that factionalism is entirely absent from the party. Whilst the incidence of factionalism is low, it nevertheless exists; individual members of the Conservative party[4] have formed groups seemingly with the purpose of winning political support for a range of policy proposals to be adopted by the party leadership. Some instances of group formation with the intention of strengthening a political position which ranges beyond one political issue include the Social Reform Committee (1911–14), the Tory Reform Committee (1943–5), the Monday Club (1961–) and Pressure for Economic and Social Toryism (1963–75). I would not, however, include the Bow Group (1951–) as a faction since it generally refrains from commitment to an overall set of policies which it wishes to persuade the party to adopt; instead it prefers to adopt a similar position to the Fabian Society, namely publishing worthwhile contributions to the political debate as a stimulant to political discussion rather than the pursuit of a partisan point of view.

The low priority placed upon ideology has already been referred to as a factor explaining party unity. Other factors are party loyalty, which Conservatives feel even to the point of jeopardising their own political careers, [5] and the cohesion within the parliamentary party arising from the similarity of recruitment patterns.[6] These all tend to curb factionalism. There are also important structural factors which limit the extent of factionalism.

First, there is the limited role of the extra-parliamentary party in policy-making. This is especially reflected in the organisation and procedure of the party's annual conference which is carefully managed by a senior group of people within the National Union, the party organisation, and the parliamentary party, who seem more concerned with achieving accord than with reflecting differences of opinion. The restricted constitutional role accorded to the National Union ensures no factional activity in the submission of resolutions for the conference, in choice of resolutions for debate, nor in mobilisation of votes on the floor of the conference. Neither is there factional concern with the election of such personnel as National Union officers or members of the National Union's General Purposes and Executive Committees. Furthermore, the National Union's functional groupings—Conservative Students, Young Conservatives, Women, Trade Unionists and local government councillors—are of limited importance and provide little institutional opportunity for political pressure of a factional nature.

Second, the constitutional relationship between the party leader and the party organisation limits the ability of factions to use the bureaucracy as a separate channel of opinion in which to challenge the parliamentary leadership. The inter-dependent relationship between party leader and senior party bureaucrats stifles factional activities.

Thus the opportunities for factions to mobilise support at alternative points in the Conservative party structure are restricted. In the Labour party, intra-party factional politics lead to pressure upon constituency parties and affiliated trade unions, which can involve the drafting of model resolutions for these bodies to submit to the annual conference, pressure upon party conference delegations, and competition amongst personnel closely related to a factional position for election to institutions of the extra-parliamentary party. In the Conservative party, such factional activity is almost totally absent. But events within the Conservative party during the period since it lost office in 1964 have provided an impetus for factionalism.

III FACTIONAL UPSURGE

Thirteen years of government naturally produced a sense of satisfaction amongst Conservatives and reinforced their belief that they were the 'natural party of government'. Since 1964 the record of only four years in office shattered that confidence, particularly since first Harold Wilson and then James Callaghan seemed intent on a conservative electoral strategy that threatened Conservative dominance. Paradoxically it seemed increasingly to be the case that the Labour party was adopting the position of the 'natural party of government', whilst the Conservative party adopted the position of 'the party of protest', representing discontented tax-payers or beleaguered whites in the inner cities. This loss of confidence amongst Conservatives was reflected in a more argumentative party in which divisions of opinion hardened into factions.

This argumentativeness has been more difficult to contain as party membership has become more meritocratic. The national expansion of higher education has had its impact. The influx of relatively more university graduates into the party has meant that many of them wish to discuss ideas and policies and are unwilling to accept the party's procedures for dealing with intra-party debate. Furthermore, the general shift in attitudes towards authority within society has had some impact within the party. Party members seem less deferential towards the parliamentarians than used to be the case.[7]

But inevitably in a political system in which Westminster so dominates party activity, it is amongst the parliamentarians that this argumentativeness has been most apparent. The parliamentary party has become increasingly rebellious. Conflict over the issue of entry into the EEC was the major factor, but the shifts in party policies between 1970 and 1974, particularly over industrial affairs, statutory curbs on wages and prices, sanctions against Rhodesia, immigration rules and the imposition of direct rule in Northern Ireland provoked a great deal of dissatisfaction amongst back-benchers. Since 1970 it has become clear that a coherent and identifiable group has emerged within the parliamentary party whose attitudes merge on a range of issues, from opposition to state intervention in the running of the economy, to support for the white Commonwealth.[8] Whereas such a group of back-benchers would become highly organised in the parliamentary Labour party (the two current factions being the Tribune and Manifesto groups), there remains a dislike for such activity by many Conservative back-benchers. Nevertheless, on the issue of entry into the EEC, the supporters and opponents of the Conservative government's policy established organisations. And since 1974 there has been further increase in organised activity amongst Conservative back-benchers.

This rebelliousness amongst back-benchers has reverberated outside the parliamentary party. Dissatisfaction with the Heath government's increasing intervention in the economy stimulated the formation of the Selsdon Group in 1973. The choice of title by this small group of economic liberals was intended as a reminder of the commitments which had emerged from the Conservative shadow cabinet's meeting at the Selsdon Park Hotel in February 1970 and on which that year's election manifesto was based.

The Selsdon Group believes economic freedom is indispensable to political freedom.

The basic principle upon which Conservative policies should rest is that what the public wants should be provided by the market and paid for by the people as consumers rather than taxpayers . . . The function of government should not be to provide services, but to maintain the framework within which markets operate.[9]

Government has three functions only—first, to maintain the value of money (although 'whether the government should have a monopoly of money is a question which has to be faced before very long');[10] second, to maintain the law; and third, to protect the country's foreign policy and defence interests. In other than these areas government direction should be withdrawn in favour of the market as a means of distributing resources and encouraging consumer choice. The group therefore proposes an end to government intervention in prices, wages and dividend controls, regional and locational policies, industrial training and job-creation schemes, employment subsidies, and investment grants and incentives. It believes that the nationalised industries should be reintegrated into the private economy by restructuring their ownership where possible, and by forcing them to raise funds on the private market. For example, the miners would take over and manage locally-organised pits on a profitability basis; so also should the railwaymen have the opportunity to own those parts of the railway system which they wished to run, and any remaining units should be allowed to disappear. No subsidies on services or commodities should be tolerated; thus, for example, transport undertakings should charge the price the market would bear, particularly for bus and air transport. Similarly, the pricing mechanism should operate in the social services. The group argues that 'it is time that the very idea of government running the social services should be abandoned'.[11] Charges should be introduced for medicine and education, and the problem of the low-income earner would be met by reverse income tax or tax credits or, in the case of education, by vouchers. Local authorities should not provide a housing service; all public housing should be automatically transferred to sitting tenants and no new public housing should be built.

Notwithstanding the support for the liberal tendency within the party leadership since Mrs Thatcher's success in 1975, the influence and impact of the Selsdon Group appears limited. It applied pressure on back-benchers in a very orthodox manner by means of meetings in the House of Commons with Conservative shadow spokesmen. Only four back-benchers are members—Nicholas Ridley, Ronald Bell, Richard Body, and Archie Hamilton—although Ian Gow, Rhodes Boyson, and John Biffen are sympathisers. A large number of back-benchers are hostile to the group, regarding members as 'ideological splitters' undermining the chances of a Conservative victory at the general election, and for this reason the group adopted a low public relations profile during 1978. It relies on pamphlets, briefing documents and individual speaking engagements as its only means of pressure within the constituency associations. It has an active membership of only 40 and a total membership of approximately 250. It has remained a small group of activists, with limited funds and no branch organisation, because of its rather academic and intellectual approach to politics and its concern not to be taken over by some fringe group, such as the National Front.

One of the dangers of a formal definition of factionalism in which one concentrates entirely upon organised groupings within the Conservative party to explain the nature of intra-party political behaviour and to assess the distribution of political power, is that significant factors which affect power relationships can be missed. For example, to concentrate merely upon the Selsdon Group might be to underestimate the impact and importance of the economic liberals within the Conservative party. Other institutions and groups not part of the formal structure of the Conservative party are clearly intent upon capitalising on external developments to influence the party in this direction.

Britain's economic problems of the late-1960s produced significant shifts of opinion within both major parties. The difficulties experienced by the 1966–70 Labour government led to a reaction within the Labour party against revisionist social democracy and the reassertion of traditional fundamental beliefs about the importance of state intervention. Support for this trend amongst many of the trade unions resulted in a shift of power within the Labour party—particularly within the annual party conference and the National Executive Committee—which resulted in *Labour's Programme 1973*.[12] A similar shift in opinion away from the social democratic consensus of the early-1960s occurred within the Conservative party. In opposition after 1964 the Conservative party began to reject some of its earlier policy commitments such as economic planning and income policies. This shift was reflected in the party's election manifesto of 1970, but when the Conservative government found it necessary to abandon some of those manifesto commitments and again to intervene to a considerable extent in the running of the economy, it produced another ideological shift and assertion of liberal values stronger than that of the late-1960s.

Mrs Thatcher's election to the party leadership in 1975 was a reflection of Conservative back-benchers' unease at Mr Heath's corporatist tendencies and his indifference towards backbenchers and party activists who challenged his government policies. Mrs Thatcher and Sir Keith Joseph, in overall charge of policy making, have made clear their own commitment to an explicit Conservative ideology, albeit a very specific and restricted one. Sir Keith Joseph announced in April 1974 that after being a Conservative MP for eighteen years he had only now been converted to Conservatism. By this he meant a commitment to reverse 'the ratchet effect of socialism' and return to a market economy of free enterprise and profitability in which the state would enforce competition, limit concentrations of power and restrict the worst excesses of individual selfishness.

The Centre for Policy Studies, founded and directed by Keith Joseph since 1974, exists as a research body to advance the cause of economic liberalism, independent of the Conservative party but clearly intended as a rival research body to the party's Research Department. The Centre's prime function is to service Keith Joseph in his public speeches, primarily on the university undergraduate circuit, but also to popularise the market liberals' case amongst party activists. It is attempting to reach a party political audience whilst the Institute of Economic Affairs concentrates upon an academic readership.

The Selsdon Group is the Conservative advance guard of the Institute of Economic Affairs and the Centre for Policy Studies. But the main effort to popularise these views amongst party activists is carried out by the *Daily Telegraph*, which has adopted a position of strong support for Mrs Thatcher's version of Conservatism. A further carrier of such opinions is the fortnightly newspaper of the National Association for Freedom—*Free Nation*. NAFF, formed in December 1975, represents a wider set of right-wing attitudes covering economic, social, and moral attitudes as well as foreign and defence policy issues. NAFF adopts an authoritarian stance on law and order issues, is pro-white in African affairs, and is anti-Soviet in foreign and defence matters. But it also campaigns for the ideas of the economic liberals and as such *Free Nation*, with a circulation of approximately eighteen thousand, is an important communicator to the party activists.[13] This political position—anti-communist, authoritarian over personal behaviour and liberal in welfare policies—used to be effectively represented by the Monday Club, which grew in the late-1960s into a significant faction actively campaigning at all levels of the party in pursuit of its policies.[14] But in 1972 the group was racked by an internal dispute over its leadership which resulted in loss of membership and almost complete withdrawal from intra-party activity for a period. NAFF emerged in 1975 to fill this political vacuum left by the decline of the Monday Club.

Six months after Mrs Thatcher's election as party leader, the Tory faction within the party reorganised; Pressure for Economic and Social Toryism, and two local groups—the Macleod group based in the north-west of England, and the Social Tory Action Group based in southern England—amalgamated into the Tory Reform Group. The group claims to represent the Disraelian tradition within the Conservative party, with its concern for the two nations in Britain (rich/poor, white/black, suburbia/inner city), requiring compassionate understanding and reform through state intervention. Robert Rhodes James, not a member of the group but a sympathiser, reflects the group's viewpoint when he writes in the group journal:

> The Conservatives still, collectively, give the clear impression that they simply do not understand what poverty, misfortune and unemployment really mean to those who suffer any or all of these afflictions . . . The Conservatives still seem the party of privilege, and not that of opportunity.[15]

The ethos of the Tory Reform Group is of partnership and cooperation between the state and the individual, between capital and labour, rather than confrontation and conflict. Clearly the group is opposed to Thatcher's style of leadership, arguing that the party 'must stand back from stridency',[16] and must reject the 'mouthing of catch-phrases about freedom'.[17] On the issue of race it has directly attacked her by arguing that '. . . to pander to basic fears and instincts in the pre-election atmosphere, as Mrs Thatcher is doing . . . is an old and ugly subtlety'.[18]

The Tory Reform Group believes that the Conservative party should commit itself to more planning and more government expenditure rather than less. The key policy area in which more planning and expenditure is required is the inner city, in order to relieve unemployment and alleviate racial problems. The group is in favour of an incomes policy which would include both statutory wage restraint and Price Commission analysis of company profits. It would help to reduce unemployment by providing temporary subsidies to non-profitable industries, and it would pay higher unemployment benefit to school leavers willing to enter community service schemes. It is very much concerned with partnership in industry rather than conflict, and thus believes in providing tax-incentives to encourage profit-sharing, and also advocates forms of worker participation. It is interesting to note that, whereas George Ward was a Selsdon Group dinner guest, the Tory Reform Group regards such employers as an embarrassment to responsible labour relations. Finally, 'power to the people' is a key theme of the group, and thus it advocates devolution and electoral reform.

Soon after its formation the group became relatively moribund and relied upon its parliamentary sympathisers to provide the group with publicity. However, such publicity was 'double-edged', since the publicists—Peter Walker, Nick Scott and David Knox— were labelled by the press as 'Heath-men' plotting to undermine the new party leader. But in 1978 the group was revitalised by a new set of leaders, primarily university graduates in their thirties. Gerry Wade, ex-chairman of the Greater London Young Conservatives and one of the leading figures in the campaign in the late-1960s to make the Conservative party more democratic, is the new chairman. The group now has a dozen branches, primarily concentrated in university towns, and approximately 1000 members. Whereas the group has been rather better at making fine-sounding but rather banal statements than at making detailed policy proposals, Wade and his new executive are intent on remedying this defect by concentrating research, long-term rather than short-term, on four areas: Europe, constitutional reform (especially electoral reform), industrial relations, and social welfare.

It is noticeable that the Tory Reform Group is not backed up by the same panoply of organisations outside the Conservative party as those reflecting the liberal and authoritarian tendencies. But that may be because parts of the National Union and the party organisation have become involved in the intra-party disputes and have adopted factional positions in a manner unknown in the past. The Tory Reform Group now relies on the support of certain sections of the party—the Federation of Conservative Students, the Young Conservatives, the Conservative Trade Unionists, and particular sections of Conservative Central Office—whilst the

Selsdon Group and the Monday Club are forced into mobilising support through extra-party organisations.

IV CONCLUSIONS

I have argued that those observers who believe that factionalism is no part of Conservative party politics are wrong; nevertheless, I do believe that a comparison of party factionalism reveals significant differences. Conservative factions are less concerned than their Labour counterparts with strategies for winning positions of political support within the party and more concerned with providing an institutional form of reassurance for those with like-minded opinions. Conservative factions exist to provide some form of meeting-ground rather than to establish a campaign headquarters. Naturally this need to provide collective reassurance is part of all factional activity. Certainly this was the case with the Gaitskellite faction—the Campaign for Democratic Socialism—which provided reassurance to individual revisionists in the constituency parties when their tenets were under attack; but its major concern was to re-establish the dominance of revisionist politics within the party. Admittedly the structures of the Conservative party make it more difficult for factions to mount such campaigns, but it remains possible to use existing procedures to influence the party's deliberations. Only one Conservative faction compares with the Labour factions in terms of intra-party activity, and that is the Monday Club. The Monday Club, before its internal dispute, used the party's procedures in an attempt to impose its views on the party leadership. It initiated resolutions for the party conference, mobilised support in the ballot to choose two resolutions for debate at the party conference, and also concentrated its attention upon parliamentary candidate selection. No other contemporary Conservative faction has adopted any of these techniques for mobilising political support and attention.

Another factor in comparing factional activity is that notwithstanding the injection of a more meritocratic element into the Conservative party, the bulk of members remain uninterested in debating and discussing political ideas and policies. The major response of party members is one of loyalty towards the party leadership irrespective of its policy shifts over time. Factionalism remains of limited importance within the Conservative party because the bulk of the membership places little importance on political argument.

As a consequence, factional activity provides little guidance to the development of Conservative policies. For example, the present dominance of economic liberalism in the party is a reflection of the mood of the electorate rather than the influence of the Selsdon Group or the Centre for Policy Studies. Examination of the electorate's attitudes reveals some popular reaction against certain basic tenets of social democracy, such as state intervention and public expenditure, to which the Conservative party has found it convenient to respond (and stimulate further) whilst in opposition.[19] On the other hand, a study of policy making within the Labour party cannot afford to ignore factional activity. For example, the strength of the organised Left had an impact, via conference decisions and NEC elections, upon the policy commitments of the Labour party in the early-1970s. No such factional impact is apparent in the making of Conservative policies.

NOTES

1. I am grateful to my good friend Lewis Minkin for his usual perceptive comments on an early draft of this paper, and to the University of Sheffield Research Fund for a grant to facilitate certain interviews.
2. R. Rose, 'Parties, Factions and Tendencies in Britain', *Political Studies*, 12(1), (1964) pp. 33–46.
3. S. E. Finer, H. B. Berrington and D. J. Bartholomew, *Backbench Opinion in the House of Commons 1955–1959* (London: Pergamon, 1961). H. Berrington, *Backbench Opinion in the House of Commons 1945–1955* (Oxford: Pergamon Press, 1973).
4. Strictly speaking I mean individual members of local Conservative associations which make up the National Union of Conservative and Unionist Associations, but for the sake of simplicity I use 'the Conservative party'.
5. For example, Sir Anthony Nutting, who resigned in opposition to Eden's Suez policy and made no attempt to justify his position because of the embarrassment it might cause the party.
6. All studies of the parliamentary party reveal that three-quarters of the parliamentarians are recruited from public schools. See C. Mellors, *The British MP* (London: Saxon House, 1978).
7. Criticisms of the party's internal procedures were contained in *Set the Party Free*, produced by the Greater London Young Conservatives in 1969. The interim report of the Chelmer Committee (1972) contained proposals for constituency associations to assess the performance of Conservative MPs. See P. Seyd, 'Democracy Within the Conservative Party', *Government and Opposition*, 10(2), (1975) pp. 219–37.

8. P. Norton, *Intra-Party Dissent in the House of Commons: The Conservative Party in Government 1970–74*, PhD thesis, University of Sheffield (1977). Norton established significant correlation in backbenchers' behaviour in the votes on EEC entry (October 1971), the annual Rhodesian Sanctions Order, the Second Reading of The Northern Ireland (Temporary Provisions) Bill (March 1972), the immigration rules for entry into the UK (November 1972), and on the Amendment to Clause 4 of The Counter Inflation Bill (February 1973).

9. *A Second Selsdon Group Manifesto* (1977) p. 3.

10. Ibid., p. 10.

11. Ibid., p. 7.

12. *Labour's Programme 1973* (Labour Party, 1973).

13. Stephen Eyres, a founding member of the Selsdon Group, is Managing Editor of *Free Nation*.

14. See P. Seyd, 'Factionalism Within the Conservative Party', *Government and Opposition* 7(4) (1972) pp. 464–87.

15. *Reformer*, 2 (Autumn 1977) p. 7.

16. *Reformer*, 1 (Summer 1977) p. 8.

17. Loc. Cit.

18. *Reformer*, 3 (Winter 1977) p. 1.

19. I. Crewe, B. Sarlvik and J. Alt, 'Partisan Dealignment in Britain 1964–1974', *British Journal of Political Science* 7(2) (1977) pp. 150–2.

11 Popular Attitudes and Electoral Strategy

Ivor Crewe and Bo Särlvik

The true Conservative course . . . is to stick as closely as possible to the centre with a slight Right incline.

(Ian Gilmour, *Inside Right*)

A choice not an echo.

(slogan for Senator Goldwater, US Presidential Election 1964).

I INTRODUCTION

When a major party of government suffers a heavy, unexpected or repeated defeat at the polls, its inner counsels usually divide into two familiar groups. On the one side—especially amongst the younger back-benchers, local activists, and publicists from the media and universities—are the 'fundamentalists'. Doubly frustrated by the party's record in, as well as its fall from office, they call for a bold and imaginative restatement of first principles, a 'choice not an echo'. On the other side—especially amongst former ministers, senior back-benchers and long-standing officials—are the 'moderates'. Made wiser by office, they urge caution, counselling pragmatism rather than doctrine and moderation rather than extremism. Electoral realities are given priority over purity of principle. In truth the lines of battle are not as clear-drawn as this, not least because of the large group of unhappy and bewildered loyalists caught in the crossfire; but a division roughly along such lines normally occurs.

The common assumption is that the Conservative party was similarly divided on going into opposition in 1974. Certainly it conducted an unusually public discussion of its future electoral and policy options, not only in the normal round of speeches and newspaper articles, but in a number of books.[1] But the debate did not run along quite the usual clear lines. Consider the two following passages written by members of ostensibly different 'sides' of the party:

> There is a very large centre group in Britain making up possibly 80 to 90 per cent of my fellow countrymen and women who have firm views on law and order, morality, personal initiative and responsibility, educational standards and discipline, and national pride. The Conservatives lose elections only when they lose contact with this central group . . . I am not talking about the soft 'centre' or the constantly shifting intellectual consensus; I am talking about the broad range of common basic beliefs that unite the vast majority of the British people.
>
> (Prologue to Rhodes Boyson, *Centre Forward*)

> A party cannot win an election unless it wins the support of a high proportion of the uncommitted voters. And as the common middle ground means the uncommitted voters, anybody who says he is not concerned with that ground is in effect saying that he does not ever want to win an election . . . for the Conservatives there is no alternative to moderation.
>
> (Ian Gilmour, *Inside Right*, p. 141)

The reader of these passages would be forgiven for feeling confused. On the one hand, in these extracts and the rest of their books, Boyson reads like the 'fundamentalist' seeking a return to first principles, Gilmour like the 'moderate' urging electoral realism. On the other hand both writers stress the importance of the 'centre', the 'common middle ground'. Their differences appear to rest not on whether to pursue 'centre' policies (the issue at stake in the Labour party in the 1950s and in the Republican party in 1963–4), but on where and what the 'centre' is. The purpose of this chapter is to clarify the terms of the debate and to bring to bear on it some preliminary evidence from academic surveys and the polls.

II THE CONCEPTS OF MIDDLE GROUND AND COMMON GROUND

To cut through the tangle of military and footballing analogies typically adopted in discussions of this sort, we propose to use the pictorial devices made familiar by Anthony Downs in *An Economic Theory of Democracy*.[2] Imagine a line representing the spectrum of positions that can be taken on any issue, running from far left to far right. On that line can be plotted:

(i)   the various positions themselves: *the ideological ground*;
(ii) the parties' position on the issue: *the campaigning ground*;
(iii) the position taken by various groups of electors—Conservative and Labour supporters, the uncommitted voter, party activists perhaps—as well as the electorate as a whole: *the electoral ground*.

Thus, although a single line is used for the purposes of display, it represents a number of quite distinct political 'spaces'. As an illustration consider the assumptions that appear to be held by the party 'moderate' who advocates the pursuit of the middle ground (Figure 11.1). In such a situation it would be electorally imperative for the Conservative party to locate itself at point X, i.e. a shade right of Centre, and well to the left of not only its activists but its normal supporters as well. And, as Anthony Downs has persuasively demonstrated,[3] the Labour party would place itself at point Y, just left of Centre, for exactly the same reasons: a middle-of-the-road consensus politics would therefore emerge. But the scene depicted above rests on two crucial assumptions: (a) that uncommitted voters take positions in between, and roughly equi-distant from, those taken by committed voters for the two main parties; and (b) that the electoral ground coincides with the ideological ground; in particular, that the electoral centre therefore coincides with the ideological centre.[4]

FIG. 11.1   The moderative Conservative's picture of the electorate

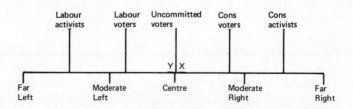

'Fundamentalists' like Boyson, however, would deny both assumptions. Their electoral picture is shown in Figure 11.2.

Fig. 11.2 The fundamentalist Conservative's picture of the electorate

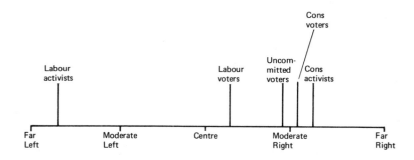

Uncommitted voters have views that come between those of Conservative and Labour voters, but nonetheless views much closer to those of Conservatives. And, more important, the electoral ground is *not* co-terminous with the ideological ground; on most issues it occupies the centre and right-hand side only, leaving the ideological left to a small minority of active socialists in the trade unions and intelligentsia. The correct electoral strategy for the Conservatives, therefore, is to locate themselves firmly on the Right, close to the position of their own activists and usual supporters, with whom the uncommitted voter, in fact, agrees on most things. Party principles and electoral advantage converge.

To speak of the middle or centre ground is one thing; to speak of the *common* ground quite another. The first refers to the *location* of a group of electors (or a party) along an electoral or ideological dimension and is best estimated by a measure of central tendency such as an arithmetic mean. The second refers to the *distribution* of the electors around that location—whether they are concentrated or dispersed—and is best estimated by a measure of dispersion such as a standard deviation. The ground occupied by five groups of electors (A, B, C, D, E) could therefore be described in one of four ways:

1. common middle ground

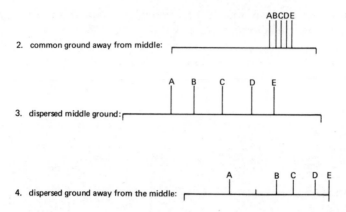

2. common ground away from middle:

3. dispersed middle ground:

4. dispersed ground away from the middle:

Which of these electoral configurations is the most common? Before coming to an answer, it is important to add some refinements to this method of proceeding. First, the 'position' on the line for any group of voters is only the average of a scatter of positions of the individuals composing the group; moreover, the degree of scatter will itself vary across issues and between groups: on nationalisation, for example, there is a greater consensus of view amongst Conservative than Labour supporters.[5] Degree of consensus has an important bearing on electoral strategy: the lower the consensus amongst a party's supporters (or the uncommitted) the more ambivalent about its position the party will need to be.

Secondly, there is no such thing as a true or objective party position. What counts is the electorate's perception of the party's position: this perception might well differ, of course, from that of the party leadership, and will vary not only between but also within groups of electors. Indeed, the degree of agreement within a group about a party's position will itself differ across groups, issues and the party in question.

Thirdly, it is unusual for a single issue to be the exclusive or decisive factor in the way any individual, or the electorate as a whole, votes. For most voters party preference is determined by a complex amalgam of issues, the precise weight of any one being difficult to gauge; and where one issue is of overriding importance it will not be the same issue in every case. Analysis therefore needs to proceed at two levels: we require the configuration for a number of issues combined and we also require configurations restricted to those electors for whom the issue in question is particularly important. And ideally, we should attempt to construct configurations that combine both.

It is also important to appreciate some of the limits to this method of analysis. For one thing, it is difficult to apply to those issues (sometimes described as 'valence' as opposed to 'position' issues) on which the electorate shares a near-identical goal and disagrees only on the relative ability of the parties to achieve it, e.g. a reduction in the rate of inflation, unemployment or strikes. For another, not all 'position' issues are unidimensional: although the issue of nationalisation can be represented by a line running from 'nationalise the lot' to 'denationalise the lot', there would be no obviously correct location for the voter who believed in nationalising some industries but denationalising others. Finally, it must be added that factors other than issues, such as a party's leadership or its overall 'image' play a part in the election outcome and these cannot be analysed in the way we adopt for issues.

There follow two electoral 'pictures', drawn from the October 1974 election, one for the issue of nationalisation and the other for that of the EEC. On both issues the subjects of the October 1974 British Election Study were asked to give their own view, and their preception of each party's position, on the two issues: there was a choice of four positions on each issue, which were scored from one to four, a low score denoting a 'left-wing' position, i.e. support for large-scale nationalisation or for withdrawal from the EEC. Committed Conservative and Labour supporters were defined as those with a 'very' or 'fairly' strong party identification, on the basis of the standard three-category party identification question:[6] there is extensive evidence from the Butler and Stokes, and Essex election surveys that the great majority of such partisans regularly turn out for their party at each election.[7] Three groups of 'uncommitted voters' were distinguished:

(a) *Conservative 'leaners'*, defined as 'not very strong' Conservative identifiers. In October 1974, 55 per cent voted Conservative, 19 per cent defected (4 per cent to Labour) and 25 per cent abstained. In other words, this group is predominantly Conservative but easily persuaded to defect and abstain: further losses of Conservative support would come primarily from this group.

(b) *Labour 'leaners'*, defined as 'not very strong' Labour identifiers. In October 1974, 53 per cent voted Labour, 14 per cent defected (5 per cent to the Conservatives) and 33 per cent failed to vote. Any

Conservative success amongst Labour supporters would first occur in this group, as would Conservative advantage from Labour abstention.

(c) *Liberal 'leaners'*, defined as 'not very strong' Liberal identifiers, of whom 54 per cent voted Liberal in October 1974, 17 per cent Conservative, 8 per cent Labour, and 18 per cent abstained. Conservative gains from a collapse of the Liberal vote at the next election could be expected to come disproportionately from this group.[8]

The two configurations shown in Figures 11.3 and 11.4 are reasonably typical of the kind that support, in turn, the case of the 'moderates' and the case of the 'fundamentalists'.

First, the issue of the EEC: this configuration has two features which support the case of the 'moderates'. First, the five groups of voters are located in the predictable ideological 'order'; indeed, in all but one case with almost equal 'distances' between them. Secondly, the five groups of voters are clustered almost exactly around the ideological centre (the score for the whole electorate was 2.51). The two parties, however, are in very different strategic locations. Labour is perfectly positioned: a shade left of the ideological centre, it is on the moderate side of its own committed supporters, very close to Labour 'leaners' and considerably less distant than the Conservative party from the two other groups of uncommitted voters. Even committed Conservative voters are somewhat less distant from Labour (.49) than from the Conservative party (.73).[9] In these circumstances it is not surprising that in October 1974 the Conservatives lost votes on the EEC: amongst February 1974 Conservative voters who (in October) considered the EEC the most important of all issues, 26 per cent defected or abstained; but amongst those who considered the issue only fairly or not very important, the proportion was 21 per cent.

For an almost exact contrast we now turn to the issue of nationalisation (Figure 11.4). Once again, the five groups of electors are positioned on the line in an ideologically predictable way, but this time they cluster around a point well to the *right* of the ideological centre (the mean position for all respondents is 2.80). And this time it is the Conservative party, not Labour, which finds itself at a clear strategic advantage, being positioned very close to both committed and 'leaning' Conservatives, and considerably nearer than the Labour party to the two other uncommitted groups

Fig. 11.3   The electoral configuration for the EEC issue, October 1974

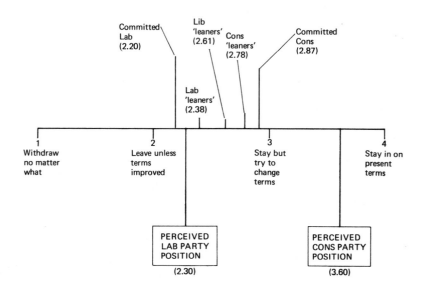

SOURCE
British Election Study, October 1974 cross-section sample.

QUESTION
'It is sometimes said that Britain should try to change the terms of entry into the Common Market and if this is not successful, get out. Which of the following statements on this card comes closest to what you yourself feel should be done?'
1 It is all right for Britain to stay in the Common Market on the present terms
2 Britain must stay in the Common Market but must try hard to change the terms
3 Britain must change the terms and should leave the Common Market unless they improve
4 Britain should get out of the Common Market no matter what.

NOTES
The perceived party positions are based on those of the respondents as a whole. Figures in parentheses indicate the point on the scale at which the group is located. The height of the vertical lines above the horizontal represent the relative size of the electoral groups.

of electors. Analysis of each group's perception of the two parties' positions revealed a similar distorting phenomenon to that found on the EEC issue (see note 9) but on this occasion it was committed

FIG. 11.4   The electoral configuration for the nationalisation issue, October 1974

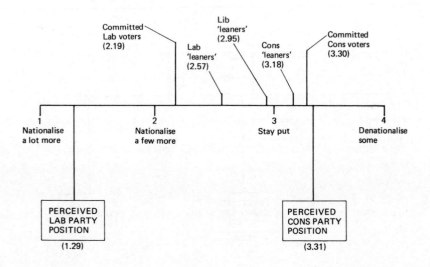

SOURCE
British Election Study, October 1974 cross-section sample.

QUESTION
'There has been a lot of talk recently about nationalisation, that is, the Government owning and running industries like steel and electricity. Which of these statements comes closest to what you yourself feel should be done?'

1 *A lot more* industries should be nationalised
2 Only a *few more* industries should be nationalised
3 *No more* industries should be nationalised but industries that are now nationalised should stay nationalised
4 Some of the industries that are now nationalised should become private companies.

NOTES
The perceived party positions are based on those of the respondents as a whole. Figures in parentheses indicate the point on the scale at which the group is located. The height of the vertical lines above the horizontal represent the relative surge of the electoral groups.

Labour supporters who 'pulled' their party towards their own less fundamentalist position.[10] Just as the Conservatives appeared to lose some votes on the EEC issue, so Labour did on nationalisation: amongst February 1974 Labour voters who (in October) considered nationalisation the single most important issue 24 per cent defected or abstained; but amongst those who considered the issue only fairly or not very important, the proportion was 17 per cent. Thus, on nationalisation the 'fundamentalist' strategy looks, for the Conservatives, the more attractive.

III THE ELECTORATE'S POSITION ON DIFFERENT ISSUES AND THE IMPLICATIONS FOR A RATIONAL ELECTORAL STRATEGY

But elections are fought on and decided by a host of issues: what are the configurations across them all? Do they generally support the moderate's or fundamentalist's assumptions, or vary by type of issue, or reveal no clear pattern at all? To answer these questions we shall analyse the large number of issue-questions included in the October 1974 British Election Study. Three kinds of issue-questions were asked:

1. *Position-issue questions*: respondents were asked to say to which of four positions on the issues of nationalisation, North Sea oil, social services, and the EEC they felt 'closest' (and, also, perceived the parties as 'closest').

2. *Social trend questions*: respondents were asked for their view on 'some of the general changes that have been taking place in Britain in the last few years'. They could choose one of five answers:

1. Gone much too far
2. Gone a little too far
3. Is about right
4. Not gone quite far enough
5. Not gone nearly far enough

The 'changes' on which judgement was invited included:

1. Equality for women
2. Leniency on law-breakers
3. Pornography
4. Declining respect for authority
5. Equality for coloured people
6. Modern methods of teaching
7. The easier availability of abortion
8. Welfare benefits
9. Cuts in Britain's defence forces

This series of questions was specifically designed to tap 'populist' resentment against modern social trends, especially the decline of traditional conceptions of authority and morality.

3. *Policy questions*: respondents were asked how important it was that the government should, or should not, carry out each of the following policies:

1. Establishing comprehensive schools
2. Repatriating immigrants
3. Increasing state control of land
4. Increasing foreign aid
5. Toughening up measures against crime
6. Getting rid of pollution
7. Encouraging worker-participation
8. Strengthening measures to curb Communist influence in Britain
9. Getting rid of poverty
10. Redistributing wealth
11. Devolving power to regions
12. Protecting countryside
13. Putting more money into Health Service

They could choose one of five answers:

1. Very important that it should be done
2. Fairly important that it should be done
3. It doesn't matter either way
4. Fairly important that it should not be done
5. Very important that it should not be done

It would be both impractical and unnecessary to provide configurations of the kind described for the EEC and nationalisation issues for each of the above. Instead we should ask: how do opinions on these issues cluster, and what are the configurations for the major clusters? A factor analysis (unrotated) of the correlation matrix for all these issues revealed three main 'clusters' (or 'factors' as they are usually termed), of which the heaviest 'loading' (i.e. contributory) issues were as shown in Table 11.1.

The primary cluster—primary in the sense that it accounts for more of the variation in public opinion than any other cluster—is the familiar socio-economic Left-Right division over the distribution of wealth and the ownership of production. The second most important cluster is more difficult to describe concisely: for want of anything better I shall refer to it as 'populist-authoritarian'. The third factor is uncomplicated, consisting of support for (or rejection of) racialist policies. It is possible, of course, to discern additional

TABLE 11.1 Unrotated factor analysis of issue questions, October 1974

Factor I		Factor II		Factor III	
Issue	Loading on factor	Issue	Loading on factor	Issue	Loading on factor
Nationalisation	·588	Measures against crime	·557	Repatriation of Immigrants	·501
Redistribution of wealth	·578	Pornography	·444	Racial equality	·457
Welfare benefits	·570	Communist influence	·406		
Social services	·564	Respect for authority	·383		
% total variance explained	17.1%		10.7%		7.3%

Fig. 11.5   Electoral configurations for three issue-clusters

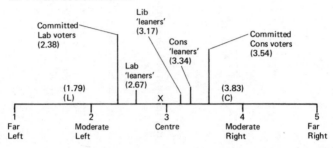

'LEFT-RIGHT SOCIOECONOMIC'

X = position of typical voter

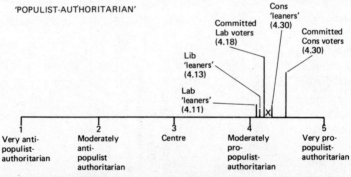

'POPULIST-AUTHORITARIAN'

X = position of typical voter

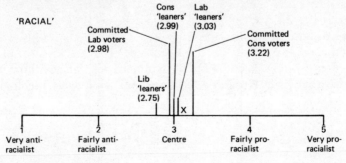

'RACIAL'

X = position of typical voter

clusters of opinions accounting for a smaller proportion of the variance; but the three described above represent the major axes by which public opinion was organised in Britain in October 1974.

How should the Conservative party respond electorally to these three opinion-clusters? Should it take a non-committal and 'moderate' position or boldly follow its ideological instincts? As the electoral configurations in Figure 11.5 show, the answer depends on the particular issue-cluster:

(a) *Left-Right socioeconomic issues.* Here the electoral configuration conforms almost perfectly to the 'classical' model: committed Labour supporters are furthest to the Left, committed Conservatives furthest to the Right, with uncommitted voters in between. The typical voter is located at almost dead centre. But whereabouts on the Left-Right socioeconomic scale do the two parties stand in the eyes of the electorate? Data on perceptions of the parties' positions are only available for two of the four issues represented by the scale: nationalisation and social services. The perceived positions of the Labour and Conservative parties on these two issues combined are denoted on the first configuration of Figure 11.5 by (L) and (C) respectively. There are a number of features to this configuration worth noting. First, both parties were placed on the 'extreme' side of their own most committed supporters—Labour to the left of theirs, the Conservatives to the right of theirs. Secondly, the committed and leaning supporters of both parties were closer to their own party's position than to that of the other party. Thirdly, it was to the clear advantage of both parties to move towards the ideological centre. A *unilateral* shift towards (but not over and across) the centre would have allowed either party to become the closer of the two parties to the Liberal leaners without becoming more distant from its own more faint-hearted supporters. Nonetheless, the Left-Right socioeconomic configuration of party and voter positions is not perfectly symmetrical. For one thing, the Conservative party is regarded as somewhat closer to the ideological

---

NOTES

Figures in parentheses indicate the point on the scale at which the group is located (i.e. its combined mean score on the issues). For each group, the score on each issue was standardised, aggregated, and divided by the number of issues. The height of the vertical lines above the horizontal represents the relative size of each electoral group.

centre (being 0.83 away) than Labour is (being 1.21 away). For another, the overall array of electoral groups is skewed fractionally to the right: Liberal leaners place themselves to the right of centre and both committed and leaning Labour supporters are closer to the centre (although to its left) than are their Conservative counterparts. As a result it would take a much smaller change of position for the Conservatives than for Labour to compete effectively for the vote of leaning Liberals or, for that matter, for the vote of uncommitted supporters of the 'opposite' party. On socioeconomic issues the rational electoral course for the Conservatives is clearly to move further towards the ideological centre. Moderation is the party's right course *not* because the electorate occupies common ideological ground but because it is symmetrically dispersed across the *middle* point of the ideological spectrum.

(b) *Populist-Authoritarian issues.* Here, on the other hand, the electorate clearly does stand on *common* ground: there is almost nothing to distinguish the views of the various electoral groups. But it is ground far to the right of the ideological mid-point: the electoral centre does not coincide with the ideological centre. On the issues that make up this cluster Rhodes Boyson's view of the electorate stands up: 96 per cent of the electorate wanted 'tougher measures to prevent crime'; 82 per cent said that the decline in 'respect for authority' 'had gone too far'; 78 per cent wanted 'tougher measures to prevent Communist influence in Britain' and 64 per cent felt that 'nudity and sex in films and television' 'had gone too far'. The electorate's positioning of the two parties on populist-authoritarian issues, however, must be a matter for speculation, since the British Election Study surveys in October 1974 did not ask respondents about the parties' positions on the issues composing this dimension. There is a small amount of fragmentary evidence from other polls and surveys. For example, each of the monthly Gallup polls from January to May 1978 asked 'Which parties do you think are particularly good at maintaining law and order': over the five months combined 42 per cent chose the Conservatives, 30 per cent Labour.[11] In February 1974 the British Election Study asked 'When it comes to dealing with Communists in trade unions, which, if any, of the parties do you think is best?': 40 per cent said the Conservatives, 25 per cent Labour. Thus the Conservatives are almost certainly regarded as closer than Labour to the electoral groups in the populist-authoritarian configuration, but *how* close is impossible to judge. It is possible, for example, that the electorate regards both parties as so remote on these issues that, much in the way that long perspective forecloses the gap between distant objects, little significant difference between the parties is discerned. But whatever the perceived party positions on this dimension, the Conservative party would appear to have much to gain electorally and little to lose by following its heart and establishing itself firmly as the party of discipline, order and morality.

(c) *Racial Issues.* Here the electoral configuration is different yet again: the electorate congregate on common ground which *is* at the ideological mid-point. The ideological and electoral centre coincide. (It is worth noting, however, that the electoral groups are not located in 'ideological order': Liberal leaners are a shade to the left of committed Labour supporters, and Conservative leaners are fractionally to the left of Labour leaners.) Once again, unfortunately, no data exist on where the electorate places the parties on the two racial issues. It is true that recent opinion polls, especially since Mrs Thatcher's remarks in January 1978 about 'swamping', have extensively covered public opinion on immigration, and on first reading suggest that the Conservatives are much the more popular party on the issue. For example, between February and May 1978 Gallup asked 'Which parties do you think are particularly good at controlling immigration?'; over the four months combined 53 per cent replied Conservative, 23 per cent Labour. There is also patchy but fairly convincing evidence that Mrs Thatcher's remarks served to distinguish more clearly the major parties' policies on immigration control, to the Conservatives' benefit.[12] But the significance of such findings should be assessed with caution. Immigration is only one aspect of the racial issue; the same Gallup polls as those referred to above also asked 'Which parties do you think are particularly good at improving race relations?'; 27 per cent said the Conservatives, 35 per cent said Labour. The rational electoral strategy for the Conservatives (and Labour) therefore appears to be to stick to the centre, certainly to avoid a Powellite line on the repatriation of immigrants or on the dismantling of race relations legislation.

IV FURTHER CONSIDERATIONS ON AN ELECTORAL STRATEGY
FOR THE CONSERVATIVE PARTY

It would be simple to end at this point with the conclusion that both
the 'moderates' and 'fundamentalists' are right: the Conservative
party's optimal appeal to the electorate would combine moderation
on the conventional bread-and-butter issues with a firm reassertion
of traditional values on the more exotic authoritarian-populist
issues (except race). Indeed, such a strategy would have the
additional advantages of appealing to the party faithful, satisfying
both the moderate and fundamentalist camps, at least in part.

Such a conclusion assumes, however, that both types of issue are
of roughly equal importance in an election, whereas the normal
view is that they are not. In the final analysis, it is said, bread-and-
butter issues are the more decisive: it is on these that the parties
campaign and the voters decide. Come an election the emotion
generated by such matters as crime, immigration, pornography and
abortion evaporates—just as it did on 'Communist influence' and
'Who Governs?' in the February 1974 campaign. Thus, the argument goes, it remains in the Conservative party's electoral interests
to abide by convention, avoid 'emotive' but essentially peripheral
issues, and take a cautious and pragmatic line on the traditional but
still salient socio-economic issues. The 'moderate' strategy should
take precedence.

But is voting quite as unaffected by populist-authoritarian
sentiments as the moderates are suggesting? Careful examination of
polls and surveys suggests that the electoral importance of at least
some of these issues—in particular race and law and order—can be
underestimated. The basis for regarding social and economic issues
as of almost exclusive importance when it comes to voting appears
to rest on figures given by the monthly polls. For example, Gallup
always asks 'What would you say is the most urgent problem facing
the country at the present time?' followed by 'And what would you
say is the next most urgent problem?'. The results since the October
1974 election are shown in Table 11.2.

On this evidence both immigration and law and order, although
slowly growing in importance over the past four years, run a long
way behind inflation, unemployment and a host of other 'conventional' economic and social issues. But in recent years Gallup
have also asked an additional question on the relative importance of
issues, which is close-ended and asks, simply, 'How important

TABLE 11.2 The Relative Importance of Issues, 1975–78 (in answer to open-ended questions)

Issue	Most Important				Next or Next most Important			
	1975	1976	1977	1978 (up to Oct)	1975	1976	1977	1978 (up to Oct)
	%²	%	%	%	%	%	%	%
Prices/cost of living	62	50	46	29	77	68	65	47
Unemployment	10	18	20	30	31	43	41	48
Strikes/labour relations	7	3	9	6	18	9	18	13
Other economic	6	10	7	7	11	16	15	14
Law and order	–	1	1	5	2	4	6	10
Immigration	–	3	1	5	–	10	5	14
Other[1]	12	12	14	15	46	40	40	41

NOTES
1. Mainly: housing, health, pensions, social security benefits, education, productivity, energy.
2. The annual percentages are an average of the monthly observations
SOURCE
Gallup Political Index, 1975 to 1978

TABLE 11.3 The relative importance of issues, Jan–May 1978 (in answer to a close-ended question)

Issue	Rank Order	% saying extremely important	Issue	Rank Order	% saying extremely important
Maintaining law and order	1	82	Increasing pensions	8	47
Controlling inflation	2	77	Improving labour relations	9	45
Reducing unemployment	2	77	Improving race relations	10	38
Controlling immigration	4	64	Improving national unity	11	36
Reducing taxation	5	55	Creating a fairer society	12	34
Protecting freedom of speech	6	51	Building more houses for owner-occupation	13	29
Protecting people's privacy	7	50			

NOTES

The percentages are the mean of the five observations for the months January to May 1978.

The answer categories were: Extremely important/Quite important/Not very important/Not at all important/Don't know.

SOURCE

Gallup monthly polls, January to May 1978

would you say . . . is at the moment?'. The results are shown in Table 11.3

On the evidence of these figures law-and-order emerges as the single most important issue to the public, and the control of immigration fourth most important. Why should the importance of these two issues differ by so much, in terms of both absolute percentages and rank order, in response to the two questions? One possibility is that the different phrasing is responsible. But a more intriguing possibility is that, unlike the first question, the second offers a 'prompt': it reminds the respondent of the existence of the issue, and to some extent 'legitimises' it. It is usually assumed that the respondent's true feelings are more likely to be expressed in answers to open-ended rather than close-ended questions, the fixed categories of the latter being regarded as imposed and artificial. But the argument can be reversed: given that election campaigns 'impose' issues on the electorate, answers to the close-ended question might be the more reliable guide to the relative impact of issues on voting decisions. A further, reinforcing, piece of evidence drawn from the British Election Study should also be considered. Respondents were asked to say which of the statements in Table 11.4 should be 'the most important general aim of a government'.

As the table shows, the maintenance of law and order (chosen by 25 per cent) was a close runner-up to the raising of living standards (30 per cent) amongst the electorate as a whole, and more or less level-pegging amongst two of the three 'uncommitted' groups, the Conservative and Liberal 'learners'. (In passing it is also worth noticing that private enterprise was bottom or next to bottom of the list for everybody other than committed Conservatives.) Thus the evidence that law and order—the core of the authoritarian-populist syndrome—and immigration could be crucial election issues cannot be lightly dismissed.

But even if populist-authoritarian and racial issues are less salient than socio-economic issues for the electorate taken as a whole, they are still the most important considerations for a minority. Indeed, the electorate can be regarded as a collection of such minorities (or 'issue-publics', as we shall call them) for each of whom a different issue assumes primary importance. Similarly, each electoral group, from committed Labour supporters to committed Conservatives, is composed of various issue-publics. These must be taken into special account in any rational electoral strategy: in particular, where views differ between those for whom the issue is important, and

TABLE 11.4　The Most Important General Aim of Government

	All respondents %	Committed Labour voters %	Labour 'leaners' %	Liberal 'leaners' %	Cons 'leaners' %	Committed Cons voters %
Maintaining law and order	25	20	18	26	24	33
Raising everybody's standard of living	30	34	26	24	27	27
Achieving greater equality	18	24	29	19	14	8
Protecting individual liberty	12	7	8	21	20	15
Protecting the weakest and worst off	10	14	13	4	8	5
Promoting private enterprise	6	1	6	6	6	13
Total	100	100	100	100	100	100

NOTES
The six answer categories were ordered differently in the questionnaire. The full question was: 'Looking at this list, could you say what the *most* important *general* aim of a government should be?'.

SOURCE
British Election Study, October 1974 cross-section sample.

those for whom it is not, the vote-conscious party will pay more attention to the former. Figure 11.6 reveals that positions on an issue can clearly differ between those who are and those who are not relatively concerned about it. For example, Labour, Liberal and Conservative 'leaners', for whom nationalisation was an important issue, all took up a somewhat more right-wing stance than those leaners for whom the matter was one of relative indifference. The electoral implication is that Conservative party can afford that much more, and Labour that much less, to maintain their respective right and left positions on the issue. On social services, however, views hardly differ between those for whom the issue is or is not important (except amongst committed Labour supporters, the concerned taking a markedly more left-wing position than the indifferent). The issues that best illustrate the importance of paying special regard to issue-publics, however, are immigration and Communist influence in trade unions. As Figure 11.6 shows, in every electoral group those for whom immigration was 'very important' clearly took a more hard-line anti-immigrant position than those for whom the issue was of little concern; moreover, this was especially true of the *uncommitted* voters. The pattern is similar in the case of Communist influence in trade unions: those to whom the matter was salient took a markedly tougher anti-Communist line. And once again, it is two uncommitted groups of voters—Labour and Liberal 'leaners'—who take a particularly large leap to the Right if they consider the issue important. It needs to be stressed that immigration is only part of the set of issues described as 'racial'; similarly, anti-Communism is only one of the four issues making up 'populist-authoritarianism'. Nonetheless, these two cases do raise the possibility that the fundamentalists' electoral strategy of robustly right-wing rhetoric on non-economic issues is based on stronger grounds than was first apparent.

There are two additional electoral advantages to the Conservative party from emphasising a fundamentalist position on populist-authoritarian issues. The first is that opinion on such issues, not only amongst the electorate as a whole but within each group of voters, is considerably more *homogeneous* than it is for socio-economic issues. This is clearly shown in the standard deviation scores set out in Table 11.5. The second electoral benefit to the Conservatives arises from the *intensity* of opinion that seems to be associated with some of these issues: as Table 11.6 shows, the proportion opting for an 'extreme' answer was considerably greater for populist-

FIG. 11.6 Electoral configurations on nationalisation, social services, immigration and Communist influence in trade unions, by importance of issue, 1974.

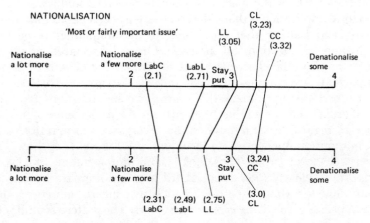

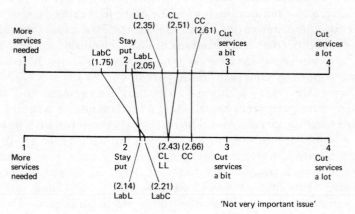

IMMIGRATION

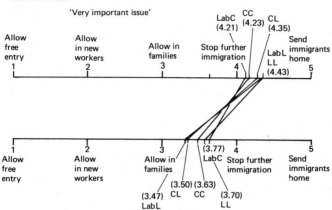

COMMUNIST INFLUENCE IN TRADE UNIONS

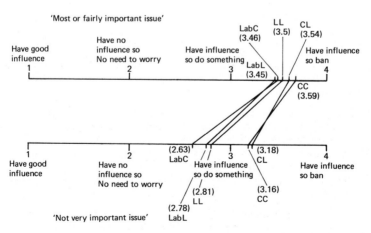

SOURCES

Nationalisation and social services: British Election Study, October 1974 cross-section sample; immigration: British Election Study, February 1974 wave of 1970–February 1974 panel sample; Communist influence: February 1974 cross-section sample.

NOTES

The question on nationalisation is given in Figure 11.4. The question on social services was: 'Now we would like to ask what you think about social services and benefits. Which of these statements do you feel comes closest to your own views?'

1. Social services and benefits have gone much too far and should be cut back a lot.
2. Social services and benefits have gone somewhat too far and should be cut back a bit.
3. Social services and benefits should stay much as they are.
4. More social services and benefits are needed.
5. Don't know, no view.

'When you were deciding about voting, how important was the question of social services and benefits (nationalisation) (Communist influence in trade unions)—the most important single thing, fairly important, or not very important?'
The question on immigration was: 'Which statements come closest to what you yourself feel should be done about immigrants?'

1. Assist in sending immigrants home.
2. Stop further immigration but allow immigrants already here to stay.
3. Allow in the immediate families of immigrants here and a few skilled workers.
4. Allow in new workers and their families.
5. Allow free entry.
6. Don't know, no view.

'How strongly do you feel about this—very strongly, fairly strongly, or not very strongly?'
The question on Communists was: 'There has been some talk recently about Communists in trade unions. Which of the statements on this card come closest to what you yourself feel?'

1. Communists should be banned from holding official positions in trade unions.
2. Even though Communists should not be banned, something must be done to reduce their influence in trade unions.
3. There is no need to worry about Communists in trade unions because their influence is rarely important.
4. Communists have some influence in trade unions and it is generally good.
5. No view/don't know.

In the case of nationalisation, social services, and Communist influence, respondents were divided into those who considered the issue not very important and those who considered it either fairly important or the most important single issue (the latter category contained too few cases for separate analysis). In the case of immigration we have contrasted those who considered the issue 'very important' with those who considered it 'not very important', omitting those in the 'fairly important' category from the analysis.

TABLE 11.5 Homogeneity of opinion of types of issue

	All electors	Committed Cons voters	Cons 'leaners'	Liberal 'leaners'	Labour 'leaners'	Committed Labour voters
Socio economic Left-Right issues	1.13	1.09	1.17	1.03	1.16	1.08
Populist-authoritarian	0.96	0.85	0.91	0.95	0.97	0.77
Racial issues	1.17	1.15	1.16	1.05	1.17	1.20

NOTE
The figures in the table are the mean standard deviation scores of an electoral group for the set of issues making up each of the three 'types' of issue.

TABLE 11.6 Proportion opting for 'extreme' answers on different kinds of issue.

% choosing 'extreme' answer category on:	All electors %	Committed Cons voters %	Cons 'leaners' %	Liberal 'leaners' %	Labour 'leaners' %	Committed Labour voters %
Socioeconomic Left-Right issues[1]	32	32	30	22	31	34
Populist-authoritarian issues	59	70	57	49	50	56
Racial issues	24	25	20	18	26	26

NOTE

An 'extreme' answer was defined as either of the two end categories of answer for any of the questions. Thus, 'Gone much too far' and 'Not gone nearly far enough' were the 'extreme' responses to social trend questions; 'Very important that it should be done' and 'Very important that it should not be done', the 'extreme' responses to the policy questions, and so on. Two of the issues-nationalisation and social services-were measured by four-category, not five-category questions. This will have slighty *inflated* the proportion of 'extreme' answers on these questions.

authoritarian than for socio-economic (or racial) issues. On populist-authoritarian issues, therefore, uncommitted voters share a similiar set of strong opinions; on socio-economic issues, on the other hand, their views are mixed and less deeply felt. It is on the latter, therefore, that the Conservatives (and Labour, of course) need to fudge, and on the former that they can be bold and clear. It is precisely on that set of issues where the Conservative party is the closer of the two parties to the uncommitted voter that it can also afford to be most assertive. But to this conclusion one important qualification needs to be made: as both Tables 11.4 and 11.5 show, the electorate is as divided and moderate on *racial* issues as it is on socioeconomic matters. For the second time in this analysis, therefore, there emerge good reasons for the Conservative party to take a much more cautious and ambivalent line on race than on the other non-economic issues. The 'fundamentalist' electoral strategy looks more promising for matters of order and traditional morality than it does for the tricky, double-edged issue of race.

There is also a good deal of circumstantial evidence from beyond polls and surveys—indeed perhaps masked by polls and surveys— that populist-authoritarian issues arouse unusually strong emotions. It is these issues which appear to crop up particularly often in anonymous, private, or informal settings which are not thought subject to the sanction of respectable or fashionable opinion—in pubs and clubs, in the conversation of families and friends, in unsigned letters and graffiti, and so on. Not surprisingly, if intensely-held but non-respectable opinions are given a sudden legitimacy through endorsement by a leading public figure—as happened after Enoch Powell's 'rivers of blood' speech—a wave of popular feeling will make itself felt, to the potential benefit of the Conservative party. In this respect it is interesting to note that two recent investigations of the impact of the immigration issue on the 1970 election have concluded that the Conservatives gained a distinct and perhaps decisive increment of the vote.[13]

Much of the material presented in this paper will come as no surprise to those familiar with the extensive literature on the 'radical right', the 'working-class authoritarian', the 'tough/tender-minded' distinction and, more recently, the differences between those with 'acquisitive' and 'post-acquisitive' values.[14] Countless academic surveys and polls have revealed the existence in Britain of majorities—ranging from substantial to overwhelming—in favour of the authoritarian reassertion of traditional ideas of morality and the national interest. The same surveys also show, consistently, that public opinion on these matters is largely independent of party preference or social class (although not level of education) and thus of opinion on the issues of economic management, distribution and ownership which have traditionally dominated election campaigns. In a large number of policy areas—foreign affairs, defence, crime, minority rights, sexual morality—the majority view aligns with Conservative rather than Labour instincts.

V CLOSING REMARKS

The puzzle is why the Conservative leadership has not exploited its electoral advantage to a greater degree. To do so would not, of course, be without political risks, notably the alienation of its liberal wing, and the possibility that the party would acquire an old-fashioned and dour image which would in turn be electorally damaging. Failure to mine this electoral seam probably stems from other factors: partly from the personal views of the three (four?) leaders preceding Margaret Thatcher, more probably from the availability of other sources of electoral support. Simplifying drastically, right-wing parties seeking to win elections in highly industrialised societies depend on attracting substantial working class support through one or more of the following means: (i) by offering the more promising economic prospect; (ii) by exploiting the residual pockets of pre-industrial values (the 'deferential' vote); or (iii) by offering the more attractive leader. The first option clearly remains, although Britain's disappointing economic record under successive governments of both parties, as well as the currently dim prospects for sustained economic growth, make it considerably more tricky than in the 1950s or 1960s. The second option is barely available as the 'deferential' vote appears to have dwindled to tiny proportions. And, judging by the polls, the third option must remain in temporary abeyance until the relative fortunes of the two parties in this respect is reversed. In these circumstances the resort to populist-authoritarian issues must seem the logical electoral strategy to the Conservative party.

NOTES

1. See, for example, Ian Gilmour, *Inside Right: A Study of Conservatism* (London: Hutchinson, 1977); Rhodes Boyson, *Centre Forward: A Radical Conservative*

Programme (London: Temple Smith, 1978); William Waldegrave, *The Binding of Leviathan* (London: Hamish Hamilton, 1978) and Maurice Cowling (ed.), *Conservative Essays* (London: Cassell, 1978).

2. Anthony Downs, *An Economic Theory of Democracy* (New York: Harper & Row, 1957).

3. Ibid, ch. 7.

4. The argument that both parties would position themselves near the mid-point strictly depends on a series of additional—but realistic—assumptions, the most notable being (a) that few committed voters or activists will abstain in protest at their party's central location; and (b) that there are approximately equal numbers of committed Labour and committed Conservative voters.

5. The standard deviation of opinions was .63 amongst Conservative identifiers and .82 amongst Labour identifiers.

6. The full wording of the question is: 'Generally speaking do you think of yourself as Conservative, Labour, Liberal (in Scotland/Wales: Nationalist/Plaid Cymru), or what?'
   This is followed by: 'Would you call yourself a very strong Conservative (Liberal, etc.), fairly strong or not very strong?' (Respondents answering 'no' or 'don't know' to the first question were asked: 'Do you generally think of yourself as a little closer to one of the parties than the others?' If they then mentioned a party they were automatically defined as 'not very strong' identifiers.)

7. See Ivor Crewe *et al*, 'Non-Voting in British General Elections 1966–October 1974' in Colin Crouch (ed), *British Political Sociology Yearbook*, vol 3, p 90.

8. There are other ways of defining the uncommitted voter. If defined as, e.g. those who defected from the Conservatives between February and October 1974 or, alternatively, those who voted Conservative in 1966 and 1970 but not in either of the two 1974 elections, the results turn out to be very similar to those presented in this paper although, of course, by using this definition it would not be possible to distinguish the partisan direction in which uncommitted voters leaned.

9. The position of the two parties is based on the perceptions of the electorate as a whole. As the following figures show, perceptions of the two party positions did differ between electoral groups: for example, committed Conservatives 'pulled' the Conservative party towards them and 'pushed' the Labour party away, such that they perceived themselves a fraction closer to their own party.

	Perception of Conservative party position on EEC (mean score)	Perception of Labour party position on EEC (mean score)	Relative closeness to Con/Lab party
Committed Conservative supporters (2.87)	3.48	2.21	.05 to Con
Conservative 'leaners' (2.78)	3.58	2.33	.35 to Lab
Liberal 'leaners' (2.61)	3.53	2.39	.70 to Lab

9 *(Continued)*

	Perception of Conservative party position on EEC *(mean score)*	Perception of Labour party position on EEC *(mean score)*	Relative closeness to Con/Lab party
Labour 'leaners' (2.38)	3.70	2.40	1.30 to Lab
Committed Labour supporters (2.20)	3.67	2.33	1.34 to Lab
All respondents (2.51)	3.60	2.30	.88 to Lab

NOTES

High scores = pro-EEC, low scores = anti-EEC
Figures in parentheses are scores for respondents' own position. 'Relative closeness' is calculated by subtracting distance from one party from distance from the other party.

10. The figures were as follows:

	Perception of Conservative party position on nationalisation *(mean score)*	Perception of Labour party position on nationalisation *(mean score)*	Relative closeness to Con/ Lab party
Committed Conservative supporters (3.31)	3.29	1.10	2.19 to Con
Conservative 'leaners' (3.18)	3.25	1.12	1.99 to Con
Liberal 'leaners' (2.93)	3.30	1.28	1.28 to Con
Labour 'leaners' (2.57)	3.22	1.44	0.48 to Con
Committed Labour supporters (2.19)	3.36	1.47	0.45 to Lab
All respondents (2.79)	3.31	1.28	0.99 to Con

NOTES

High scores = anti-nationalisation, low scores = pro-nationalisation. Figures in parentheses are scores for respondents' own position. 'Relative closeness' is calculated by subtracting distance from one party from distance from the other party.

11. See *Gallup Political Index*, nos 211–15, February to June 1978. It should be added that these figures cannot be explained as simply a reflection of the Conservatives' greater overall popularity: the average Conservative lead over Labour in the Gallup polls for this period was only 3.6 per cent. An August 1978 MORI poll, published in the *Daily Express*, produced a similar result: 42 per cent thought the Conservatives 'had the best policies' on law and order: 24 per cent thought Labour had.

12. A Gallup Poll in February 1978, conducted shortly after Mrs Thatcher's remarks, asked 'If the Conservatives/Labour won the next general election do you think there would be more or less immigration, or wouldn't things change?' The figures were:

	Under Con Govt	Under Lab Govt
More	6	25
Less	71	13
No change	14	54
Don't Know	9	9
	100	100

The same pair of questions was asked of nine other 'items'—unemployment inflation, taxation, etc. On no other item was there such a consensus of view about Conservative policy or such a low proportion of 'Don't knows'.

13. See Donley Studlar, 'Policy Voting in Britain: The Coloured Immigration Issue in the 1964, 1966 and 1970 General Elections', *American Political Science Review* 72(1) (March 1978) pp 46–64; and W. L. Miller, 'What was the Profit in Following the Crowd? Aspects of Labour and Conservative Strategy since 1970', paper presented to PSA Conference, March 1978, University of Warwick.

14. On the 'radical right' see Daniel Bell (ed.) *The Radical Right* (Garden City, NY: Doubleday, 1964) and Seymour Martin Lipset and Earl Raab, *The Politics of Unreason* (London: Heinemann, 1970); on working class authoritarianism see S. M. Lipset, 'Democracy and Working Class Authoritarianism', *American Sociological Review*, 24 (1959) pp 482–502; on 'tough' and 'tender-minded' personalities see H. J. Eysenck, *The Psychology of Politics* (London: Routledge & Kegan Paul, 1954) and on acquisitive and post-acquisitive values see Ronald Inglehart, *The Silent Revolution* (Princeton, New Jersey: Princeton University Press, 1977).

Select Bibliography

P. Abrams and A. Little, 'The Young Activist in British Politics' *British Journal of Sociology*, 16 (1965) 315–33.

F. Bealey, J. Blondel, W. McCann, *Constituency Politics* (Faber, 1965).

S. Beer, *Modern British Politics* (Faber, 1965).

R. Behrens, 'Blinkers for the Carthorse: The Conservative Party and the Trade Unions 1974–78', *Political Quarterly*, 49 (1978) 457–66.

A. Beichman, 'The Conservative Research Department: The Care and Feeding of Future British Political Elites', *Journal of British Studies*, XIII (1974) 92–113.

H. Berkeley, *Crossing the Floor* (Allen & Unwin, 1972).

H. Berrington, *Backbench Opinion in the House of Commons, 1945–1955* (Pergamon, 1973).

R. Blake, *From Peel to Churchill* (Fontana, 1972).

Lord Blake and John Patten (eds.), *The Conservative Opportunity* (Macmillan, 1976).

G. Block, *A Sourcebook of Conservatism*, Conservative Political Centre (1964).

J. Blondel, 'The Conservative Association and the Labour Party in Reading', Political Studies xx (1958) 101–19.

S. Brittan, *The Treasury under the Tories, 1951–64* (Penguin, 1964).

Lord Butler, *The Art of the Possible* (Hamish Hamilton, 1971).

Lord Butler (ed.), *The Conservatives: A History from their Origins to 1965* (Allen & Unwin, 1977).

D. E. Butler and M. Pinto-Duschinsky, *The British General Election of 1970* (Macmillan, 1971).

D. E. Butler and D. Kavanagh, *The British General Election of February 1974* (Macmillan, 1974).

——, *The British General Election of October 1974* (Macmillan, 1975).

D. E. Butler and D. Stokes, *Political Change in Britain* (Macmillan, 1969).

R. Churchill, *The Fight for the Tory Leadership* (Heinemann, 1964).

D. H. Close, 'The Growth of Backbench Organisation in the Conservative Party', *Parliamentary Affairs*, XXVII, 4 (1974) pp. 371–83.

M. Cowling (ed.), *Conservative Essays* (Cassell, 1978).

I. Crewe, and B. Sarlvik, and J. Alt, 'Partisan Realignment in Britain 1964–1974' *British Journal of Political Science*, 7 (1977) pp. 129–90.

A. D. R. Dickson, 'MPs Readoption Conflicts: their Courses and Consequences', *Political Studies*, XXIII (1975) 62–70.

R. Eccleshall, English Conservatism and Ideology, *Political Studies*, XXV (1977) pp. 62–83.

L. P. Epstein, 'Politics of British Conservatism', *American Political Science Review*, XLVIII (1954) pp. 27–49.

——, 'British MPs and their Local Parties: the Suez Cases', *American Political Science Review*, LIV, 1960, 374–91.

L. Fairlie, 'Candidate Selection Role perceptions of Conservative and Labour Secretary/Agents', *Political Studies*, XXIV (1976) pp. 281–95.

S. E. Finer, H. Berrington and D. J. Bartholomew, *Backbench Opinion in the House of Commons 1955–1959* (Pergamon, 1961).

N. Fisher, *The Tory Leaders: Their Struggle for Power* (Weidenfeld & Nicolson, 1977).

——, *Ian Macleod* (Andre Deutsch, 1973).

P. Foot, *The Rise of Enoch Powell* (Penguin, 1969).

R. C. Frasure, 'Backbench Opinion Revisited: the Case of the Conservatives', *Political Studies*, XX (1972) pp. 325–8.

R. C. Frasure and A. Kornberg, 'Constituency Agents and British Party Politics', *British Journal of Political Science*, 5 (1975) pp. 459–76.

Andrew Gamble, *The Conservative Nation* (Routledge & Kegan Paul, 1974).

I. Gilmour, *The Body Politic* (Hutchinson, 1969).

——, *Inside Right: A Study of Conservatism* (Hutchinson, 1977).

H. Glickman, 'The Toryness of English Conservatism', *Journal of British Studies*, I (1961) pp. 111–43.

P. Goodhart, *The 1922: the Story of the 1922 Committee* (Macmillan, 1973).

Lord Hailsham, *The Conservative Case* (revised edition 1969).

N. Harris, *Competition and the Corporate Society* (Methuen, 1972).

J. Hoffman, *The Conservatives in Opposition* (London: MacGibbon & Kee, 1964).

R. T. Holt and J. E. Turner, *Political Parties in Action: the battle of Barons Court* (Collier-Macmillan, 1968).

D. Hurd, *An End to Promises: Sketch of a Government 1970–1974* (Collins, 1979).

R. J. Jackson, *Rebels & Whips* (Macmillan, 1968).

R. R. James, *Memoirs of a Conservative: J. C. C. Davidson's Memoirs and Papers, 1910–37* (Weidenfeld & Nicolson, 1969).

——, *Ambitions and Realities: British Politics 1964–70* (Weidenfeld & Nicolson, 1972).

B. Jessop, *Traditionalism, Conservatism and British Political Culture* (Allen & Unwin, 1973).

A. King, 'How the Conservatives evolve Policies', *New Society* (20 July 1972).

Z. Layton-Henry, 'The Young Conservatives, 1945–70', *Journal of Contemporary History*, VIII (1973) pp. 143–56.

——, 'Constituency Autonomy in the Conservative Party', *Parliamentary Affairs*, XXIX (1976) pp. 396–403.

——, 'Race, Electoral Strategy and the Major Parties', *Parliamentary Affairs*, XXXI (1978) pp. 268–81.

——, 'Democracy and Reform in the Conservative Party', *Journal of Contemporary History*, 13 (1978) pp. 653–70.

J. Lees and R. Kimber, *Political Parties in Modern Britain* (Routledge & Kegan Paul, 1972).

T. F. Lindsay and M. Harrington, *The Conservative Party 1918–1970* (Macmillan, 1974).

R. T. McKenzie, *British Political Parties* (London: Mercury Books, 2nd revised edition, 1963).

R. T. McKenzie and A. Silver, *Angels in Marble* (Heinemann, 1968).

L. W. Martin, 'The Bournemouth Affair: Britain's First Primary Election', *Journal of Politics*, XXII (1960) pp. 654–81.

C. Mellors, *The British MP* (Saxon House, 1978).

N. Nicholson, *People and Parliament* (Weidenfeld & Nicolson, 1958).

E. Nordlinger, *The Working Class Tories* (MacGibbon & Kee, 1967).

P. Norton, *Conservative Dissidents: Dissent within the Parliamentary Conservative Party, 1970–1974* (Temple Smith, 1978).

N. Nugent and R. King, *The British Right* (Saxon House, 1977).

N. O'Sullivan, *Conservatism* (Dent, 1976).

F. Parkin, 'Working Class Conservatives: A Theory of Political Deviance', *British Journal of Sociology*, XVIII (1970) pp. 278–90.

M. Parkinson, 'Central Local Relations in British Parties: a Local view', *Political Studies*, XIX (1971) pp. 440–6.

M. Peston, 'Conservative Economic Policy and Philosophy', *Political Quarterly*, XLIV (1973) pp. 411–24.

M. Pinto-Duschinsky, 'Central Office and Power in the British Conservative Party', *Political Studies*, XX (1972) pp. 1–16.

——, 'Stratification and Policy in the British Conservative Party', *American Behavioral Scientist*, XVII (1973) pp. 285–92.

R. M. Punnett, *Front-Bench Opposition* (Heinemann, 1973).

J. Ramsden, 'The Changing Base of British Conservatism' in C. Cook and J. Ramsden (eds.) *Trends in British Politics since 1945* (Macmillan, 1978).

——, *The Age of Balfour and Baldwin 1902–1940* (Longmans, 1979).

A. Ranney, *Pathways to Parliament* (Macmillan, 1965).

R. Rose, 'Tensions in Conservative Philosophy', *Political Quarterly*, XXXII (1961) pp. 275–83.

R. Rose, 'The Bow Group's Role in British Politics', *Western Political Quarterly*, XIV, 4 (1961) pp. 865–78.

——, 'The Policy Ideas of English Party Activists', *American Political Science Review*, LVI (1962) pp. 360–71.

——, 'Parties, Factions, and Tendencies in Britain', *Political Studies*, XVII (1969) pp. 413–45.

——, *The Problem of Party Government* (Macmillan, 1974).

——, *'Studies in British Politics* (3rd edition) (Macmillan, 1976).

A. Roth, *Enoch Powell—Tory Tribune* (Macdonald, 1970).

M. Rush, *The Selection of Parliamentary Candidates* (Nelson, 1969).

T. Russel, *The Tory Party* (Penguin Books, 1978).

J. E. Schwarz, 'The Impact of Constituency on the Behaviour of British Conservative MPs', *Comparative Political Studies*, VIII (1975) pp. 75–89.

J. E. Schwarz and G. Lambert, 'Career Objectives, Group feeling and Legislative Party Voting Cohesion: the British Conservatives 1959–68, *Journal of Politics*, XXXIII (1971) pp. 399–421.

D. E. Schoen, *Enoch Powell and the Powellites* (Macmillan, 1977).

P. Seyd, 'Factionalism within the Conservative Party: the Monday Club', *Government & Opposition*, VII (1973) pp. 464–87.

——, 'Democracy within the Conservative Party', *Government & Opposition*, X (1975) pp. 219–37.

D. Studlar, 'British Public Opinion, Colour Issues and Enoch Powell', *British Journal of Political Science*, 4 (1974) pp. 371–81.

D. Urwin, 'Scottish Conservatism: a Party Organisation in Transition', *Political Studies*, XIV (1966) pp. 145–62.

W. Waldegrave, *The Binding of Leviathan* (London: Hamish Hamilton, 1978).

D. J. Wilson, 'Constituency Party Autonomy and Central Control', *Political Studies*, xxi (1973) pp. 167–74.

——, *Power and Party Bureaucracy in Britain* (Saxon House, 1975).

D. J. Wilson and M. Pinto-Duschinsky, 'Conservative City Machines: The End of an Era', *British Journal of Political Science*, 6 (1976) 239–44.

Peter Walker, *The Ascent of Britain* (Sedgwick & Jackson, 1977).

Lord Woolton, *Memoirs of the Rt. Hon. Earl of Woolton* (Cassell, 1959).

Index